The Cornett-Whitley Gang

Violence Unleashed in Texas

David Johnson

Foreword by Doug Dukes

Number 21 in the A.C. Greene Series
University of North Texas Press
Denton, Texas

Printed in the United States of America.

10 9 8 7 6 5 4 3 2 1

Permissions:
University of North Texas Press
1155 Union Circle #311336
Denton, TX 76203-5017

The paper used in this book meets the minimum requirements of the American National Standard for Permanence of Paper for Printed Library Materials, z39.48.1984. Binding materials have been chosen for durability.

Library of Congress Cataloging-in-Publication Data

Names: Johnson, David (David D.), 1950- author.
Title: The Cornett-Whitley gang : violence unleashed in Texas / by David Johnson ; foreword by Doug Dukes.
Other titles: A.C. Greene series ; 21.
Description: Denton, Texas : University of North Texas Press, [2019] | Series: Number 21 in the A.C. Greene series | Includes bibliographical references and index.
Identifiers: LCCN 2019008278| ISBN 9781574417685 (cloth : alk. paper) | ISBN 9781574417784 (ebook)
Subjects: LCSH: Cornett, Brack, 1860-1888. | Whitley, Bill, 1864-1888. | Outlaws--Texas--Biography. | Criminals--Texas--Biography. | Brigands and robbers--Texas--Biography. | LCGFT: Biographies.
Classification: LCC F391 .J643 2019 | DDC 364.1092/2 [B] --dc23
LC record available at https://catalog.loc.gov/vwebv/search?searchCode=LCCN&searchArg=2019008278&searchType=1&permalink=y

The Cornett-Whitley Gang: Violence Unleashed in Texas is
Number 21 in the A.C. Greene Series

The electronic edition of this book was made possible by
the support of the Vick Family Foundation.

Jacket and page design by Joseph Parenteau

Dedication

This book is dedicated to the master of Texas history, Donaly E. Brice, whose knowledge, friendship, and skill are unparalleled.

Contents

Foreword by Doug Dukes vii

Acknowledgments x

Dramatis Personae xii

Introduction xvi

Chapter 1 ✢ At the Mustang Pen in Butler's Pasture 1

Chapter 2 ✢ Demonic Laughter 21

Chapter 3 ✢ The Headwaters of Ugly Creek 37

Chapter 4 ✢ Without a Single Train Robber 53

Chapter 5 ✢ Fiendish Atrocities 67

Chapter 6 ✢ Immunity from Unpleasant Consequences . . . 83

Chapter 7 ✢ A Stream of Fire 100

Chapter 8 ✢ I Will Make Things Lively 116

Chapter 9 ✢ Wild, Woolly and Hard to Curry 132

Chapter 10 ✢ Prefer Them Dead 148

Photo Gallery . . . . after page 162

Chapter 11 ‡ Lawless and Violent 163

Chapter 12 ‡ The Wages of Sin 182

Appendix 1 ‡ Editorial in the *Fort Worth Daily Gazette,* May 24, 1887 200

Appendix 2 ‡ "Song of the Train Robbers" 202

Appendix 3 ‡ Editorial in the *Fort Worth Daily Gazette,* June 20, 1887 204

Appendix 4 ‡ Jim Stephens's letter to *Fort Worth Daily Gazette,* December 12, 1888 206

Appendix 5 ‡ Buck Powell in the *Galveston Daily News,* July 10, 1892 208

Endnotes 213

Select Bibliography of Sources Consulted 259

Index 274

Foreword

Brack Cornett, Bill Whitley and those who composed the Cornett-Whitley gang were deadly, dangerous, mean men. They were the worst Texas had to offer. Their sadistic tendencies toward promiscuous violence were matched only by their desire for easy money with no more effort than a quick pull of the trigger. As is the case today, their families were not always aware of the type of men they truly were. As more and more contemporary accounts and records become available, the truth is slowly becoming apparent as to who and what these men really were. Thanks to Dave Johnson, the reader is transported back into a time and place that some will not always find appealing, and most will be glad to return from to their own world. Yet without Dave, the truth of these men would not only go untold but it would not be told in such a truthful, insightful, and entertaining manner.

The name of Bill Whitley first came to my attention while researching law enforcement in Central Texas during the nineteenth century. Being a retired Law Enforcement Officer from the Austin Texas Police Department, it was always my intent to learn about both Austin City Marshal, and former Texas Ranger, James Lucy and Williamson County Sheriff John Olive. Both men were involved in the pursuit of John Barber, Bill Whitley, Brack Cornett, and others following the robbery at the McNeil train station located just a few miles north of Austin. Noted United States Marshal John Rankin also pursued the gang according to the news coverage concerning the robbery. The fact that both John Barber and Will Whitley were later indicted for killing Williamson County Deputy Sheriff Bill Stanley quickened my interest and started an entirely new research venture into the gang.

Except, perhaps, to his family, Bill Whitley was not a nice guy. His death at the hands of Marshal Rankin is a tale of two cities coming from the viewpoints of both his family as opposed to law enforcement officers. While researching Whitley, I learned that descendants had both his rifle and pistol in their possession. After chasing down Whitley's relatives, I located and photographed both his pistol and rifle.

From the family I learned that subsequent to Whitley's death, his widow, Cordelia Lucinda Cox Whitley, married John Wilson Swinney. Together they had several children including William Rance "Willie" Swinney. Knowing a Captain Wilford Swinney, who had also retired from the Austin Police Department, I contacted him and learned that his father was said William Rance Swinney. Through Captain Swinney the final point of irony was brought to light. While the Captain spent 39 years with Austin Police, his father was also a policeman, but only for one year. The pistol Whitley carried as a train robber, bank robber, and generally bad man was used by William Rance Swinney during 1924 in his job as an Austin Police Officer. Thus the conundrum of good and bad, the yin and the yang of not only a specific pistol but that of the men who used it shows the marked opposites of the individuals.

Hunting Bill Whitley in the present day provides insight into the diligence one must have to hunt the entire gang. Dave Johnson is no stranger to the Wild West as well as the ins and outs of navigating the world of researching it. His book on *The Mason County "Hoo Doo" War, 1874-1902,* is the quintessential book on the complete story of Mason County and the story of the struggle between the German immigrants and those who opposed them. *John Ringo, King of the Cowboys His Life and*

Times from the Hoo Doo War to Tombstone is in multiple editions and is considered be the complete cradle-to-grave story of this well-known gunfighter. His work on the Horrell brothers, *The Horrell Wars: Feuding in Texas and New Mexico* radically enhanced our knowledge of these men.

Unlike some authors, Dave Johnson has no agenda. A true historian, he reports what happened and leaves it up to the reader to fill in the blanks. He digs for records more than some and reports everything he digs up: the good, the bad, the ugly, the warts and all. While this can be dangerous, it is the best way for a historian to operate. Johnson provides the reader all the information and tells all that happened, not just the good, making up the rest. Even though he may live outside the great State of Texas, Dave has availed this book with contemporary newspaper accounts, official reports, and other contemporary records to support his work. It is not unusual to have a single page with eight to ten endnotes and quotes. Dave is an excellent researcher and goes out of his way to find and present the most up-to-date data and stories to support his work. This volume is no different. His documented resources will show that this work is the most definitive work on the Cornett-Whitley Gang to date.

Doug Dukes

Acknowledgments

As with any book the author is indebted to numerous individuals for their help and support. No book on Texas history could be complete without the aid of the master researcher Donaly E. Brice who has forgotten more Texas history than most of us will ever learn. An extra special thanks to his wife Clare whose tolerance for those of us who vicariously live in the 1800s remains one of the modern wonders of the world.

For matters of legal procedure and hands on experience dealing with criminals the author has relied upon three notable historians and retired law enforcement officials. Bob Alexander provided much insight into the criminal mind and pointed the way to a number of sources on the gang and their associates. Longtime friend and former police officer and county attorney Rick Miller provided a number of sources in addition to his tongue-in-cheek humor that is always welcome. Historian Doug Dukes, a former police lieutenant, aided my understanding of the gang and corrected an old saw concerning honor among thieves. "I have never found there to be honor among thieves. There are only thieves among thieves." The author is fortunate to have them as friends.

Historian Chuck Parsons, a close friend for forty years or more, provided both archival assistance and support. Mike Koch, veteran Cornett-Whitley researcher, tracked down the true identity of Charley Ross through dogged determination and a lot of hard work. Also indispensable to this book was Dave

Turk, historian of the U. S. Marshal's office, and Bob Ernst, an expert on the lawmen who operated out of Fort Smith.

Last but hardly least are those family members who provided family stories, histories, and much more. These include Lynn Cornett, Roger Cornett, Keith Reed, Mike Buck, Terry Wooten, Gaylon Powell, Mary Beth Marchant, Liz Hancock, Tom Cloud, Mo Braum, Ken Drope, Keith Brown, Peg Engeldow, Richard Lucy, John Henry Pickren, Jr., Carl Jacobs, Chris Butterworth and many others. A special thanks too to Peggy Engledow of the Caldwell County Historical Society.

Dramatis Personae

The Cornett-Whitley Gang

Barber, John Toliver
Cloud, Isaac Kennedy "Ike"
Cornett, Braxton E. "Brack"
Powell, James Asberry "Bud"
Reeves, Edwin James "Ed"
Secrest, Sion Searcy alias Charley Ross
Whitley, William Henry "Bill"

Gang Affiliates

Bennett, Joe
Brown, John (or George)
Butler, Newton Green
Cresswell [sic: Crisswell], John
Day, Martin
Harrell, Eli
Harrell, Will
Herrin, Jim
Holloman, J. H.
Humphreys, William
Insall, John
Jacobs, Will
Jones (Montgomery?), Tom
Kelly, Henry Peter
Neff, Sam
Queen, Samuel DeKalb "Kep"
Rogers, Bob

Standley, Eugene	
Standley, Hamp	
Stephens, Jim	

Texas State Officials

Hogg, James Stephen	*State Attorney General*
King, Wilburn H.	*Adjutant General*
Ross, Lawrence Sullivan "Sul"	*Governor*

Law Enforcement

Allee, Alfred Young	*Deputy Sheriff*
Aten, Austin Ira	*Texas Ranger*
Bailes, Tom	*U. S. Deputy Marshal*
Bailey, W. C.	*Railroad detective*
Bell, J. W.	*U. S. Deputy Marshal*
Bonnell, W. H.	*Missouri Pacific detective*
Boyd, John H.	*Sheriff of Johnson County*
Brady, C. J.	*City Marshal of Georgetown*
Connelly, Barney	*Deputy U. S. Marshal*
Daugherty, W. C.	*Sheriff of Frio County*
Ellis, George W.	*Sheriff of Harris County*
Erichson, Albert	*Deputy Sheriff of Harris County*
Evans, James W.	*Sheriff of Fannin County*
Furlong, T. K.	*Chief Detective Missouri Pacific*
Grimes, Albert C.	*Texas Ranger*
Hornsby, William M.	*Sheriff of Travis County*
Hughes, John R.	*Texas Ranger*
Hume, James B.	*Wells Fargo detective*
Jones, Frank	*Texas Ranger*
Jones, William E.	*Sheriff of Gonzales County*
Kegans, Ben	*Deputy Sheriff of Harris County*
Lewis, Andrew Jackson	*Sheriff Milam County*
Lewis, Nathaniel	*Sheriff of Bexar County*
Lucy, James E.	*City Marshal of Austin*

McDade, Thomas S.	*Sheriff of Waller County*
McMurray, Sam	*Texas Ranger*
McNeil, J S.	*Deputy U. S. Marshal*
Olive, John Thomas	*Sheriff of Williamson County*
Platt, Sam	*Deputy Sheriff Travis County*
Rankin, John Taylor	*U. S. Marshal*
Reynolds, N. O.	*Sheriff of Lampasas County / former Texas Ranger*
Rudd, William L.	*Sheriff of Karnes County / former Texas Ranger*
Sanders, Ed	*Sheriff of Cherokee Nation, Oklahoma*
Schmitt, George	*Texas Ranger*
Scott, William	*Texas Ranger*
Sieker, Lamar P.	*Texas Ranger quartermaster*
Smothers, A. J.	*Sheriff of Lavaca County*
Stanley, William	*Deputy Sheriff of Williamson County*
Stevens, Ed	*Constable in San Antonio*
Thacker, John	*Wells Fargo detective*
Thomas, Henry Andrew "Heck"	*Deputy U. S. Marshal*
Townsend, James Light	*Sheriff of Colorado County*
Van Riper, William	*U. S. Deputy Marshal*
West, Duval	*Deputy U. S. Marshal*
Wolf, John W.	*Sheriff of Burnet County*
Yglesis, Eugene	*Deputy U. S. Marshal*
Zapp, Brutus Lytt	*Sheriff of Fayette County*

Railroad Personnel

McNeil Station

Cook, William	*porter*
Ely, Samuel R.	*railroad agent / telegrapher*
Glidden, William	*engineer*
Hawkins, W. E.	*conductor*

Northacker, A. J.	*express messenger*
Spangler, Samuel H.	*fireman*
Spaulding, S. R.	*postal clerk*
Walker, C. D.	*brakeman*
Woods, J. S.	*postal helper*
Flatonia	
Pickren, Ben	*engineer*
Lyons, Jesse K.	*conductor*
Wright, S. L.	*fireman*
Folger, M. E. "Frank"	*expressman*
Hart, -----	*baggage master*
Allen, A. N.	*butcher*
Johnson, Charles	*porter*
Verdigris River Bridge	
Bentley, J. T.	*brakeman*
Codding, A. B.	*express messenger*
Colton, Willis P.	*mail clerk*
Rasback, Wallace H.	*engineer*
Ryan, Henry	*newsboy*
Harwood	
Everett, Milton	*ticket agent*
Greeser (Glaisor, John?)	*fireman*
Saran, Ed	*mail agent*
Shackford, E. E.	*conductor*
Toomey, Dan	*engineer*

Introduction

Since the era of the horseback outlaws following the Civil War, when jayhawkers and guerrillas roamed the West, the public has been fascinated with their exploits, both real and imagined. It was exciting stuff to be sure, and during the late nineteenth and early twentieth centuries, dime novels flourished by recounting the exploits of these men, which in turn aided and abetted their behavior. Credit for the first dime novel is given to Erastus Beadle who published *Malaeska: Indian Wife of the White Hunter* in 1860. The book was swiftly successful and the chase was on. The genre expanded as entrepreneurial Americans entered the market and in Europe such novels became known as penny dreadfuls.

In general, the dime novel focused on the dramatic exploits of a single character. Many of them focused on a western theme. Frequently they included real people such as Buffalo Bill Cody, Kit Carson, and outlaws such as Billy the Kid, Rube Burrow, and Jesse James. Nor was the sensationalism confined to the written word. There were ballads about folk heroes such as Sam Bass and Jesse James, and with the dawn of motion pictures Hollywood glamorized outlaws and lawmen alike, thrusting such individuals as Butch Cassidy, the Sundance Kid, Wild Bill Hickok, and twentieth-century creation Wyatt Earp into the limelight with numerous others. Biographies and pseudobiographies have been written concerning all of these men along with many others. Perhaps the genre is best summed up in the title of John E. Hallwas's book, *Dime Novel Outlaws: The Notorious Maxwell Brothers*.[1]

Despite the national and international recognition that the Cornett-Whitley gang garnered during their heyday, from media such as the *Auckland Star* in New Zealand and the *Western Gazette* in England, there was never a dime novel devoted to them. On the surface, the gang has all the elements required. They were bold and daring. They achieved an international recognition that arguably was never achieved by most outlaws. They also concentrated their efforts on trains.

Following the Civil War, train robbery blossomed in the United States. Those who had learned their skills during the Civil War, and those who had simply figured out that a train carrying large sums of money was a vulnerable target, put their criminality to use. The robberies in themselves could be singularly violent, as was the robbery of the Ohio and Mississippi train on May 5, 1865, by Confederate guerrillas who derailed the train some fourteen miles from Cincinnati.[2] This has never been considered the first peacetime railroad robbery for obvious reasons. Nor was the January 1866 train robbery of a train between New Haven, Connecticut, and New York which, from the accounts, was more of a burglary conducted on a train.[3] Instead, the Reno brothers claimed the dubious distinction of the first postwar train robbery. The outlaws boarded the train as passengers, then walked to the express car. None of the passengers were molested.[4]

Writing of such men, the late historian John D. Tanner offered, "For cowhands who lived with the reality of earning a 'million dollars in a million days,' however, the glitter of gold at the end of the railroad's rainbow continued to tantalize."[5] It was not only cowhands who sought easy money. Eugene Bunch was well educated, a teacher who traipsed down the wrong path. Bill Miner, on the other hand, was a career criminal who served prison time in both the United States and Canada. Both of these men and many others have been the subject of books and articles. Many of them were enshrined in dime novels, and not a few of them were the subjects of movies and even television shows.

Adding to the notoriety that the Cornett-Whitley gang garnered internationally, county sheriffs, city marshals, U. S. Marshals, and the legendary Texas Rangers all pursued them, adding their own reputations to the outlaws' infamy. Among the pursuers were legendary ranger Ira Aten and his protégée, John R. Hughes, later one of the Four Great Captains.

So the question of their relative anonymity returns to the Cornett-Whitley gang. To date the gang has been addressed in two articles, both written nearly fifty years ago by the late British historian Jeff Burton. There has also been a biography of Bill Whitley authored by his granddaughter. Given their prominence, both domestic and international, at the time the question becomes why. The answer, in the author's view, may be summed up in a single word: Flatonia. The train robbery devolved into an orgy of sadistic wanton violence as the outlaws tortured their way through the passengers. It was an act that in the modern world would be termed terrorism. Yet these men made no claim to a purpose higher than self-gratification. This train robbery established not only who they were but, far more importantly, *what* they were: sadistic, brutal psychopaths.

Most of the gang was composed of alpha males, and as such having a cohesive unit was never possible. Like a malignant cancer, they spread throughout Texas and Oklahoma leaving destroyed lives in their wake exploiting and exposing the weaknesses not only of their adversaries but of the media of the day. They were the Cornett-Whitley gang, and they would break all of the rules.

Chapter

1

At the Mustang Pen in Butler's Pasture

Some were wary of the others as they gathered, predators taking in both their surroundings and each other, evaluating those who had come. Some were eager, excited, blinded by the lure of fast money and unmindful of the risks they would undertake. Others regarded their new companions with caution, their cold eyes gauging those present, calculating the odds and who they would kill first if things went sideways. Some were misguided heading down a path from which they could never return. Some were cruel, hard men growing harder with every passing breath. One of them was mad, a sociopath whose sadistic and violent tendencies were frequently at the forefront, a killer whose conscience, if he ever had one, had long since fled his mortal frame. They were not friends but necessity had drawn them together in early 1887 to accomplish their purpose. There were seven of them and none of them had known the others long. Ed Reeves recalled their meeting well:

> I met Brack Cornett in Kansas [*sic*: Karnes] County, at the mustang pen in Butler's pasture, in February 1887. Bud Powell, or more properly Jim Powell, was present. Charley Ross brought Cornett up there. I had know[n] Charley Ross only two or three weeks prior to this time. . . . I met John Barbour [*sic*: Barber] and Bill Whitley about a week before the McNeil robbery, in De Witt County, about seven miles east of Cuero, in the woods close to Joe Bennett's house. I went to that place with Brack Cornett, Charley Ross, Ike Cloud and Bud Powell.[1]

Joe Bennett was loosely affiliated with the gang. Bennett provided aid to the outlaws at times but never participated in their raids. In an unrelated matter, during 1893 he was convicted of cattle theft. He drew a three-year sentence but was pardoned the following year.[2]

Those who gathered were not a pack bonded by extreme loyalty and devotion to the group, as are wolves. Rather they were solitary predators—sharks—concerned only with their own wellbeing. At best this was the formation of a gang, and like sharks whose social hierarchy is defined by survival of the fittest, these men had a hierarchy of sorts, one established instinctively by their own natures and their recognition of the natures of the others.

There are challenges in the identification of these men, even knowing their names. That all of them were liars is no surprise, but it goes beyond that. Even today some of their families refuse to discuss these men. Most, if not all, used aliases at one time or another to cloak their identities and not a few of them assumed multiple identities. Only Ed Reeves left a statement discussing the original gang, a statement that is limited in many ways. They did not trust one another nor confide in their companions. They did, however, need each other, at least for the moment.

Ed Reeves

Ed Reeves, who provided the only account of the gang's formation, was born Edwin James Reeves around 1857 in Arkansas to Green William Reeves and Elizabeth Courtney. The couple had been married in Montgomery County, Alabama, on July 7, 1846. Elizabeth was nearly fifteen years Green's junior.[3]

The Reeves family did not linger in Alabama. According to family records, their oldest child Mary Francis "Fannie" was born July 6, 1848, at Big Springs, Arkansas. Between Fannie's birth and 1858 the couple produced five more children. Following their sixth child's birth, the family moved to Bowie County, Texas, where they were enumerated on June 23, 1860. The census shows that the oldest four children had all attended school within the previous year. Green is listed as a farmer with $500 in real estate and a valuation of $1020 in personal property. In Bowie County the Reeves family had two more children. Three years later, on November 6, 1866, Green Reeves died.[4]

Perhaps it was fortuitous that one of Green's younger brothers, Jesse Winchester Reeves, was recently widowed. Almost hastily, Elizabeth married Jesse. It appears likely that their marriage on January 24, 1867, in Coryell County, Texas, began as one of practicality.[5] The union would produce several more children.[6]

By 1870 the Reeves family was in Davis (present-day Cass) County, Texas, where Ed Reeves is recorded as twelve years old.[7] One account notes succinctly that Reeves "was born in Arkansas, but moved to Texas with his parents when he was quite young. He has lived in Ellis, Hays and other counties. He married in Ellis County in 1879, and has one boy about 8 years old. He has a sister, a Mrs. [Rachel Matilda Reeves] Hamilton, who lives near Round Rock, and she has charge of his son, his wife having died several years ago."[8] Ed Reeves was living in Ellis County, Texas, during 1879 when he married Emma (or Inez)

Burt on September 18.[9] Emma, eighteen, was the daughter of John and Margaret Jane Abbey Burt, and had been born around 1861.[10] The 1880 census confirms Ed and Emma Reeves living in Ellis County along with Reeves's brother James H.[11]

Here the records become less clear. Emma, listed as age eighteen in the 1880 census is noted as Inez in the 1870 Navarro County, Texas, census. Sometime after June 1, 1880, when the census was enumerated, Emma gave birth to a son.[12] Contemporary sources state that Emma died prior to 1887, but this appears erroneous. The couple separated, and Hill County, Texas, marriage records indicate that "Miss Ines Burt" married James Page on December 9, 1880, possibly without divorcing Reeves.[13] Ed and Emma's son was left in the care of Ed's sister Rachel, apparently indicating that Emma and her family wanted nothing to do with Ed Reeves.[14]

The reasons Emma left Ed Reeves can only be speculated. Perhaps they were simply too young when they married, but it appears more likely that Reeves's chosen vocation was the cause. When Ed's stepfather Jesse died in October 1881, Ed Reeves was already well on his way to establishing a reputation. U. S. District Attorney Jack Evans later stated that he had "known of Reeves and his exploits for a number of years and regards him as one of the hardest tough citizens whose daring has led him into many horse-thieving expeditions."[15] Reeves did not confine himself to horse theft. On October 3, 1883, Ed Reeves was convicted for theft of a steer in Ellis County and sentenced to two years in prison.[16] On October 11, 1883, he and a number of other prisoners were transferred to Rusk Penitentiary in Cherokee County by J. D. Snow. "They are from Ellis county, and all claim to be native Texans" reported the *Galveston Daily News*. Among them was Ed Reeves's brother James, also convicted for "theft of steer."[17] Prison records state that Reeves entered prison on October 11, 1883, as convict

1479. His nativity is incorrectly given as Texas and his birth around 1858.[18] One contemporary description notes:

> A casual glance at Reeves would detect nothing to indicate a desperate or dangerous man, but a close study of his face and head and eye and movements will disclose much combativeness, firmness and nerve.
>
> He is one of—those men if he plans a train robbery, or joins in with others to accomplish the pleasing pastime, is going to do his share toward making it a success.
>
> He is poorly educated, but has a deal of horse sense, coupled with much cautiousness![19]

In his prison record Reeves stated his residence was Waxahachie in Ellis County and claimed that he was married, although his wife had left him years earlier. The records give his age as twenty-eight and his birthplace as Texas. Descriptions of Reeves vary. Penitentiary records show that Ed Reeves was six feet three quarter inches tall, 155 pounds with a fair complexion, blue eyes and black hair at the time of his incarceration. Reeves arrived at the penitentiary with twenty-five cents to his name. He was distinguished by a bullet scar on his rump. Both Ed and James drank and smoked, and both had only a limited education. James had two dollars on his person when he entered the penitentiary.[20]

Three years later Wells Fargo provided another description: "Ed Reaves, alias 'Pat;' 32 years old; about 6 feet high; weight 180 pounds; red complexion; ring-worms on face; black hair; big black moustache." The same circular that described Ed also contains the statement that "His brother was killed by a constable at Breckenridge, in Karnes Co., a few months ago."[21]

This incident is described in one contemporary newspaper account. On February 12, 1887, a man using the name Jim

Butler "got his hide full of Karnes county tangleroot" and rode his horse into the freight depot in Breckenridge. When the local constable approached Butler and ordered him to surrender, he "made a bad break, but [Manuel] Espizer got there first" and dropped Butler from his horse after the third shot. The constable surrendered himself at Helena to authorities, and on February 13 he, Sheriff W. L. Rudd, three deputies, and William Green Butler rode to Breckenridge to examine the body. Not only was Butler not dead, but he was not a son of William Green Butler as he had claimed. An examination of his papers indicated that his name, possibly, was Sparks. His wound was not considered fatal at the time.[22]

Sheriff Rudd prudently distributed an inquiry through the media.

> BRECKENRIDGE, Feb. 14.—A man giving his name as Butler was shot here Saturday night by the Constable. Description as follows. Five feet 10 inches high, dark brown eyes, black hair, dark mustache, about 25 years old, weight, about 160 pounds. In his memorandum book is the names J. Thorp and J. S. Sparks. Any information of above will be gladly received, as he is a suspicious looking character. W. L. Rudd, sheriff of Karnes county.[23]

From this description, "Butler" appears to be Reeves's brother James. Upon his entry to the penitentiary in 1883, James was described as twenty-two, six-feet one-inches tall, 160 pounds, dark complexion, black hair, and grey eyes. James had a large wart on his right hand.[24]

Ed Reeves was neither the leader nor the brains of the gang, and evidence suggests that he was likely recruited by Bud Powell. When he rendezvoused with the others at Butler's pasture Reeves was one of the least deceptive, using his real name. Not all of them did.

Bud Powell

While some apologists might cite the death of Reeves's father as a reason for his descent into outlawry, no such claim can be made for Bud Powell. To look at him Powell appeared out of place among the others. Wells Fargo describes James Asberry Powell as a "small man with florid complexion; light hair; dark eyes; little, thin, light, downey [*sic*], boyish moustache; about 27 years old; weight about 140 pounds."[25] Commonly known as Bud Powell, he was born February 21, 1859, to Samuel S. and Agnes Stone Powell in De Witt County. Both of his parents were alive and well when he headed down the outlaw trail.[26]

Samuel and Agnes Powell had a number of children before their move to Texas in 1854. Unfortunately the family chose to settle in DeWitt County, which would become a battleground of the Sutton-Taylor War following the Civil War. Here more children, including Bud Powell, were born.[27] By 1870 the census indicated Samuel Powell was a small farmer with a total personal and property value of $1000.[28]

Bud Powell's family background is deceiving, for he himself did not enjoy a good reputation. As a child he had heard a great deal concerning the infamous Sutton-Taylor War where violence and lawlessness were perpetrated by a Reconstruction government that ruled a disenfranchised populace. In DeWitt County the infamous Jack Helm provided a brand of justice best described as murderous, helping to fuel the war and an unhealthy disregard for the law, which in many cases was as bad or worse than the outlaws they claimed to suppress.[29] Tempting as it might be to claim that Powell was collateral damage arising from the feud, it appears that he had simply fallen into bad company. In 1883 he, Eli Harrell, and a number of others went into a Karnes County church armed with pistols.[30] Had Powell confined himself to this youthful indiscretion very likely he would not be known today. He did not.

> It is known here that shortly before the McNeil robbery Reinhardt Schneider, Will Kelley, Will Jacobs and Bud Powell were in their old range near the line of this Karnes & Gonzales Cos that horses were stolen from this neighborhood one of which is said to have been found near the place of the robbery. Since then they have again been reported as again in this country and immediately preceding this last robbery another lot of horses have disappeared. These facts and the knowledge I have of the character of these men suggest a possible clue to these robberies which you can consider with other information you may have of the matter.[31]

Jacobs was later involved with the gang. Wells Fargo adds that one of Powell's sisters was "the wife of the notorious Rheinhardt Sneider. [*sic*: Reinhardt Schneider].[32] At the time Schneider was an escaped convict and well known as a horse thief.[33] Powell was a follower, drawn to the gang by the siren's lure of fast and easy money. Like Ed Reeves he was probably recruited by John Barber.

Ike Cloud

Like Powell, Ike Cloud came from good stock. Cloud was the youngest son of William Augustine Cloud and his wife Elizabeth Kennedy, who was Tennessee-born. His father had come to Texas via Alabama and Louisiana. In Alabama, William lived in Cypress Creek with two of his brothers, working as a merchant.[34] The Clouds had three children while living in Alabama, the youngest of whom, Mary, lived only one day.[35]

Perhaps it was Mary's death that prompted the Cloud family to leave Alabama. During 1839 William had been serving as a justice of the peace in Alabama, but in 1840 the family moved to Union Parish, Louisiana. Here a number of Cloud children were born.[36] Fate dealt the family a cruel blow during the summer of 1850 when three of their children died within a month. The death of these three children so closely together may indicate one of the summer plagues.[37] William's health also deteriorated, and the family resolved to move west. When they reached Williamson County, William's health abruptly improved. The Cloud family settled near Bagdad where their youngest son, Isaac Kennedy Cloud, was born on August 15, 1860. Texas appears to have improved the family's luck, and the 1860 census notes William as a farmer. He again served as a justice of the peace.[38]

William Augustine Cloud died on May 27, 1870, of a prostate condition and his son Thomas assumed the farming responsibilities.[39] By 1880 Ike was living with his mother and brother George close to the home of Penelope Cloud, his oldest brother James's widow.[40] Elizabeth Cloud died on May 9, 1881.

No physical description of Cloud has been located to date, but like Powell he was already in trouble with the law in Williamson County. When he arrived at Newt Butler's horse pasture he was under bond on two separate charges of theft and receiving stolen property, one of which was augmented by driving livestock from their accustomed range.[41] It is possible he had partnered with John Barber in some of these affairs.

Sion Secrest, alias Charley Ross

Charley Ross trusted none of the others. Reeves was clearly suspicious concerning Ross's real identity, noting, "I only knew him as Charley Ross."[42] He recalled Ross as "about 140 to 145 pounds, has dark skin, black hair, brown moustache, dark hazel eyes." Reeves added that Ross lived in Kerrville for roughly three years, 1884 through 1887, which is undoubtedly what Ross told him and the others. Tax records, however, show no one named Ross in evidence in Kerr County during this time period.[43] His uncle, Abraham Francis Secrest, was living there however, and Ross may have been living with him under yet another assumed name.

Reeves's suspicions were shrewd. Ross's father was Tennessee-born Thomas Carroll Secrest who had married Mariah Bird Dismukes.[44] In Arkansas a number of children were born to the Secrest family, but by 1850 they had moved to Fayette County, Texas,where the census enumerated on October 6 notes Thomas Secrest as a small farmer.[45]

During the decade from 1850 to 1860 the Secrest family prospered significantly. Financially their holdings increased from $400 to a combined value of $9200. Texas was good to them, and during this decade three sons were born to them. On December 12, 1859, the man later known as Charley Ross was born to Thomas and Mariah Secrest. His parents christened him Sion Searcy. His name appears for the first time on legal records as Sion S. aged six months in the 1860 census.[46]

The Civil War apparently had little financial impact on the Secrest family. Their finances remaining much the same in 1870 as they had been in 1860.[47] The family's relationship had deteriorated however, and following the 1870 census Thomas and Mariah were divorced. On January 29, 1874, Thomas married Martha M. Paddock.[48] The same year, one of Sion's older sisters, Barbara Allen, died, probably due to complications of childbirth.[49] Mariah remained in Fayette County, and in 1880 "Searcey Sun" was enumerated as a farm hand living with his mother.[50]

Sion Secrest was no ordinary farm hand, however. Local lore has it that he was shot in the leg by a man named Polk while attempting to steal a yolk of oxen from Polk's cow lot.[51] Early on some of the Secrest family acquired a hard reputation. One history reports that while most young men of the time had fist fights, "there were some, like the Secrest boys, that were always beaten in their fistfights and resorted to the pistol and the fast draw." Sion Searcy Secrest was not the exception and was known locally as "one of the fastest gunmen in the area."[52] It appears likely that it was this penchant for fighting that led to Secrest's first killing. On September 24, 1879, Sion Secrest had a confrontation with eighteen-year-old Samuel Merkin. Secrest shot Merkin in the head, killing him instantly. On November 20, 1879, a jury rendered a not guilty verdict for the killing.[53]

Available records indicate that Secrest fell into bad company. The following year Secrest added cattle theft to his reputation as a man killer. On June 22, 1880, Secrest, his brother Bud, Hamilton "Vic" Dickson, and Short Day were rounding up stray cattle when they passed the ranch of Robert Ragsdale.[54] The men decided that the stray beeves they were hunting included a number of cattle from Ragsdale's cattle pen. Unobserved by the thieves Ragsdale's son James saw them taking the beeves. When Bob Ragsdale returned home from business in Hallettsville that night, James told him about the theft and the identities of the thieves.

Ragsdale was having none of it. "Ragsdale stood under six feet and weighed about 180 pounds. He was a real man, not afraid of anyone."[55] The following day, June 23, Ragsdale set out alone to recover the cattle, a courageous but foolish act. He caught up with the men at a public cattle pen close to the Secrest home. When he demanded the cattle he was met by a flurry of bullets. Ragsdale attempted to flee but was run down and shot from his horse.[56]

The killers attempted to hide the body, but the brazen murder could not go undetected for long. Secrest prudently fled, and at this point he began sporting the alias Charley Ross.[57] Those charged with Ragsdale's death included Secrest, his brother Thomas Abraham "Bud" Secrest, Short Day, and Vic Dickson. None of them were ever convicted, but fate was not kind to them. Bud Secrest committed suicide on July 8, 1880.[58] Day apparently fled with Sion Secrest and was killed the same year in a knife fight in Mexico. Dickson was killed on August

21, 1882, by Robert Deal. An erroneous report had it that Secrest had died in Lavaca County "from the effects of a pistol shot wound inflicted by his brother, 'Bud' Secrest at the time Ragsdale was murdered."[59]

How Sion Secrest fell in with Brack Cornett is unknown, but it appears likely he and Cornett were involved in horse stealing in west Texas. That they knew each is certain, Reeves recalling that "Charley Ross brought Cornett up there."[60]

John Barber

John Toliver Barber embraced a criminal career early in life. Family lore places Barber's birth in Lampasas County, Texas, on January 18, 1860, but the 1860 census enumerated on July 9 placed the family in neighboring Burnet County.[61] In addition to his parents, Isaac and Joanna, four older siblings were counted in the census. With the benefit of hindsight, John Barber's parents may have wished that they had stopped at four children. Like the other families, the Barbers were of good stock. By 1850 Virginia-born Isaac Barber was living at the home of John W. Finny in Carroll County, Arkansas, where he gave his occupation as farmer.[62] Here he met Joanna Petty. The couple married young, and by 1853 they were living in Texas where their children were born. In 1860 Isaac Barber gave his occupation as stock raising, the family having a personal estate listed at $680.[63]

The 1860s were not kind to the family. Little less than a year following the census enumeration daughter Sarah died on July 2. On January 5, 1862, the Barbers were blessed with another child, Samuel D., but their joy was short lived as Samuel died on November 15 of that year. Their worst tragedy remained alive and well, for John Barber would bring grief to the entire family. By 1870 the Barbers had relocated to Williamson County where Isaac gave his occupation as a farmer.[64]

Wells Fargo described John Barber as "5 feet 8 or 9 inches high; weight about 150; black hair and moustache; brown eyes. His right arm is badly scarred from injuries received in a cotton gin, and the wrist is so badly scarred that he wears a knitted wristlet to hide them. He wears a heavy plain gold ring on the forefinger of the left hand and handles his pistol with his left hand."[65] In addition to being the only southpaw in the gang, Barber was brash and flippant. His sister Attie Hunt testified, "when I asked him where he was going, he generally says to see the girls."[66] Ed Reeves recalled contemptuously that Barber "is looked upon as a bad man, but he wasn't. He was the best runner in the crowd and that's what we thought he would do when the pinch came."[67] In time Barber would sport a breastplate to augment his running abilities.[68] Barber also possessed the less than endearing trait of thoughtlessly causing trouble for his family to an uncanny degree, particularly his brothers.

John Barber may have been in Oklahoma during 1877 when a man calling himself Tom Barber and John Barber decided on Christmas Day to force Henry Rigney to drink with them. When Rigney objected, Tom Barber opened fire. No one was killed and the Barbers were charged with intent to kill although John's name was later dropped from the indictment.[69] Regardless if this was or was not John T. Barber, by 1880 he was back in Williamson County working for his father as a farm laborer.[70] All indications are that Barber was the brains of the gang, but not the leader. It was probably Barber who recruited most of the gang.

One family story concerning Barber is that Isaac Barber was killed by the Williamson County sheriff and that John "swore that on the day he turned 21 years of age that he would kill that Sheriff. When his 21st birthday came he put on his gun and went and got his man."[71] The story is garbled, for Isaac outlived his wayward son. What is not garbled is that he was a particular "pal" to the sixth man in the group, Bill Whitley.[72]

Bill Whitley

Bill Whitley was the anomaly of the gang. While he has leant his name to the gang, apparently he used the alias John Hill during these early meetings.[73] Reeves recalled Barber and Whitley well. "They were unquestionably the most dangerous couple in the gang. They mated well. Whitley didn't know what fear was."[74]

Like the others, the Whitley family, with the exceptions of Bill and his brother Jasper, whom we will hear about later, was made up of good people. Whitley's father, William Taylor Whitley, married Elizabeth Henry in Fayette County, Alabama, on January 30, 1869. By the time William Henry Whitley was born in Itawamba County, Mississippi, on September 7, 1864, the family had numerous children.[75] Four of the children died prior to the family's final move to Texas following the Civil War.[76] Wells Fargo described him as "5 feet 8 or 9 inches high; weight about 150; florid complexion; blonde hair; light colored moustache."[77]

Whitley was unique among the gang's members. He is the only member of the gang about whom a biography exists. While Whitley's biography is a commendable effort, the author based much of Whitley's life upon stories she heard as a child from her aunts who were children themselves when the events transpired. The book ascribes his turn to outlawry as having begun at a horse race in Coryell County. According to the stories, Jasper Whitley, an older brother of Bill, attended and won the horse race.[78] While heading home, Jasper rode ahead of the others. "Bill, who was seventeen years old, and several other boys rode along with a friend of Jasper's. The friend was upset about losing the race and called Jasper a son-of-a-bitch." According to this account, Bill told Jasper about the insult. Jasper then went to his friend's house and killed him. Jasper Whitley then went into hiding, and Bill and a friend took clothes and food to Jasper's hideout. Unbeknownst to them "a deputy sheriff followed them and shot and killed Jasper without giving him a chance to surrender. Bill and his friend swore they would get the deputy who killed Jasper."[79]

As with the Barber family story, there is a kernel of truth in this account, but the details became garbled over the years or, perhaps, were considered too sordid for a young woman to hear. The reality of the tale is more sordid. It began September 8, 1882. Jasper Whitley was in Palo Pinto where he encountered Peter Laughlin. Laughlin was foreman of a construction job and had taken a break to have a drink. Jasper Whitley offered to buy him one, but Laughlin politely declined. Whitley then drew his pistol to "make him drink." In the scuffle that ensued Laughlin disarmed Whitley. Jasper then drew his knife and stabbed Laughlin in the heart.[80] Jasper did not know Laughlin, and there was no insult to avenge. Jasper simply killed Laughlin in a drunken row.

Nor is the tale of Jasper Whitley's death correct. In late September 1882 Jasper and Bill Armstrong were overtaken by deputy sheriffs from Bosque County while stealing cattle in Tarrant County. The pair resisted and in the ensuing gunfight Jasper was killed outright and Armstrong wounded.[81]

Another product of this garbled tale is the assertion that Jasper's killer was later killed himself. "Bill Whitley heard that the law wanted him for the death of the deputy sheriff who had killed Jasper." According to the story Whitley believed his sister-in-law had done the killing. Despite attempts to get him to surrender voluntarily, Whitley refused.[82] Of course Whitley had no reason to surrender himself to anyone since no deputy had been killed in revenge for Jasper's death. Aside from this family story, there is no evidence that Bill Whitley made any attempt to avenge his brother. There is some truth underlying this tale linked to the Barber family story, but that came later.

The second circumstance separating Whitley from the others was that Whitley was not a wanted outlaw at the time. Bill

Whitley married Cordelia Lucinda Cox in Williamson County on December 14, 1883.[83] Their first child, Minnie Margaret "Eliza" Whitley, was born on November 18, 1884, in Bell County, Texas, followed by Temperance Alice "Tempie" on March 15, 1886. Family tradition recalls that Bill was a family man. "He loved and played with his girls more than a boy played with a pup."[84] Wells Fargo confirms his earlier honest life, noting that he "was driver of the mail hack between Cuero and Goliad."[85] Perhaps it was a combination of his own poor prospects and his growing family that put him on the outlaw trail, but it appears more likely that he fell prey to the slick tongue of John Barber, when they crossed paths, according to Whitley's granddaughter and biographer.[86] John Barber was persuasive, and Bill Whitley had been swayed. Ed Reeves recalled:

> He was a wonder. We looked upon him as the nerviest man of the gang. He would look straight into the muzzle of a six-shooter, expecting it to go off every minute, and wouldn't blink his eye. . . . Whitley had no nerves that I ever heard of. He swore that he wouldn't be taken alive, and we knew he was telling the truth.[87]

Brack Cornett

Perhaps Reeves was correct, but there is no doubt that Brack Cornett stood unchallenged at the summit of the gang, a violent, sadistic sociopath born Braxton E. Cornett on January 29, 1860, in Goliad County, Texas, to Laban E. Cornett and Cornett's second wife Cordelia Ann McGinty.[88] His first wife was Mary Elizabeth Wooten by whom he had three children: John William born December 13, 1851, Sarah born c. 1852, and Elizabeth Agnes born March 4, 1853. The couple separated, Mary taking the children with her. Later she married

William R. Mapes. It is unlikely that Brack Cornett ever met his half-siblings.

Why Laban and Mary separated is unknown, but Laban relocated to Texas where he married fourteen-year-old Cordelia Ann McGinty, literally, a child bride and thirteen years Laban's junior.[89] Brack Cornett was their first child, named for his uncle Braxton A. Cornett with whom he is sometimes confused.[90] Laban and Cordelia also had a daughter, Cordelia Lucretia, born on June 28, 1862.

At a casual glance Cornett appears similar to the others, but factually he was cut from a far different cloth. The late historian Jeff Burton, an acknowledged authority on train robbers, authored two papers on the Cornett-Whitley gang. Commenting on Cornett, Burton wrote that he "was neither the boldest nor the brightest among them—but he was certainly the meanest, and definitely the leader."[91] Raised in Goliad County during the bloody turbulence of the Sutton-Taylor War, Cornett seemingly had all the disadvantages a child could have.[92] Even before the death of his father Laban from pneumonia on January 5, 1870, his family and neighbors provided an education and example for Cornett, as if the Sutton-Taylor War was somehow lacking.[93] On November 2, 1866, his uncle Peter M. Miller was indicted for murder and livestock theft, the latter charges in company with James Patterson.[94] Patterson was also charged with horse theft in July 1867.[95] On November 5, 1866, his uncle Braxton A. Cornett was indicted for murder along with James P. Miller and A. McCarty.[96] Then too another of Brack Cornett's uncles, J. R. "Dock" Cornett, only nine years Brack's senior, was charged with the robbery of Seeligson's bank in Goliad during 1876.[97] All of them stepped up to help raise Brack Cornett, and by the age of eighteen Cornett had amassed an impressive criminal record of twelve indictments in Goliad County.[98]

Brack's earliest recorded run-in with the law came in 1878 when he and Steve Bell were captured while driving stolen horses.[99] Following a guilty plea, Cornett entered the penitentiary as convict 7141.[100] Bell also plead guilty and joined him as convict 7142.[101] Prison records describe Cornett as 5 feet 10 inches with blue eyes and light hair. He was unmarried and did not use tobacco.[102] Wells Fargo adds, "He is now about 30 years old; 5 feet 10 inches high; weight about 150 pounds; light sandy moustache; light brown hair; quick and active in his movements."[103]

A far more glamorous description is provided by the *Daily Globe-Democrat*. "He was of a decidedly handsome type—small, regular features; white, even teeth; keen, dark-blue eyes; light, curly hair, and sweeping golden mustaches. He was most elegantly proportioned, stood 5 feet 10 in his stockings, broad-shouldered and thin flanked, and was as lithe and graceful, as quick and strong in his movements as a panther. He was utterly devoid of fear, and was with the 6-shooter and rifle, the weapons of his boyhood and manhood, a phenomenal hand."[104] Less adoringly, another newspaper bluntly asserted that he was "the boldest and worst man in the gang."[105] One might add to that the fact that he was vicious and brutal.[106] Topping all of this with Cornett's sadistic tendencies provides a full portrait of Brack Cornett's less than sterling qualities.

Cornett proved difficult to hold. Dissatisfied with prison life, on December 6, 1878, he escaped from a chain gang. He was recaptured the same day after stealing Gus Walker's horse near Flatonia.[107] On November 27, 1880, the opportunity to escape arose again and he took it along with others of his ilk.[108] During 1888 it was reported that he and two other convicts had "fought and whipped a sheriff's posse," very likely at this time. No contemporary account of this fight has been located to date.[109]

Perhaps Cornett decided that honest work was now in order although the probability is slim. Using the alias Bill McGinty, his grandfather's name, Cornett brazenly took a job as a prison guard overseeing chain gangs working on the Union Pacific railroad. Law enforcement was less than amused, and when he was discovered he fled again.[110] Cornett migrated to south Texas and resumed his vocation of stealing horses, still using his grandfather's name as an alias. Here he ran a horse theft ring in conjunction with T. J. Hargrove.[111] Another report states that "Cornett stole fifty head of mules in one of the western counties."[112] It was probably around this time that Cornett made the acquaintance of Sion Secrest—usually called Charley Ross—who later brought him to the meeting in Karnes County.

Cornett was more than a simple stock thief. Allegations have been made that he killed several men. One of the victims specifically named is Gus Lewis in Atascosa County.[113] Lewis was killed on December 1, 1882, but Cornett's involvement is questionable.[114] One account states "One Lewis, supposed to have attempted to stop nine men, who escaped from the Atascosa county jail, was missed from home. His wife sent a young man to hunt him, and the body was found half a mile from his residence perforated with Winchester bullets."[115] Another paper reported, "A. M. Lewis a sheepman was found dead near Pleasonton on Monday. The supposition is that he was murdered by one of the men who escaped from the Atascosa County Jail a short time ago."[116] It has also been alleged that Cornett killed a man in Louisiana, but this has not been verified.[117] Still another report states he killed a wealthy stockman named Brown in Kansas and that Brown's relatives "made strenuous efforts to capture him."[118] There are other claims of murder as well, but at least one of them is provably false.

Cornett had lost his uncle Braxton A. Cornett prior to the gathering due to smallpox on January 22, 1886.[119] Considering the man, it is unlikely that he had grieved prior to his arrival at Butler's horse pasture in 1887. Secrest brought him to Karnes County where Ed Reeves first made his acquaintance.[120] Like

Secrest, Cornett sported an alias confirmed by Wells Fargo. "He is now known among his fellows as Bill Bradley; is an escaped convict, and has been 'dodging' for two or three years."[121] Cornett trusted none of the others, a fact confirmed by his numerous aliases, among them Harrington, Jones, George Lacy, and James W. Johnson.[122] Had anything been amiss at this meeting in his twisted mind Cornett had no reservations about killing to break free. Cornett was a brutal, psychopathic sadist whose indiscriminant, unprovoked violence inspired terror in both his victims and the rest of the gang.

These were the Cornett-Whitley gang. In later years Texas Ranger Ira Aten somewhat generously recalled that the gang "were just bad boys raised in that country, stole cattle when young, you know. And that wasn't big enough, they went to train robbing." He couched this recollection with the addendum "those were real bad men."[123] Aten was correct, but the Cornett-Whitley gang was different from the start. They would break all the rules and add their own savage, brutal twists to train robbing techniques doing as they damned well pleased. Within months they would achieve international prominence. To paraphrase the ancient prophets, they would become a plague upon the land.

Chapter 2

Demonic Laughter

They had not selected the mustang pen at Butler's on a whim. According to federal documents, there were others involved with the gang, among them the Harrell brothers Will and Eli, both employees of Newt Butler the land's owner.[1] Whitley's biographer states that the Harrell brothers were cousins of Bill Whitley, but such is not the case. Nor was the Harrell family near-kinsmen of the Horrells of Lampasas County.[2] Records indicate that William Carroll Harrell and his first wife, known only by the initials M. J., were in Gonzales County by 1860 arriving via Louisiana where the older Harrell listed his profession as stock raiser.[3] This changed during the 1860s, and in 1870 the forty-year-old Harrell gave his profession as "Minister of the Gospel."[4] It was not a career that his oldest two sons chose to follow.

William Carroll "Will" Harrell was born in 1858, younger brother Eli Y. following in 1861. By 1885 they had established reputations of their own. During a dance at the home of John McGraw, the Harrell brothers became engaged in a drunken quarrel with Harry Patton. Both of the Harrell brothers and

Patton were seriously wounded, and for a time their lives were feared for.[5]

As noted, the Harrell brothers were in the employ of the powerful Butler family. Following the shootout at McGraw's, the brothers were again involved in a violent confrontation, this time at Daileyville, Texas, that left three lawmen and two innocent bystanders dead.[6] Reeves makes no mention of the Harrell brothers being involved in the McNeil train robbery, but it appears probable that they provided a secure hideout for the men. Federal officials saw matters differently from Reeves, indicting the original seven gang members along with Will and Eli Harrell.[7] Nor was their employer, Newton Green Butler, innocent of involvement with the gang.

Butler had one advantage none of the others had. Born December 7, 1858, to William Green Butler and his wife Adeline Riggs Burris, Newton Green "Newt" Butler's father was the wealthiest landowner in Karnes County.[8] Writing of Newt Butler, one historian points out that he had troubles with the law "but they were nothing that daddy couldn't bail him out of."[9] The family as a whole had a violent history. Emmett Butler, a brother of Newt's, had killed Sheriff Edgar Leary while terrorizing Helena, Texas. Emmett was killed as he attempted to flee.[10] Newt Butler was charged with cattle theft in Atascosa County at the time.[11] He too was involved in the troubles at Daileyville during 1886 when five men were killed.

During the gathering at Butler's mustang pen, the gang decided on a common purpose: "We agreed at this time to rob the Sunset train at Flatonia" in southwestern Fayette County.[12] By the mid-1880s stage robbery in Texas had largely given way to a new criminal enterprise, train robbery, largely due to the fact that "the longer stage lines had been largely replaced by railroads."[13]

Around May 10, 1887, the outlaws descended upon Flatonia's graveyard. Barber, Whitley, and "Ross" (Secrest's name most of the time) came together by way of Cuero, meeting at the graveyard as planned. The plan was thwarted by a freight train that passed at nearly the same time. Concerned that they would stop the wrong train, the attempt was abandoned. The men camped overnight then split up, Cornett and Whitley heading out, followed a short time later by Powell. Barber and Reeves paired up as did Ross and Cloud.[14]

Train robbery was a relatively new but not unknown crime for Texas, but in the east where the railroads had been established for some time it was far more common. While credit is generally given to the Reno brothers for the first post-Civil War train robbery in the United States, indefatigable historian Rick Miller determined that a train was robbed in January 1866 between New York and New Haven, Connecticut.[15] Miller notes, "this has not been acknowledged as a 'bona fide' train robbery."[16]

It was not until October 6, 1866, that John and Simeon Reno, accompanied by Frank Sparkes, boarded the Ohio and Mississippi Railway train as it left the depot in Seymour, Indiana. The haul netted the gang roughly $16,000.[17] While these robberies were nonviolent, in 1873 the James-Younger gang deliberately wrecked the train near Adair, Iowa, killing both the engineer and fireman. The outlaws netted roughly $2,000.[18] In Texas noted outlaw Sam Bass had worked the railroads during 1878.[19] In the 1880s noted train robber Eugene Bunch embarked on his own train robbing career while living in Texas although he confined himself to trains in Mississippi and Louisiana.[20] In north Texas Rube Burrow and his gang had successfully robbed a train at Bellevue in Clay County on December 11, 1886. Burrow followed this up with another robbery at the Gordon depot in Palo Pinto County on January 23, 1887.[21]

In one sense the railroads had drawn trouble on themselves. At the time railroad companies generally served as a symbol of capitalism that forced ranchers and farmers to cede land and right-of-ways to them. In the public mind there was something glamorous about armed men overcoming a powerful locomotive, and robbing an express company was viewed as a crime against a corporation. Texas was then in transition, parts of it still the wild frontier while the eastern region had a flowering economy due in part to the railroads who improved commerce.

In general two techniques were employed by train robbers. If there were only a few outlaws, they concentrated on the express car. The men would board the train, overpower the agents in charge, and pilfer the car before dropping off the train. This was the technique employed by the Reno brothers and Frank Sparkes in Indiana. If the gang was large enough, the train was halted and both the express car and passengers robbed as the James brothers did near Adair, Iowa. The latter was more difficult as the larger number made their trail easier to follow and generated more witnesses who could identify them.[22]

The key to a successful holdup was controlling the train. The violent means used by the James gang were the exception. Generally the outlaws were out for plunder, not a wholesale massacre that could trigger not only legal but extralegal vigilante vengeance as did the Gage train robbery of 1883 near Silver City, New Mexico. The outlaws managed to successfully derail the train without killing anyone, but then opened fire, killing the engineer needlessly. Two members of the gang were summarily lynched.[23]

Typically gangs halted the trains by barricading the tracks and flagging them so the crew would halt. This was the tactic used by the gang responsible for Samuels train robbery near Horseshoe Bend in west Texas in 1891.[24] While this gang was swiftly run to ground by the Texas Rangers under the command of Frank Jones, others were not.[25]

The Cornett-Whitley gang's original plan was nothing new, using techniques perfected by others in the preceding twenty years. Some of the men were to wave torches at the passenger train so that the engineer would stop at the next station where Cornett, Whitley, and Reeves would board the engine.

Fayette County was unaware of their close brush with history. Newspapers provide no indication that the gang was noticed. In LaGrange the Fayette County prohibition convention met on May 8.[26] On the eighteenth of May the unsuspecting "citizens of Flatonia" entered into a contract with the San Antonio and Aransas Pass Railroad Company "to build their line to Flatonia."[27] One newspaper noted that a "contract has been signed by which the Aransas Pass Road agrees to go by Flatonia on its way to Waco."[28] Fayette County was booming, or appearing to. "Booming towns on all sorts of pretexts and denouncing men who have money for not putting it into all kinds of rash enterprises is now the rage of newspapers and public-spirited citizens who are ever ready to do the wind work in public affairs," the *Galveston Daily News* wisely commented, adding:

> The La Grange people got to running Uncle Tom Menafee a little too hard the other day, bantering him to take shares or make subscriptions to street railroad, manufactories, poor-houses, etc., all for the good of the city. He quietly remarked that he would subscribe to one thing—"to fence in the city and call it an insane asylum and keep all the La Grange folks inside it."[29]

The gang departed peacefully, and everything remained calm. Fayette County's luck would not hold, however. Like locusts, the gang would return. For the moment they came away from the aborted holdup with only one thing: a plan for another train robbery.

One contemporary newspaper account describes McNeil Station as "a nominal place. There is a depot and the next building is a farm house, a quarter of a mile distant. It would be a stretch of courtesy to call it a hamlet, and indeed none of the Williamson county rustics that occasionally stray there, do call it so. The country round about is broken and brush covered, very sparsely inhabited and affords every facility for the business that night transacted."[30] McNeil Station served as a crossroad for the Missouri-Pacific Railroad and a small narrow-gauge railroad that ran to Burnet and Marble Falls that was used to transport red granite blocks to the capitol building then under construction. The passenger line conveyed passengers, mail, and express company funds from San Antonio to Dallas. Isolated as it was, there was small chance of outside interference, and it was this very isolation that drew the gang's attention. From their perspective it was a good choice.

Following the aborted Flatonia robbery, John Barber suggested that the gang move north and rob the train at McNeil Station. On May 15, 1887, the outlaws rendezvoused on the west side of the tracks near the crossing. Here the outlaws took stock of their situation and prepared for the robbery. Some of their horses were "rode down" and on the morning of May 16 Barber and Cornett rode to the home of Barber's brother Joel to obtain fresh mounts.[31]

Joel Barber, commonly called "Joe," had married Attie Lee Swinney on December 25, 1879, in Williamson County.[32] Joe Barber was both a farmer and a solid family man with four young children at the time of John's unwelcome arrival with Cornett.[33] No indication has been located that Joe Barber had been in any serious difficulty prior to this, but younger brother John would soon change all that. Joe was not at home when John and Cornett arrived, which was fortunate, for the brothers were not on good terms. Here the outlaws exchanged the spent horses for two fresh mounts.[34] Barber also took the opportunity to visit his pregnant sister, Attia Hunt, who made a lunch for the men.[35] While Barber and Cornett were absent, Cloud and Powell left to visit some of Cloud's family, probably Barbara Emily Cloud Mitchell.[36]

All of the outlaws returned to their camp on May 17. Along the way Barber and Cornett stopped to eat the lunch Barber's sister prepared for them. The meal was wrapped in a piece of newspaper with the name of their father, Isaac Barber, on it, and the men thoughtlessly discarded the paper after they finished eating. When they returned, Cloud and Reeves rode to a nearby shepherd's home. After they had eaten, the pair asked if the family could cook some bread for them. The family was unprepared to cook and advised them to go to the section house where bread would be available without waiting.[37]

On May 18 the gang tied their mounts southwest of the station and finalized their plans. It was a dark night, the moon was waning midway between the third quarter and a new moon.[38] Secrest walked to the station to learn when the train would arrive, returning with the news that the train was due in the next fifteen or twenty minutes. It was around 9:45 in the evening, and Brack Cornett led the gang as they moved towards the station.[39]

Unaware of their approach, railroad agent Samuel R. Ely was attending to his duties in the station.[40] With Ely was J. B. Rickett, a geologist from Birmingham, Alabama, who was waiting to take the train.[41] Both men were caught by surprise as the outlaws entered with guns drawn.[42] Reeves described what happened as a simple heist. "When we reached the station house we threw our pistols on the agent and passenger (Mr. Riggles), Cornett broke the telegraph instrument and robbed Riggles of a gold watch, chain and charm."[43] The outlaws robbed Ely of sixty-five cents, but the station attendant's luck held for the moment. "He had $256 in another pocket, but the robber got his hand in the wrong one."[44] Rickett was less fortunate losing not only his watch and chain, but $150 he had on him.[45]

Contemporary accounts provide a darker picture than Reeves's sanitized version of the robbery. After Cornett smashed the telegraph instrument, the gang cut the telegraph wires. The train had not yet arrived, and the outlaws felt the need for amusement. The "robbers laid hold of the operator and shoved him around apparently for mere fun," the bullying broken by "occasional demonic laughter." Shoving the helpless agent around was apparently not enough for one of the gang, probably Brack Cornett, who abruptly drew his pistol "and hit the luckless lightning slinger a blow over the head, which did not quite fell him to the floor, but stunned and made him see sparks."[46] Fortunately for Ely the outlaws heard the train's approach, and whatever further frivolity the outlaws intended was abruptly cut off. Minutes later the train pulled into the station. Cornett and Barber swiftly covered the engine while Secrest pulled cross ties onto the tracks.

Driving the train was thirty-seven-year-old, Irish-born William Glidden.[47] The fireman with him in the cab is identified in contemporary accounts simply as Spangler but probably was Samuel H. Spangler, aged twenty-nine.[48] Along with Ely and Rickett the men were herded off toward the smoker car.

Contemporary accounts of the robbery vary. According to at least one news release, none of the outlaws wore masks. Another stated that all of them wore masks. Still other reports state that some of the gang wore masks but the leader did not.[49] Ely later described them simply as "border ruffians."[50] Most reports at the time claimed that from thirteen to twenty men were involved in the McNeil Station train robbery, and that is the information carried in the exchanges to non-Texas newspapers.[51] Considering the antics that unfolded, the time and the astronomical conditions, this error is understandable in retrospect. The most reliable account was and remains that of Ely and Rickett who stated that they were alone "when they were waited on by a deputation of an even half-dozen strangers."[52] Few if any of the train crew or passengers were in a position to make an accurate count.

The first man on the train to encounter the outlaws was the train's porter, William Cook. The unsuspecting Cook clambered down from the train and "went ahead, as usual, to flag the train over the crossing." Abreast of the baggage car he encountered Ely and Rickett followed by Ed Reeves who had his pistol drawn. Reeves ordered Cook back onto the train. Undaunted, Cook, believing Reeves was a tramp, was having none of it. Reeves cursed and struck him, and the angry Cook "clinched" with Reeves, who fired at the porter, very likely in conjunction with Ike Cloud who was also on the east side of the train.[53]

Because Cook was a black man, his valor was both questioned and derided by some of the media. According to J. S. Woods, a "helper" in the postal car, Cook encountered all of the outlaws "a short distance in advance of the engine." In fairness Woods obtained this information second hand, stating that all of the gang opened fire on Cook who "ran back, crying out as he did so: 'Don't shoot! Don't shoot! I'm not a convict,' evidently supposing the mob to be a party in search of escapes." Woods confirmed the hearsay stating candidly that he was in the postal car tying a package at the time.[54] Ed Reeves also refuted the account of the fleeing porter and confirmed bluntly that he had "a tussle" with Cook.[55] After Reeves fired, Cook broke away and prudently scrambled under the car to the west side of the train pursued by an angry Reeves who crossed the car's platform. Here Cook again "clinched with him, and after quite a scuffle got loose from him, blew out his lantern and escaped back into the cars."[56]

Cook provided his version of the events much later. "I met the operator and a man coming toward me, and behind them a man with a pistol; he ordered me to go back; I said I wouldn't, and he cursed me and threatened to kill me; he struck me, still ordering me to go back; I clinched with him, but got away from him and got back," adding "I was abreast of the baggage car when I was stopped; the mail car was in front of this car."[57]

Conductor W. E. Hawkins saw Cook scuffling with Reeves and another man "and started towards them with my pistol in my hand." He was swiftly intercepted by a man armed with a Winchester, either Powell or Whitley, who ordered him to drop his pistol. Hawkins complied but the cocked pistol discharged "and he fired at me. I retreated and as I did so, was fired at again." Who fired at Hawkins is uncertain, but from circumstantial evidence available the likely shooter appears to have been Whitley.[58]

Hawkins was not the only man aiming for the front of the train. Brakeman C. D. Walker was also confronted by one of the outlaws. The feisty Walker "smashed him in the face with his lantern. Thereupon the robber shot at him, the ball striking just over the brakeman's eye, not hurting him much, but the war ceased right there."[59]

Media of the day generally credit the shot fired at Cook as opening the fusillade that followed, but it is more likely that the combined shooting from various points triggered it.[60] Startled by the sudden shots, passengers started leaning out of the cars to see what was happening. Hawkins recalled that the robbers, whom he believed numbered ten or twelve, "kept yelling at the passengers to keep their heads in the car, and now and then firing their guns off."[61] The gunfire appears to have been more to indulge their violent natures rather than for mere intimidation. Woods testified flatly that it was "indiscriminate."[62] The *Galveston Daily News* referred to it as "promiscuous."[63] At least one of the outlaws recognized it as well, shouting, "don't shoot any of our own men."[64]

In the postal car, clerk S. R. Spaulding and Woods were working when a bullet fired by John Barber crashed through the car. Woods was "tying up a package, and had just leaned to one side to get a knife with which to cut the string. While in this position a bullet crashed through the side of the car and whistled past me; I should say within four inches of my face. Had I been standing erect I would have been in direct line of the shot, and would have caught it in my head."[65] Charles W.

White, of Waco, claimed that "about 100 shots" were fired "into the coaches to help keep up the quietness of the passengers," which qualifies it as promiscuous and implies that at least some of the outlaws needed to reload to continue the fusillade.[66]

Austin resident Oliver Brush, travelling with Sherman Drake to California, also had a close call.[67] In a letter to his brother George from Fort Worth, Oliver stated in part that he was talking with Charles White when the shooting began.

> Only one man got shot; he was in the sleeper; the ball went through the top of his left hand and out through the window on the opposite side above the washstand. I was sitting on the washstand until I went in to see Charlie.[68]

The luckless passenger was Harry Landa.[69] Diverse accounts of how Landa was wounded exist. One report states that Landa was sleeping "in a coach with his arm out of the window. The robbers believing he had a pistol in his hand ordered him to take his hand in. He did not hear them and they began firing, shooting him in the hand."[70] Landa himself told reporters that when he heard the shots he "raised his window and looked out, when an order was given him to draw his head back and close the window. Before he had time to comply he was wounded in the arm and badly powder burned by a shot fired in close proximity."[71] Another report added that Landa "was a little slow in obeying the order, and the next second a bullet struck his hand, tearing it open between the wrist and knuckles. He dodged just in time to miss another one that would doubtless have plowed through his head." Reeves was unsure who shot Landa but believed it was either Bud Powell or Bill Whitley.[72] Even in the dim light of the waning moon, it would have been clear that Landa did not have a weapon at point-blank range. As noted, none of the passengers or train crew was in a position to accurately count the attackers. Between thirty and one hundred shots were fired into the cars and the passengers prudently took cover on the floor.[73]

Luckier than others, R. H. Arnold of Carson County, Texas, told reporters that he had an "intimate acquaintance with the border and personal contact with that class of citizens supposed to be 'tough.' " Arnold was in the smoker as the train came to a stop and "a volley of pistol shots rang out. Thinking that maybe it was a lot of the boys having a little frolic, as I've seen 'em occasionally at Mobeetie, Tascosa, and other towns of the breezy west. I jumped off to the ground on the side farthest from the depot, to watch proceedings a minute." He immediately spotted Cornett, Reeves, and Secrest by the express car, realized the train was being robbed and started to retreat, "two or three bullets that came whizzing along my way emphasized the importance of rapid motion." As he retreated he ran into another one of the outlaws, who was very likely Ike Cloud based on his armament and position, pistol drawn, who ordered him back onto the train. Arnold prudently did not argue and boarded the sleeper.

> By this time all the passengers on the sleeper, most of whom were women, were keenly alive to the realities of the episode. Most of the ladies were terror stricken, and not a few of the men turned several shades whiter. Then the hiding of money and valuables began. But the preservation of property was soon lost sight of in the first law of nature—the preservation of existence itself. The sleeper was at that moment surrounded by the bandits, who began firing indiscriminately through the car. That was the most exciting time. The passengers, men and women, prostrated themselves along the aisle and hid under the seats. Some of the ladies cried and one fainted.

Reportedly another passenger futilely attempted to locate a pistol to fight the outlaws.[74]

While the passengers were under siege, the outlaws moved on the express car. Express messenger A J. Northacker, realizing what was happening, locked the express car's door.[75] Cornett and Reeves initially missed the express car and accosted Spaulding and Woods in the mail coach. The men pointed the proper car out to them. Secrest demanded to know if they had any registers handy, but the others quickly intervened. "We don't want to run against Uncle Sam; we just want to tap Jay Gould a little bit." One account adds that Cornett took the clerk's hat and gave it to Reeves who had lost his in the tussle with Cook.[76] Another newspaper quotes a dialogue demonstrating that Reeves himself demanded the hat and some tobacco from Spaulding:

"Any tobacker, pard?"

"Nary a scrumption, don't chaw, specially at such times as this."

"Damn you, get me a chaw anyhow, and gimme that hat of yours. I've just lost mine," said the bandit.

The hat and tobacco were both forthcoming.[77]

At the express car Northacker refused to open the door even after several shots were fired into it. Secrest broke down the door, and Cornett and Reeves stormed in. When Northacker attempted to resist, Cornett hit him on the head with his pistol. An angry Cornett wanted to kill Northacker, but Reeves's intervention prevented the murder.[78] "The leader of the crowd, a tall, slender man, with light whiskers that looked in the dim light to be a false beard, ordered the door to be broken open, which was done, and a portion of the gang jumped into the car, striking the messenger over the head with their pistols as they did so."[79] Their success in entering the car put the outlaws in good frame of mind, "and while getting their booty laughed and talked."[80]

Charles White later stated that Northacker informed him that he either would not or could not tell him the amount the outlaws seized from the train. According to White, Northacker told him, "When I saw the fellow start out with the silver, which was a bulky package, I thought I was safe, but when they returned and commenced looking for the currency I knew it was all up with me."[81] Woods added that "the tall man" whom he believed was the leader stopped at the mail car and demanded an empty mail pouch. One of the others swiftly protested that "If we take anything out of that car we might as well take all of it, that's United States mail."

It was probably this lack of a means to transfer their plunder that led Northacker to comment that they were likely "green hands" at train robbing.[82] Experienced robbers would have brought something to carry their loot. White, on the other hand, believed they "understand their business very thoroughly."[83]

With their booty secured, the outlaws removed the barricade and ordered the train to pull out. They waited at the station until the last car had passed before retrieving their mounts and fleeing the scene. The entire robbery had taken around a half hour.[84] The outlaws rode west half a mile where they built a fire and hurriedly divided the money. If Reeves's recollection is correct, the gang netted somewhere between $5,000 and $6,000. Then the gang split up after agreeing to meet back at Butler's pasture. Barber and Whitley, who had hit it off, headed for Joe Barber's home. Secrest and Cloud paired off aiming for Kerrville while Cornett, Powell, and Reeves headed east.[85]

In later years Ira Aten recalled how he and U. S. Marshal John Rankin might well have put an end to the gang before they truly got started.

> One night the train was robbed there four miles below Round Rock, and the joke was, it was the very night

> I was going to Austin. John Rankin, United States Marshal at San Antonio came up on the train with me. I was a deputy U. S. Marshal under him. He said, "Come and go with me, Aten," and I says, "No, I have to stop in Austin." And he said he would stop, too.
>
> That very train was robbed at McNeil.

Aten continued that if he and Rankin had been on the train "we would have had a fight because those were real bad men." Almost regretfully he concluded that they would have had the "time of our lives."[86]

Aten accurately assessed both the gang and his might-have-been partner. At the time of the holdup Aten was an experienced lawman.[87] Illinois-born, coincidentally Aten was raised at Abingdon, Illinois, within miles of where twentieth-century creation Wyatt Earp, contrary to the heroic versions of him popular among revisionist historians, "was already treading the crooked road of criminality."[88] The Aten family relocated to Texas in 1876, and in 1883 he enlisted in Company D of the Texas Rangers.[89] In 1886 Aten killed outlaw Wes Collier, and was recruiting John R. Hughes, later named as one of the Four Great Captains.[90]

Aten was a good judge of character, and John Taylor Rankin was no exception. Rankin's first clash with violence came at a dance in 1869 when Walter Holt killed his brother Patten H. Rankin.[91] On February 26, 1875, Rankin married Olivia Perkins. In 1882 he was elected sheriff of Fayette County. The following year he captured Dick King in Mexico. King had been involved in the murder of one Dietrich Mueller ten years earlier.[92] He served as sheriff until 1886 when he was appointed U. S. Marshal for the western district of Texas. By all accounts, Rankin was a fine U. S. Marshal.

For veteran career lawmen such as Aten and Rankin, there were clear signs at the McNeil train robbery, portents of things to come. The bullying and pistol-whipping of Ely was gratuitous, violence indulged in for its own sake. As a whole the gang was trigger happy, firing several promiscuous volleys into the train.[93] The outlaws did not care if anyone was hurt or killed. Nor did the bandits shoot high to frighten the passengers. Rather, the gang fired at a height where someone could easily have been killed, as the experiences of Woods, Brush, and Landa demonstrate. Landa was not hit by a stray bullet. Given that his hand was powder burned it is unlikely that the man who shot him thought he had a pistol, and the shot fired into the window immediately afterwards was not simply to intimidate Landa. Nor was the shot that nearly killed Walker a stray bullet. Rather the gang was announcing what they were: brutal, sadistic, brazen, and violent. Experienced lawmen recognized the symptoms, obscure as they were. Not everyone did, however, the media among them.

Chapter 3

The Headwaters of Ugly Creek

While the outlaws made their escape, the train continued to Taylor where Sheriff John Olive of Williamson County was immediately notified by telegraph.[1] Olive, no stranger to man-hunting, responded swiftly "and in a few hours he and his deputies, with the bloodhounds were on the spot of the robbery."[2] Prior to the McNeil Station robbery, Olive had served as a deputy sheriff before being elected sheriff of Williamson County in 1884 and being reelected in 1886. Another telegram reached Austin at about 10:30 p.m. from where a "large posse of sheriffs, officers of the city police and Federal marshals left about midnight last night on the special train, taking their horses with them."[3] The posse was led by Austin City Marshal James E. Lucy.

The anger and humiliation that the McNeil Station train robbery caused is incalculable. State Attorney General James Stephen Hogg was reportedly "exasperated."[4] Nor was he the only one, for the *Austin Statesman* reported on the delay in the posse's departure from Austin that:

> A crowd was speedily gathered, but some delay was experienced in getting horses, and a still further delay in obtaining Winchesters. Application was made to the adjutant general's office, but Captain Seiker [*sic*] declined to furnish the weapons, it is said, alleging, as a reason, that the state had already lost so many guns by loaning them out that he did not feel warranted in complying with Captain Lucy's request. This necessitated the troublesome work of getting arms from private parties, but at length the posse got off, about 12 o'clock.[5]

This story was fake, or at best highly garbled, news. Sieker had done nothing to warrant the insult, nor would he allow the charge to remain unanswered.[6] Sieker could honestly claim that Texas Rangers who knew him would verify his "honor, sobriety, honesty, and valor, also my perfect willingness to discharge every duty put upon me."[7] That Sieker had served with distinction is beyond question, as was his inevitable response to the *Statesman*'s inaccurate account. Exactly what was said is unknown, but the *Statesman* wasted no time in correcting their account. "In the report yesterday morning, it was stated that Captain Sieker, of the adjutant general's office, had refused to loan guns to the posse. This does an injustice to that officer, who states that he did not furnish the guns because he did not have them. His remark to Captain Lucy was that the state had loaned out so many guns and never got them back, that she was now without any to loan."[8]

The two posses converged on McNeil Station from opposite directions. Austin City Marshal James E. Lucy's posse consisted of United States Marshal John R. Rankin, Deputy Sheriff Sam Platt, and Sergeant Palmer, and Officers Rundell,

Gissoway, Jake Platt, Anglin, Bracken, Montgomery, and Walter Robinson. Sheriff Malcolm M. Hornsby of Travis County was too ill to accompany them.[9] With Sheriff Olive's posse was Georgetown City Marshal C. J. Brady and telegraph operator J. B. Shea.[10] The railroad sent a special train to Hearne to obtain the loan of Colonel Charles Lewis's pack of "famous bloodhounds" to assist in the chase. The dogs arrived around 11 a.m. on May 19, and while they were able to pick up the scent initially, the trail was far too cold for their effective use.[11]

The trail was followed to where the gang had divided their loot. Lawmen at first believed that the outlaws had turned west toward Burnet County, the general direction that Cloud and Secrest had taken. Then they discovered a trail heading east towards the Yegua bottom, a heavily wooded area that "furnishes plenty of timber for hiding." One newspaper boasted confidently, "Whatever way they went it is not probable they will long elude the vigilance of the officers."[12]

On May 20 Attorney General Hogg left for Round Rock in Williamson County "with his stenographic clerk, accompanied by County Attorney Barnhart, Justice Calhoun and Constable Thorp."[13] Here he and District Attorney Robinson (or Robertson) provided assistance in working up the case.[14] Very likely they were gathering statements from those that they could before the memories faded, and while Hogg's personal appearance may have amounted to overkill, it was a sound investigative technique. In Austin Adjutant General Wilburn H. King remained in his office late into the night, but there was no news concerning the robbers.[15] The news media, describing Hogg's reactions, poked a bit of gentle chiding at his personal involvement. "If Gen. Hogg had been in office here as long as Gen. King, he would have learned to take such incidents as the train robbery at McNeil more serenely."[16]

The two posses rounded up three or four locals, but all of those detained proved an alibi and were swiftly released.[17] The first real break in the case came when a Lee County farmer told authorities that he had seen "a gang of men riding at a trot about 2 a.m. on the morning after the robbery about twenty miles from the scene." Two of the outlaws' horses were "ridden down" and abandoned by the outlaws.[18] Later in the day another farmer spotted Cornett, Reeves, and Powell and tried to catch up with them. The outlaws increased the speed of their mounts to keep a safe distance from him.[19]

The officers trailed Cornett, Reeves, and Powell down Brushy Creek to the Yegua River bottom some forty miles from the scene of the robbery, but hopes for their capture had dimmed. The *Waco Daily Examiner* reported that "once safe in the Yegua bottom their arrest will be almost an impossibility."[20] The fugitives knew it as well. Marshal James Lucy informed one reporter that "the pursuit had been carried over hills and through thickets into the Brushey bottom. They cut fences as they went along, and led their pursuers a merry chase, finally eluding them in the density of the Yegua thickets." Three miles from the bottom they lost the fugitives.[21] The *Waco Daily Examiner* knew the region well. "The Yegua lands are very favorable to concealment, being covered with chaparral and dense Yapon growth all interlaced with briars and threaded with a labyrinth of paths, the region being vast and possessed of limitless opportunity to persons familiar with its intricasies [*sic*] as are these robbers, no doubt."[22]

In Austin the excitement was intense and rumors spread freely. One rumor was that a fight had occurred between the outlaws and their pursuers in which Sheriff John Olive was killed.[23] Another was that one of the outlaws had been left "mortally sick" in a cabin on Brushy Creek.[24] Still another rumor was that "the bandit chief who gave his orders to the gang at McNeil with such coolness and in such tone of accustomed command was none other than the celebrated Frank James. The chief foundation for this belief is that it was announced some time ago that James was coming to reside in North Texas."[25] It was also rumored that the robbers had apparently known of another train: "the day before the robbery about $300,000 came down the road. It is supposed it was that that the outlaws were after, but missed it by a day, and pounced upon the other train as the next best thing."[26] None of them were true, and as the posses returned empty handed to their homes, the disappointment of the media was evident. They had anticipated that the outlaws would be crushed "within the folds of a great anaconda. There are officers in the pursuing party who are artists at man hunting."[27] Instead, the posses had failed to capture any of the outlaws and the press who had foolishly predicted a crushing blow was left with the proverbial egg on their faces and an anger that it had happened, not at their own foolish predictions but at the law's "incompetence" in capturing the gang.

What the news media failed to note was that despite the outlaws having significant advantages, James Lucy and John Oliver had organized a remarkably coordinated effort by law enforcement at the federal, state, and local level in combination with private entities. Officers had drawn together in the proverbial brotherhood of the shield disregarding where their local authority ended to ensure the safety of the citizens and apprehend the gang.

The press had bragged on these lawmen only days earlier. Now they changed their collective fickle tune. The *Austin Statesman* noted in part that the robbery created a big sensation "which is considered the more funny because it occurred under the very nose of the state government."[28] Under the headline "Train Robbers" another wrote:

> Lone Star State—All train robbers will please disband and follow some lawful pursuit.

> Train Robbers—Not much we won't; we are well organized and have the power; we intend to go right along with our business; we have got you.
>
> Railroad Superintendent—Boys, this is all wrong; you ought to be ashamed of yourselves for stopping our trains and robbing our passengers.
>
> Train Robbers—What are you kicking about; just stopping a train a few moments? That's nothing; we don't hurt you, and don't intend to. All we do is to rob passengers and express. You let us alone and we will let you alone.[29]

Adding to this, northern newspapers wired their correspondents "to send full particulars of the robbery."[30] The McNeil heist made national headlines from coast to coast. *The Daily Northwestern* in Oshkosh, Wisconsin, published the exaggerated claim that the outlaws had captured between $21,000 and $55,000.[31] Still another newspaper placed the haul at around $12,000.[32] In Los Angeles one reporter raged, "The robbers are supposed to be new hands at the business, and yet they got away with the booty. If trains can be brought to a halt and the robbers get away with the sack as easily as they have been doing lately, we shall look to see the stage gentry transfer their attention from mountain roads and mud wagons to the lonely plains where the iron horse drags behind him the treasures of transcontinental commerce."[33] Still another newspaper heralded the robbery under the banner "Wednesday Night's Train Robbery in Texas a Success."[34] In Indiana *The Daily Journal* reported that "One Hundred Shots Fired into the Coaches to Make the Passengers Keep Quiet."[35] It is no surprise that the Texas newspapers carried the story, but the exchanges catapulted it across the country.[36]

One of those who did not care about the gang's rise to national prominence was Harry Landa, who was shot during the holdup. Originally it was believed that Landa's wound was not serious, and he got off the train at Taylor to return to San Antonio on May 19.[37] Here physicians determined that amputation of several fingers was necessary. Rumors soon spread that he was thought to be dying.[38] One newspaper reported that Landa's hand was amputated.[39] On May 21 it was reported that Landa was doing well but there was still a danger of lockjaw.[40] Landa survived the ordeal.

Samuel Ely likely did not care either. The operator survived his ordeal more or less intact, most of his money being overlooked.[41] Doubtless the train's crew considered themselves fortunate that the trigger-happy outlaws had not killed them. Express messenger A. J. Northacker, reportedly was "weak from the loss of blood and the effects of the blows" he received from Cornett and Reeves, but he survived.[42]

The railroad and express company immediately offered a reward of "$500 for the arrest and conviction of each of the robbers."[43] Governor Ross was not far behind issuing a proclamation of "$500 per head for their capture."[44] Governor Ross was as angry as Hogg. Since Rube Burrow and his gang had robbed a train at Bellevue on December 11, 1886, two more train robberies, including McNeil Station, had taken place and none of them had been solved. The press wasted no opportunity to chastise law enforcement and the government, and the Adjutant General King was irritated. He called Aten to his office, and in later years Aten recalled:

> I was there in Austin and the Adjutant General told me to take the trail of these men and get them.
>
> I went and saw John Hughes and asked him if he would go with me. He wasn't a Ranger yet, but he went with me. We trailed them through Lampasas and out to the edge of the trail, then back over toward Corsicana.[45]

This assignment may well have prompted the *Fort Worth Gazette* to report, "It is understood that the whole police machinery of the state will be put in motion to catch them."[46]

The string of successful train robberies wore thin on the public, or at least upon the press who used them as their catspaw, and "questions were asked about when the robbers would be caught." Whether the questions originated with the public or a petulant press is uncertain.[47] What is certain is that public officials felt the pressure to apprehend the robbers. The pressure, provided by the media, combined with their own sense of civic responsibility and, not unnaturally, their pride and desire to be reelected. Rewards were offered, and Adjutant General King had dispatched Ira Aten, his "go to" Ranger, in pursuit. Aten had his own favorite and solicited John R. Hughes, who was not a Ranger at the time but would become one of the four great captains, to join him in the pursuit.[48] Federal U. S. Marshal John R. Rankin and his deputies were also on the hunt although the outlaws in all accounts had avoided touching the United States mail. J. S. Woods stated that the "tall man, the leader" had "stopped at the door of the mail car and demanded an empty mail pouch, but another of the robbers remarked: 'If we take anything out of that car we might as well take all of it, that's United States mail.'"[49]

The gang's mistake was that while they did not molest the mail, they did, despite the warning voiced by one of them, rob the postal clerk. Woods testified that "One of them asked me for a chew of tobacco, and made me give him my hat, saying he had lost his own.[50] It was more than enough, and on April 27, 1888, federal indictments were finally filed for John Barber, Ed Reeves, Bud Powell, Brack Cornett, Ike Cloud, Will Whitley, and "Charley Ross" (Secrest) as the perpetrators, throwing in Joe Barber, Eli Harrell, and Will Harrell for good measure.[51]

With the alarm raised, a posse started for McNeil Station from Austin under the leadership of Austin City Marshal James

E. Lucy, an experienced, career lawman. He had served under Texas Ranger Jesse Lee Hall from July 15 through August 31, 1877, then enlisted under Captain Dan Roberts in Company D of the Texas Rangers, serving from 1877 through 1880.[52] Accompanying Lucy were a host of lawmen from different backgrounds including U. S. Marshal John Rankin, Deputy Sheriff Sam Platt, "Sergeant Palmer and Officers Rundell, Gissoway, Jake Platt, Angling [*sic*: Anglin], Bracken, Montgomery and Walter Robinson."[53]

John Olive sent to Hearne for a pack of bloodhounds to help trail the fugitives, but the dogs did not reach McNeil Station until the trail was far too cold for the dogs to catch their scent.[54] Several local men were arrested on suspicion. All of them quickly proved alibis and were released.[55] Despite these initial setbacks, the press confidently predicted the speedy arrest of the outlaws. As if in response, arrests were forthcoming within days. On May 21, Sheriff Olive arrested Joe Barber at his home.[56] His suspicion was not unfounded. Joe Barber, rightly or wrongly, was believed to be part of his younger brother's gang.[57] These charges have never been proven, but the stigma brought by John Barber remained with Joe throughout his life. Barber's arrest was uneventful. John Olive later testified that "When I arrested him he was trying to catch a horse in the field. He had a mare saddled just outside the fence." He further testified that the horse in the field looked as if it had been ridden hard.[58]

This was not the first time that John Barber had caused trouble for his family. Inevitably reckless in his actions, Barber was considered responsible for luring his brother Austin into trouble for horse theft in 1886. The clemency petition for Austin Barber states bluntly, "Your petitioners are informed and believe that the said Austin Barber committed the offenses aforementioned under the influence of his older brother, who has escaped punishment, the said Austin Barber being quite young at the time of the commission of the offense."[59] Austin Calloway Barber, born January 8, 1859, in Burnet County, Texas, had married Ida Elizabeth Stapp in Lampasas on May 18, 1882.[60] In 1886 he was convicted of "unlawfully, fraudulently branding a horse" in Burnet County. Austin Barber entered Huntsville Penitentiary as convict 4259 on December 10, 1886, leaving his wife with two young children.[61]

Austin Barber's problems did not end with his discharge in 1891. A month later he was arrested for theft of a horse in Williamson County—the very animal he had been convicted for in 1886. Fortunately for Barber, executive clemency was sought and obtained by the citizens of Burnet and Williamson County.[62] When the matter was finally cleared, Austin Barber prudently moved his family to California where he died on December 7, 1930, at Sacramento.

Nor were the unwanted attentions of John Barber confined to his family. In later years rancher John Henry "Jack" Juby informed Ernest Langford that whenever Barber and Whitley rode up to Mr. Juby "they would get off their horses and engage him in conversation. They were constantly on the alert, looking this way and that, knowing that they were wanted men." Juby recalled that on one occasion his horse strayed away with its saddle on. Barber and Whitley offered to find the mount for him and did. Juby offered to pay them but they refused. Later Juby was summoned before the grand jury in Burnet and "questioned at length about his associations with Barber and Whitley." Juby was fortunately not charged as the jury "agreed with him."[63] His association with the men did not tarnish his reputation in the long run, the *Burnet Bulletin* noting that he "was widely and favorably known."[64]

In his classic comic strip *Li'l Abner*, cartoonist and satirist Al Capp created a character known as the world's worst jinx: Joe Btfsplk. It was inevitable that this John Barber, the early day Joe Btfsplk, would bring trouble to John's brother Joe's door.[65] Joe Barber's arrest coincided with the contemporary belief that "the bandits were from the Travis and Williamson county hills."[66] Nor was Barber's arrest based solely upon suspicion. During the pursuit the posse had discovered solid, if circumstantial, evidence when they found John Barber and Brack Cornett's camp site where the outlaws had thoughtlessly discarded the newspaper scrap that had "J. I. [*sic*: Isaac Jones] Barber" written on it.[67] On May 26 Joe Barber was transferred from the city jail to the county jail while two detectives searched his home.[68]

Four more arrests were made at Luling, Texas, in Caldwell County on May 22. The luckless men were identified as Ab and James Ussery and Cheed and John Craft.[69] Fort Worth's *Gazette* confidently predicted that "Other arrests are likely to follow."[70] The prediction proved correct, and on May 26 Charles Buckley was brought in to Austin. Buckley was arrested near Luling on suspicion "of complicity in the late train robbery at McNeil." Officers cautioned the press that the evidence against Buckley was circumstantial.[71] Buckley's arrest created a small rift between Sheriff Nat Lewis of Bexar County and "the United States officials."[72] What created the rift is unknown, but it may be linked to the report that the evidence against Buckley was circumstantial. It may also have been Lewis's own inexperience on the job. He had been elected sheriff of Bexar County in 1886 but only served until 1888.[73]

Ironically the McNeil train robbery occurred near the grave of another train robber, "the notorious Sam Bass."[74] Unlike Bass, however, the capture of the suspects did not involve a violent shootout. The Ussery and Craft brothers were taken on the morning of May 22 between 9 and 10 a.m. "at the railroad water tank four miles from Luling." Like Joe Barber, the men offered no resistance.[75]

Cause for suspicion of both the Ussery and Craft brothers came from a source other than the circumstantial evidence that netted Joe Barber, due, indeed, to their own allegedly criminal histories. The Ussery brothers were two of the sons of Mastin and Sarah Jane Ussery. James Welcome Ussery, born November 14, 1847, in Tennessee, was over thirteen years his brother Abner's senior. By 1860 the Ussery family had relocated from Tennessee to Guadalupe County, Texas, where James's brother Abner Mastin Ussery was born on March 3, 1861. The family remained in Guadalupe County, and the 1870 census shows James working as a farmer with his father.[76] James married Annie Elizabeth Hensley on January 1, 1874, in neighboring Caldwell County, Texas.[77] His younger brother Abner married Elizabeth Manila "Bettie" Ketchum in Caldwell County on April 8, 1885.[78]

To all appearances the Ussery family was no different from hundreds of others that settled in Texas, but trouble found them in 1883. On September 6 one Sam Brown killed Mastin Ussery and attempted to kill his wife as well. Brown had come to the Ussery home to ask for permission to marry his daughter. Mastin Ussery was insistent that Brown obtain a marriage license and wed the girl at the Ussery home. Angered at Ussery's terms, Brown abruptly drew his pistol and killed Mastin, then turned the pistol on Mary Jane who barely knocked it aside and escaped with a powder-burned face. Brown fled but was so closely pursued by enraged citizens that he surrendered to Sheriff William A. Clark at Lockhart.[79] In October 1883 Brown was brought to trial.[80] On January 21, 1884, Brown was hauled out of the jail at Lockhart and lynched. "His body was mangled in a most horrible manner."[81] Abner Ussery was suspected along with others.[82] All of the cases against Brown's alleged killers were dismissed in October 1884.[83]

Linked to the Usserys are the Craft brothers, John and Archalaous "Cheed" Craft, sons of Archalaous and Lucinda Mathis Matthews. Both of the brothers were implicated in the Sam Brown killing.[84] John, the elder of the pair, was born around 1851. He married Catherine "Kitty" Ussery, a sister of the Ussery brothers. His younger brother Cheed was born around 1867.[85]

Under the Fourth Amendment of the Constitution probable cause is a requirement that must be met before the law can make any arrest, conduct a search, or receive a warrant. In general it requires a reasonable basis for believing that a crime may have been committed. This was nothing new. Despite the fact that the evidence involving them in the train robbery was circumstantial and the process of probable cause well known, that was not how the press viewed the arrests, as trial by media began in earnest.

At Clarksville the *Standard* reported that "The two Crafts are brothers, as are the young men, Ab and Jim Ussery. The youngest of the party is about 27 years old and the oldest not over 35. They all live in the neighborhood of Luling, and are *ostensibly* [italics added] farmers. When arrested they appeared cool and indifferent and are very reticent."[86] The *Times-Picayune* added, "The prisoners are a desperate set of men and capable of engaging in almost any crime. They have been suspected for a long time, and Buckley, who is a very bad man himself and an ex-convict, was employed to get their confidence and expose their operations."[87] In the media's minds the men were already guilty, and the blatant attacks on their character were meant to sway public opinion. Legal justice is, however, far different from the mob law practiced in San Saba County or trial by media.[88]

Shortly after the robbery, numerous men arrived in Austin to investigate the train robbery. W. C. Bailey, a Missouri Pacific detective, was in Austin on May 21, and "assistant special agent" W. H. Bonnell arrived the same evening.[89] Joe Barber's arrest, combined with U. S. Deputy Marshals W. J. Bell, Ed Van Riper, and Thomas O. Bailes nabbing five suspects, was sensational news.[90]

All in all, law enforcement had mounted a well-coordinated pursuit of the outlaws, disregarding rank, position, and jurisdiction and concentrating their law enforcement skills to protect the public and willingly accepting the aid of private entities. In more recent times it is known as the Brotherhood of the Badge, and while this was not the first time coordinated efforts had been made, the pursuit further served to solidify that bond.

The press knew all of this, but then as now they could not resist castigating both public and private sector officials, utilizing eagle-eyed hindsight to make their determinations. The *Times-Picayune* published a blistering editorial castigating both government and the railroad, which was picked up by Texas newspapers. The editorial begins simply with "Train robberies in Texas and Missouri occur almost as often as did the stage coach robberies in the days of the 'gentlemen of the road.'" After pointing out the obvious differences between stage and train robbery, the editorial continues, "Thus nothing is simpler than plundering a railway train, and apparently no enterprise is attended with less danger to the robbers, while they are sure of a rich harvest to pay them for their trouble." The editorial then proceeded to take both the state and railroads to task. "The strangest part of the entire affair is that no efficient and systematic effort is made by either the state or by the railways to crush out this evil or to protect passengers and shippers and their property." The *Picayune* concluded tersely that "If the corporations are not liable and the state is powerless to give the needed protection, all railway travelers ought to take to be authorized and even required to carry arms for their own defense. The Texas laws now disarm travelers and place them at the mercy of the robbers."[91]

The media's criticism notwithstanding, reliable information on the outlaws was developed by the authorities. Despite the original estimates of thirteen to fifteen outlaws, veteran man hunter James Lucy believed that "there were not over eight or nine men in the robbing party, most of whom were green hands."[92] Ely the station agent agreed, stating there "were just six in number." Spaulding believed there were only five men in the gang.[93]

The authorities also knew that the gang had scattered, three of them heading toward the Yegua bottoms while others (Secrest and Cloud) struck southwest in the direction of Burnet.[94] The train's crew consistently stated that from the dress of the outlaws they were either farmers or stockmen. None of the gang was masked when they entered the station. Rankin reported early on that "the men were undisguised and will probably be recognized."[95] Ely and Rickett described the gang as "young men, without masks, and roughly clad. Only one had a long beard, and he was the most elderly of the lot."[96] All of the descriptions indicated that the gang was composed of young men, one newspaper announcing, "It was reported at 1:45 this morning that the robbers were young men, undisguised; were dressed generally in dark clothes and wore spurs. They were armed with Winchesters and shotguns."[97] Some of them donned masks when they robbed the train itself. Witnesses reported that "some of the men were masked but the one that did the ordering was unmasked, tall and dressed like a cowboy."[98]

The outlaw who drew the most attention was the man the victims believed was the leader. The *Fort Worth Daily Gazette* noted that "The leader of the gang was unmasked. He seemed not to care."[99] The outlaw "showed himself to be a bad man from the headwaters of Ugly creek."[100] Another report states, "The leader of the robbers is described as a tall man, wearing a long sandy beard, supposed to be false from the peculiar way in which it hung from his face. He was perfectly cool and spoke with a voice and air of habitual command. He seemed to be obeyed with the utmost alacrity."[101] Another newspaper adds that the leader "understood his business, and planned his attack with coolness and skill."[102] All that they lacked, for the moment, were the identities and good descriptions of the gang.[103]

The law also knew one further thing. The cases against Joe Barber, the Crafts, and the Usserys were largely circumstantial, hardly enough to justify holding the men for trial. Some of them had doubts as to the defendants' guilt but were content to allow the law to take its course. What all of them knew was that if these men were not guilty, the "bad man from the headwaters of Ugly creek" would return, and when he did, things were going to get worse.

They were going to get a lot worse.

Chapter 4

Without a Single Train Robber

Joe Barber's hearing before United States Commissioner Ruggles began on June 1 at 2:10 in the afternoon. The prosecution's first witness was S. K. Spaulding. Spaulding testified that his first intimation that the train was being robbed was when he heard one of the outlaws snarl "get back into the car there," followed immediately by gunfire. Spaulding opened the door when commanded but the robbers did not rifle the mail. Spaulding further testified that he did not believe that he could recognize any of the robbers. Most importantly for Joe Barber, Spaulding stated, "I don't think I ever saw the defendant before to-day." Spaulding stated that he saw five of the outlaws at one time, but none of them had entered the mail car.[1]

The prosecution then called conductor W. E. Hawkins who testified that he had seen the porter "sculling with two men" and started for them with his pistol drawn. Another of the outlaws had quickly accosted him, demanding he drop his pistol.

Hawkins wisely complied, but the pistol fired when it hit the ground. When the weapon discharged the outlaw fired at him as he retreated onto the train. As with Spaulding, Hawkins also testified that he did not believe he could identify any of the outlaws. Under cross examination an important clue did develop, however. Hawkins stated that "the defendant looks very much like the man who had the rifle drawn on me; he had on a white hat and a coat; I could not say positively that this is the man, but this man is about the same size and general appearance."[2] It may well have been this failure to identify Joe that prompted one newspaper to report, "Joe Barbour, the man on trial yesterday, is not connected with the gang."[3]

G81 Denison resident A. J. Northacker was then called to the stand. After testifying about his beating, he added that two of the men who entered the car were masked but the third was not. Northacker further stated that "I do not recognize the prisoner as one of the men who was in my car; I think I could recognize the men if they were fixed as they were that night." He also provided a description of Cornett, the man who had done most of the pistol whipping:

> The man who struck me was about 5 feet 9; small, sandy moustache; his beard had grown on his face perhaps seven or or [*sic*] eight days; was short and stubby, sandy in color. His hat was pulled down over his eyes; he weighed perhaps 165 pounds; wore no mask; was pretty active; by the language he used I should say he was a southerner, uneducated; looked like a cowboy; I have not seen him since; would know him if he was dressed as he was that night.[4]

Nor could William Cook identify Joe Barber, stating candidly, "I could not distinguish any of them; do not identify the prisoner; the man I had the tussle with had a longer beard than this man. I can't say that I would be able to identify any of them. They might have been masked."[5]

How suspicion had fallen upon Joe Barber was provided under oath by Sheriff John T. Olive. Not unnaturally Barber denied any involvement with the robbery but admitted that he took both the *Austin Statesman* and the *Georgetown Sun*. Olive testified that he had known Joe for about three years. At McNeil he had tracked the outlaws to where they had eaten their meal and found part of a copy of the *Georgetown Sun* of May 5 with the name I. J. Barber on it. Olive testified that they trailed the outlaws northwest to where the outlaws had split up. He also identified Joe as I. J. Barber's son.

Postmaster S. B. McLaue of Florence confirmed Olive's testimony, noting that Joe's father had left for the Cherokee Nation a month before the robbery and had his mail forwarded to Joe. McLaue noted that he delivered the newspapers to him, adding that Joe "got no papers in his own name; the old man was the only one who took papers." J. E. Cooper, publisher of the *Georgetown Sun* confirmed that the paper was mailed to I. J. Barber at Florence.

Both Olive and James Lucy testified that Barber maintained his innocence. Lucy further testified that Barber told him

> that he did not know and could not explain how the piece of paper got to the place. He said he bad wrapped up no lunch or meat for anyone in the paper. I asked him the question if he had given anyone meat or grub in that paper. He said he had not, and at that time did not attempt to explain the finding of it. Subsequently he intimated that his brother had been at his house within a couple of weeks, and he might have taken the paper. He acknowledged that the paper was one part of one which he took. He said that he did not see his brother when he came.

Joe Barber did not attempt to connect John Barber with the newspaper that had been found, but he did know that John had been at his sister Attia Hunt's home a week or two before the holdup although he did not see him.[6]

By now the suspicion had dawned on Joe Barber as it had on Olive and Lucy that the key to unravelling the McNeil robbery lay in the newspaper found near the crime scene. Joe hired W. A. Crowder, who shared his cell, to visit his wife "and have her explain about the piece of the *Georgetown Sun* found near the robbery, and which had Barbour's [*sic*: Barber's] father's name on it, saying it was unexplained damaging evidence to his case." Crowder, who had been in jail "for carrying a pistol," was promised $10 and a horse for the service. Crowder testified that he gave the request to his cousin J. C. Martin.[7]

Of interest is what Barber told Crowder. He asked Crowder to see his wife and "find out if she could tell anything about it."

> He told me to tell his wife to see his sister; he told me he wanted me to tell his wife if she could not explain it to get her sister to see if she could; *he did not ask me to do anything wrong* [emphasis added].[8]

Martin confirmed this and stated that he went to visit Attia Barber Hunt and delivered the note. According to his testimony Sheriff John Oliver asked Martin "to get into the confidence of the family" and get any clue relative to the robbery "and to arrest John Barbour [*sic*: Barber] at any event." Martin was the prosecution's last witness. The *Galveston News* confidently predicted, "The case will close tomorrow and it is tolerably certain the accused will be held over."[9]

Barber's defense had other ideas and produced a thorough rebuttal. W. R. Jackson testified that he sold Joe some goods at 6 o'clock in the evening the day of the robbery some sixty miles from McNeil and produced his books as evidence. Jackson was not sure, but thought Joe had gone to the post office from his store adding that Joe Barber "was riding a mare that had a young colt following." He concluded, "I can't say if it is possible to ride from my place to Round Rock by 8 or 9 o'clock at night; I don't know, but think it would take a good horse to do it."[10]

The next witness was Joe Barber himself. Joe stated that he was at home on the night of May 17 and during the day on May 18 where he hoed corn in the morning and went to a neighbor named Lamar's home during the afternoon to borrow a cotton planter but could not get it. Around four in the afternoon he had gone to Florence riding a mare with her colt in tow. His testimony confirmed what Jackson had said. On his return home he met "two men named Shoffner and Deer" whom he spoke to for a few minutes. A little further on he met Steve Kirk and his son and were talking about crops when they were joined by John Kennedy. After parting with the men he returned home to his wife and children. "I have four children; the oldest is about six years old; the youngest child was a year old on May 18; my wife and I spoke of its being the baby's birthday."[11]

Barber continued his testimony detailing his activities until the time of his arrest. "Mr. Olive was the first man who told me of the robbery when he came to arrest me." He then discussed the horse that had been ridden hard. Barber had three horses, his mare and colt and a "bold faced bay pony" that he freely admitted belonged to his brother John. John Barber had left the horse with his brother during the fall of 1886. During the spring of 1887 the horse got away "and I did not get him back until about three weeks before I was arrested." Joe agreed with press releases that noted the mount had been ridden hard at the time he found him adding that the mount was bare footed when it escaped and shod on the front hooves when recaptured.

Barber's testimony reflects his agitation. He was taken to Florence before being jailed at Georgetown. "No one went to the house to tell my wife I was arrested." Joe asked if he could fetch his coat from the house and was told he would not need it. At Florence he wanted to have an examining trial but the officers took him to Georgetown and from there to Austin on the train. Here the officers attempted to get him to make a statement. Olive allegedly offered Joe "$1,000, and if I was sent to the penitentiary, and he couldn't get me out any other way, he would break me out."[12] John Olive may well have made the statements Joe Barber credited him with in an effort to obtain a confession from Joe Barber. It is highly unlikely that Olive either intended or seriously considered breaking Barber out of prison if Barber was convicted.

As the hearing drew on Joe informed the court that his father was in Oklahoma at the time of the robbery and had forwarded both his mail and newspaper subscriptions to him. He freely admitted that he had no idea how the newspaper had arrived at McNeil although he did know that one of his sisters had taken some of them. Joe also corroborated Crowder's testimony. "I told him to tell my wife that they connected me with the robbery by a piece of paper, the Georgetown Sun; I did not tell him to tell her to fix up a story about the paper, but to tell her if she remembered anything about it to keep it until the day of the trial." It was a strong point on his behalf, and the prosecution attempted to negate it under cross examination. Barber's response was consistent. "I did not employ him (Crowder) to go to my wife and concoct some scheme about the paper; I thought the paper was good circumstantial proof against me, and I was anxious to know if anyone had carried a paper from my house." Nor was this point lost on the defense, and under redirect examination Joe reiterated his statement. "I told the man in the calaboose that I thought the piece of paper was what they connected me with the robberies: Olive told me he found the paper where the express packages were broken open; I told Crowder to tell my wife that if she knew how the paper got from my place to remember it to the day of the trial."[13]

The testimony created a stir that was swiftly picked up by the exchanges. The *Philadelphia Inquirer* reported that Sheriff Olive "offered $1000 to confess that he was connected with the robbery, and promised that if convicted and sent to the penitentiary he would be released therefrom, even if force had to be used."[14] This was a charge bordering on corruption that left reporters salivating. What the media did not do was attempt to clarify Barber's testimony with the principals involved. At best it was sloppy reporting. At worst it bordered on slander.

When Joe Barber was arrested, $100 had been found in his wallet which the prosecution attempted to prove had come from the train robbery. Barber admitted that the money had been given to him by his brother John who hoped to obtain a pardon for his brother Austin. The prosecution further charged that Joe Barber told Charles Buckley while the men were in jail that he was involved in the robbery. Joe's response was decisive. "I did not say to Buckley in jail that this money was given me by my brother, and was part of what was gotten at the robbery of the train; did not tell him my brother was at my house just before the robbery and had wrapped up provisions into this paper." The evidence of the money was corroborated by prosecution witness James Lucy who stated: "He said the money was given him by his brother, who was a fugitive, some months previously, for the purpose of paying Sneed, Pendexter & Burleson to endeavor to secure a pardon for a brother who was in the penitentiary. The money looked like it had been in an express package, but not recently for several months at least."[15] The attorney Joe had hired, Thomas Sneed, confirmed Joe's story as well stating that he had been hired around the last of March or the beginning of April to obtain the pardon for Austin.

Joe's cross examination by the prosecution was what might be expected. There were attempts to get him to impeach his testimony, but in the end they failed. Joe readily admitted that his sisters, "Mrs. Smart,[16] Mrs. Moore,[17] and Mrs. Hunt"[18] regularly visited the Barber home and were welcome to the newspapers.

As his testimony continued, Joe's view of his brother John becomes clear. "John is evading arrest; he was last at my house four or five months ago . . . I told John I did not like for him to come to my house; if the officers knew of it they would get me into trouble." In the end his testimony remained unshaken. "I suppose they wanted me to tell the truth; I told nothing, for I knew nothing to tell . . . I was not present when the robbery occurred; know nothing about it, nor anyone connected with it living or dead; knew of nothing whatever about it; never heard of it till I was arrested."[19] Both the prosecution and defense understood that the case against Joe Barber was going south, and following his testimony the case was abruptly delayed to hear the charges against the Ussery and Craft brothers.

Hard on the heels of the first part of Barber's preliminary hearing, a second sensation occurred, one that the media leaped upon with both feet. The headline in the *Times-Picayune* said it all: "One of the Train Robbers Turns State's Evidence."

> AUSTIN, Tex., June 1 – [Special.] – Today John and Cheed Craft, Ike and Bill Ussery, and Charles Buckley, the McNeil train robbers, had a hearing before the United States commissioner. Buckley, to the disgust and astonishment of the other men, turned state's evidence, and before he got through with his testimony disclosed that he was in the employ of the sheriff of Bexar, and had been for some time.
>
> He had been detailed to watch the men, and he and they had planned to rob a bank at Luling, a town on the Sunset Route. This, however, was abandoned, and on May 4 they planned the McNeil train robbery. A fellow named Hill was captain of the gang, and he and the Crafts, the Usserys and others not known to Buckley committed the robbery. Buckley

> was not with the gang, but was at his mother's at San Antonio. The robbery was to occur on the 16th, but from some cause was delayed until the 18th.
>
> The cases will be resumed tomorrow.[20]

Buckley's testimony was damning, at least as far as the press was concerned. After the attorneys agreed that all of the evidence taken in the Barber case "as the same relates to the detention of the mail, the robbery or attempted robbery was to be taken as true," the prosecution opened by entering a *nolle prosequi* against Buckley and placed him on the witness stand. The *Statesman* noted that "It had been whispered around for several days that one of the prisoners would turn state's evidence, and the introduction of this man, of course, put the crowd in attendance on the tip-toe of expectation."[21]

Buckley's story was indeed incriminating. After stating that he was a resident of San Antonio, Buckley testified that he had been with the defendants at Jim Ussery's home near Luling. Buckley claimed that he had come there with John Hall and two men named Johnson and Copps. He claimed that these men had conversations relative to robbing a train. The men first agreed to "rob a train on the Sunset road at Three Mile tank, near Luling" but the plan was abandoned because there were too many trains on the road and that made it more hazardous.

Undeterred at entering a budding life of crime, the men proposed robbing the Luling bank, which apparently required more men since another man named Wilburn was added to the gang according to Buckley. This scheme, too, fell by the wayside when "it was learned that the bulk of the money had been shipped off." Someone then suggested that the crowd rob a train up by Round Rock. According to Buckley the scheme was plotted at Jim Ussery's home and in Luling where the gang "would knock around the bar-rooms and hold conferences in the cellar of a vacant house." Buckley claimed that John Hall was the leader of this gang.

Buckley also advised that he was a "special officer" employed by Sheriff Nat Lewis of Bexar County. He further claimed that he unfolded the plot to Deputy Marshal W. J. Bell who engaged him to "stand in with the crowd" and give the game away at the right moment along with Sheriff Lewis. The group had agreed to meet at Ussery's home on May 15.

Not surprisingly, Buckley conveniently became sick upon his return to San Antonio. Under oath he testified that "later on he saw an account of the robbery, and supposed it had been done by this gang." Apparently he was also too sick to notify either Bell or Lewis about the holdup plans although one story stated that he told one Chris Miller to inform Bell about the robbery. To add credence to his testimony, Buckley also claimed that he had been threatened while in the Austin jail by Joe Barber and the Craft brothers if he turned state's evidence. He further claimed that he was attacked and beaten while in the jail cell although he could not tell if the Ussery and Craft brothers were among his attackers.[22]

As in the Barber case things were not what they first appeared to the press. The attorney for the defense was the famous William M. Walton. Walton was a noted politician, former Confederate officer, and attorney.[23] Walton immediately attacked Buckley's credibility. Under direct examination Buckley admitted the fight could have been due to the fact that he "had won money from some of them."[24] Buckley also admitted serving two terms in the state penitentiary, five years from Menard County and eight years from Bosque County.[25] Buckley then proceeded to lie on the stand concerning his terms in prison: "witness thought he had received a pardon in this case, but admitted to having escaped and been out some time; Col. Goree, however, testified that no pardon had issued to him on the second case, and he had served the full term, less commutation for good behavior."[26] With that unnecessary lie on the record, counsel for the prosecution may well have anticipated that all of the cases were on a downhill slide, and they were right. It was going to get worse. It was going to get a lot worse.

Over the next few days a line of witnesses testified at the preliminary hearing. One witness was James Anderson, a conductor of a stock train that had to side track at McNeil on May 15 to wait for the south-bound passenger train. "While waiting there about twenty minutes he saw a party of men around a camp fire, near the track; there were eight or ten of them; one of them got up and walked towards the train; witness took the party to be rangers, because they all seemed to be well armed; he was unable to recognize any of the defendants, as the man who walked out, the only one he saw clearly; the camp fire was about 400 yards south of the depot building."

Deputy Marshal W. J. Bell also took the stand and advised that Bexar County Sheriff Lewis, who had allegedly recruited Buckley to infiltrate the train robber gang, was after a horse thief while Bell pursued the train robbers. "Buckley was authorized to get in with the gang and ferret out the offenders . . . The arrangement with Buckley was *not* (emphasis added) for the purpose of working up a train robbery, but to get in with the gang of outlaws and place any of them who were wanted by the law officers in the way of arrest." Then the motives for Buckley's startling claims became clear. Bell told Buckley "that, so far as he was concerned, all rewards for arrests made by his aid and assistance he could claim."[27] Had there indeed been thirteen to fifteen men, the rewards would have more than doubled what the outlaws had taken. As it was, if Barber, the Ussery brothers, and the Craft brothers had been convicted Buckley would have netted $5,000. It appears that Buckley had concocted all of the testimony.

As it turned out, both the Ussery and Craft brothers could prove their whereabouts at the time of the robbery. So could

Joe Barber, and his sister explained how she had packed a lunch for their brother John. John had arrived and stayed only a few minutes and departed before her husband returned. Mrs. Hunt gave him a lunch of biscuits and preserves and "wrapped them in a paper—it was either The Statesman or the Sun. I don't know which."[28] In what the media implied was a desperate bid to save the case, the assistant U. S. Attorney tried to impeach the witnesses by charging that a party had carried information to them.[29] The charges proved groundless and could not be sustained.

Defeat was in the air, and the media sensed it. One of the mildest comments came out of Fort Worth. "A beautiful rainbow was clearly visible in the sky Saturday night, but it is not thought to have had any connection with the train robbery."[30] The *Galveston Daily News* castigated Attorney General Hogg for his "invasion" on the "province of the local authorities of Travis County." The *Statesman* fired back that the attack was both uncalled for and unjust.[31] The heaviest blow came with the discharge of the cases. The *Statesman* pronounced bitterly that the whereabouts of the accused had been "clearly established."[32] In the end, the evidence was insufficient to bind over any of the prisoners to trial.[33]

The failure to hold over a single one of the men for trial was galling to the media, but not for the professional lawmen. Olive had followed the clues and uncovered a strong lead to one of the train robbers, John Barber. Bell and Lewis had also followed leads that on the surface appeared credible, but their witness was fatally flawed. Moreover, had the officers had the time to properly investigate the alibis of the accused, it is unlikely that any of those charged would have been brought before the court in the first place. The press had been eager for blood, and the officers had hurried their investigation. None of the lawmen would make the same mistake again. The media proved far less introspective, and the castigation and mockery began swiftly.

In Fort Worth the *Gazette* published the "Song of the Train Robbers," which featured as one verse:

> After we take a train we go right into town,
> Upon a soft spring mattress lay us gently down.
> We hear about the officers and how they run all night
> Without a single train robber being in their sight.[34]

Adding to what appeared an endless litany of successful railroad heists, on June 4, 1887, the Rube Burrow gang struck a train at Benbrook Station in north Texas.[35] Under the headline "HOW LONG, OH! LORD!" the *Gazette* ran an article covering the holdup that reflects the growing aggravation of the media with train robbers and the government's seeming lack of ability to deal with them. In the same issue the paper editorialized. "What with train robbers, fence cutters and rotten eggers, Texas must strike the average man as a cross between a 'robber state' and a 'highly civilized' community in which free speech and free thought are tolerated only so long as they accord with the prevailing opinion. If Texas keeps on it will surpass both Missouri and Iowa."[36] What the train robberies did accomplish was to divert attention from the infamous San Saba County War, then in full swing, a conflict far more violent than the train robberies. The killings in this feud had begun in 1869, and the government, despite sporadic and repeated efforts, had failed to suppress it. The press failed to do the hard, investigative work on the feud when train robbery glittered before their eyes like a child's bauble.

For the moment, however, the train robberies dominated everyone's attention. The Waco newspaper confidently predicted "Other Trains Will be Robbed." Given the fact that the outlaws allowed "reasonably fair intervals between just enough for the public to catch its breath and get over the shock before the next attack," the paper continued, "Whether the bandits are mounted or on foot, the result has been the same in every instance and for all practical purposes they might as well have taken wings and soared up to the moon from the scene of their crime. Of course this apparent immunity will make the bandits bolder and there is no reason why each successive robbery may not be more and more daring and startling . . ."[37]

One thing was not apparent to those concerned with hunting the outlaws. "A train is robbed near Austin, in a week's time four or five men are arrested, and an examining trial drags along for weeks, with the defense piling up proof of alibis; suddenly nearly two hundred miles away another train in the same way is robbed. Are they a part of the McNeill [Station] gang, or are they other hardened men, made bold by the immunity of the McNeill robbers?"[38] No one truly knew that there were two separate gangs operating in Texas, the Cornett-Whitley gang and that of Rube Burrows.

Prophetically one editor wrote, "The train robberies in Texas have really been very small affairs, but they go out to the world as fearfully exaggerated outrages."[39] The Cornett-Whitley gang would prove obliging. The next outrages would not be "fearfully exaggerated." If anything, they were understated. Within two weeks the gang would catapult themselves into international infamy.

Chapter 5

Fiendish Atrocities

The assignment of Captain George H. Schmitt, commander of Company C of the Texas Rangers, to investigate the McNeil train robbers appears fundamentally sound on the surface. The decision failed to consider the seriously flawed Schmitt's less than sterling qualities, however. Much of Schmitt's life remains a mystery, and he was never considered one of the great Texas Rangers.[1] What has been determined is that Schmitt was born in Bavaria around 1836.[2] It is possible that Schmitt may be the George Schmitt incarcerated in the Huntsville Penitentiary for mail theft in 1859, but this is by no means certain.[3] What is certain is that Schmitt served as sheriff of Comal County from 1876 through 1882, where he acquired a reputation "ripe with controversy and contentiousness."[4]

Over the many decades that the Texas Rangers have existed, there have been many great rangers, from Jack Hays through the Four Great Captains who carried the Rangers into the twentieth century to modern-day Captain Jack Dean.[5] Schmitt was never one of them. On the contrary, George Schmitt was arrogant, argumentative, and self-aggrandizing, swift to criticize others while defending even the least significant decisions that he made. Opinionated, Schmitt was frequently critical of his fellow officers. One of them was Captain William Scott upon whom he "expended a great deal of vitriolic energy over several years."[6] His main qualification for the Ranger position appears to have been that he was a personal friend of then-Governor John Ireland who literally forced him upon the Rangers. In short he was a political hack. With the benefit of eagle-eyed hindsight, Schmitt criticized other lawmen's operations liberally while he held an exceptionally high opinion of only one Texas Ranger: himself. It was not an opinion shared by other Rangers. In 1883 Company D, to whom he was first assigned, circulated a petition asking for his resignation.[7]

In typical Schmitt fashion and without knowing any particulars, Schmitt now voiced the opinion that the McNeil train robbers were "outlaws from Atascosa County." Committing his thoughts to the adjutant general, Schmitt further stated that "the leader in that robbery was in Taylor the morning of the robbery and passed through the southbound train that morning. Schmidt [*sic*] says there are ten or fifteen men in the gang, who are murderers and thieves." Except for the unexceptional pronouncement that the gang was composed of murderers and thieves, Schmitt was wrong on every assertion. Nonetheless, Schmitt offered the personal opinion that he stood "a good show of getting the right parties."[8]

Apparently Adjutant General King accepted Schmitt's confident boast, responding to him on June 14, "I trust you will be able to capture some of them, and especially if a few of these train robbers meet the fate of the Mexicans you killed the action of the rangers will be very commendable."[9] Three days later King again advised Schmitt that he wanted "to have captured or killed the gang of outlaws of whom our [Will] Jacobs seems to be the leader."[10]

What none of the authorities knew was that the gang had already fractured. Ike Cloud understood after the McNeil robbery that he had gotten into far more than he had bargained for, and from his actions it appears that he may have feared Cornett and the others. Following the McNeil Station robbery he and Secrest had partnered up and headed west. Reeves later stated that Secrest and Cloud soon separated and admitted that he had not seen Cloud since the robbery.[11] Ike Cloud was not the only one who had misgivings about his new companions, as time would demonstrate.

Unmindful of Schmitt's braggadocio, the gang was already planning its next robbery. Around June 1, 1887, the Cornett-Whitley gang again rendezvoused in Newt Butler's pasture in Karnes County. Barber and Whitley arrived last, having initially hidden out in the vicinity of the homes of Joe Barber and Joe Bennett.[12] Present at the time were Cornett, Whitley, Powell, Reeves, and Secrest in addition to a recent recruit, man-killing Will Jacobs, alias "Speckled Bill" due to his freckles. Jacobs, whom Schmitt believed was the leader, was in fact the newest member of the gang.[13] In 1885 he and his cousin Alfred Y. Allee had been involved in the killing of Frank Rhodes. While on the run, Jacobs killed Deputy Sheriff Lee Pool near Rockdale, Texas.[14]

The killing of Lee Pool created major problems, not only for Jacobs but for his friends as well. Pool was a particular friend of Sheriff Andrew Jackson Lewis of Milam County who posted a reward of $250 for Jacobs, a reward that Governor Ross was swift to match. Lewis was not a man to be trifled with, and as lawmen went he was relentless. In 1881 he became a deputy sheriff and was elected in 1886 as sheriff of Milam County. He was a career lawman and a good one.[15]

The furor over Pool's murder nearly resulted in violence. On April 12, 1887, Sheriff Lewis arrested four men on suspicion of harboring Jacobs. Almost immediately he and the officers were confronted by a crowd of armed men. The officers prevented the men from lynching the suspects.[16] Company C of the Texas Rangers had to spend June 6 through June 10 hunting Jacobs from their base in Brownwood, and it was likely this hunt that convinced George Schmitt, at least in part, that Jacobs was the gang's leader.[17] That the gang had recruited another member, particularly one wanted so badly, may have caused some dissention. Secrest already had serious misgivings about the original gang members. Adding a new comrade known for having killed a lawman intensified his doubts.

There were others at the rendezvous as well. Reeves recalled that Eli Harrell provided the gang with false beards that Newt Butler had purchased for them. Newt Butler had come as well. "The robbery was talked over between Newton Butler and us in the pasture," Reeves admitted. Here the gang planned their next robbery, a return to Flatonia, although sometime during the discussion Butler and Harrell decided not to participate. When the gang finally left for Flatonia they were still a man down. Like Ike Cloud who never rejoined them, Ross (Secrest) abandoned the gang.[18] It proved to be a prudent move.

Nor did Jacobs make the robbery. "Six of us—Cornett, Barbour [*sic*], Whitley, Powell, Jacobs and I started to the Flatonia robbery, but Jacobs weakened when we reached a swollen stream on the way, and turned back." After crossing the San Antonio River, the gang separated after agreeing to meet at the Flatonia graveyard. They arrived there on Wednesday, June 15. Reeves states that they intended to rob the train on Thursday night, but it left before Cornett and Barber could board it. Unlike their first trip to Flatonia, this time the outlaws patiently waited to hit the train the following day.[19]

Newspaper accounts place the Flatonia train robbery as between midnight and 1 o'clock a.m. on June 18. Whitley's biographer states that "Bill and Cornett boarded as passengers in Flatonia. About a mile out of town, Cornett clambered over the tender and held a pistol on the engineer, telling him to slow down so his partner, Bud Powell, could get on."[20] This is disputed by contemporary witnesses' accounts.

As the train pulled out of Flatonia, Barber and Cornett rushed the engine. One of them managed to board the coal tender where Georgia-born Ben Pickren, the engineer, first noticed him. Pickren believed the outlaw was either a tramp or a drunkard crawling up on the coal tender and demanded what his business was.[21] His answer was a drawn pistol and the command to be quiet. "Just as the train pulled out a man boarded the engine, the second man missing his hold. The train proceeded almost one hundred yards when the man who had boarded the engine with drawn pistol ordered the engineer to stop until his partner could catch up and get on, when they ordered the engineer to pull out."[22] The outlaw then called out to "Dick" who had mounted the train between the coal tender and the express car. The second outlaw scrambled over the coal tender with a drawn pistol. Under cover of two pistols, Pickren and his fireman complied, halting the train on a bridge roughly a mile and a half from Flatonia where a campfire had been built close to the tracks.[23] A solitary report had it that seven men had boarded the train at Flatonia, and as the train pulled out two of them went forward over the tender and covered the engineer and fireman, but the report was discounted.[24] The pair were in good humor, but that would change quickly.

When the train halted on the trestle, conductor Jesse K. Lyons put his head out of the window of the car nearest the engine and called, "What is the matter, Ben?" Pickren replied quickly that the train was in the hands of robbers who had ordered it stopped.[25]

As with the McNeil robbery, the initial estimates of how many men attacked the train near Flatonia were vastly inflated. Early accounts stated that eight or ten men, all armed with Winchester rifles, were lurking at the robbery site, but the conditions were not optimal for anything resembling an accurate count. There was no significant moonlight, the moon being in a waning crescent and nearly dark, the only other light being provided by the fire the outlaws had built. Burton also theorizes that at least eight or ten men were involved in the holdup, adding the names of Tom Jones (also known as Tom Montgomery), Milton Day, William Humphreys (or Humphries), Henry Kelly, and Will Jacobs.[26] Problems with these identifications exist, however, as will be shown.

The gang planned the robbery well. While the engine, express, and mail cars were on one side of the bridge, the passenger cars were secured on the trestle. Pickren and the fireman, S. L. Wright, were herded off the engine while the outlaws took up their positions. Ed Reeves later claimed that the outlaws covered the length of the train. "I was stationed at the hind end of the cars, Whitley and Powell went into the express car. Barbour guarded the outside."[27] With the train trapped on the trestle, five men were more than enough to control the situation. What transpired shocked the world. Historian Rick Miller refers to the Cornett-Whitley gang's "brutal method" of robbing trains.[28] Brutal is a mild word to describe it. The gang demonstrated a vicious cruelty that had not been seen in train robberies. They moved through the train with promiscuous, pitiless violence, as uncalled-for as it was inhumane.

The outlaws herded the train's crew to the express car, which doubled for carrying baggage. Here they met "stout resistance" in the form of Wells Fargo expressman M. E. "Frank" Folger.[29] At first Folger refused to open the door of the car, hiding some money in the stove and tossing away the keys to the safe. After a quick consultation with the baggage master, a man named Hart, the men opened the door. Two or three of the outlaws entered the car and demanded that Folger open the safe. He refused and told them that he had thrown away the keys.

The outlaws did not receive the news well, and whatever "good humor" they exhibited evaporated swiftly. Enraged at Folger's defiance, the outlaws began a "severe pounding on the head and body with pistols."[30] J. H. White, sheriff of El Paso County and a passenger on the train, later informed reporters that the outlaws "wreaked vengeance on him by beating him over the bead with their revolvers and cruelly splitting his ears with pocketknives."[31] In later years the torture was detailed, although with what accuracy is unknown, that Folger's "ears were cut, underbit in the right and fork. And slope in the left."[32] A more grisly version was provided years after the event. Commenting on Brack Cornett (alias "Captain Dick"), the *Omaha Daily Bee* commented, "On one occasion he cut off the ears of an express messenger who had resisted him, and subsequently mailed them to his victim."[33] The torture was succinctly summarized by one newspaper: "They beat him over the head with pistols until he was insensible, split his ears, and left him for dead."[34] Whitley's biographer identifies the two men who tortured Folger as Cornett and Reeves.[35]

In the end, Folger's heroic efforts proved futile. The outlaws found the keys and emptied the safe.[36] That completed, they turned their attention to the mail, cutting open every bag and scattering the mail on the floor.[37]

With their primary target disposed of, the gang turned their attention to the passenger cars. By all accounts three of them boarded the lead car. Jesse Lyons provided descriptions of the trio who entered the coaches:

> There were three men came in the train. The one who came first they called captain. He had no mask on. They all had large white hats on. The one with the mask had a heavy mustache, and his beard was about two week's growth and sandy. He had on a brown pair of overalls, brown coat, a dove-colored

> shirt, a large pair of spurs, was about 5 feet 8 inches high and weighed about 165 or 175 pounds. The other one that came through had on a mask, beard and mustache. The mustache was very large, beard brown, and dressed as the one described above, had a white handled revolver stuck in a belt in front. The one who stood in the coach door had a black cloth tied over the bridge of his nose, his eyes showing above. He was dressed as described above, but not so stout as the first man mentioned. The first man was a little stooped, broad shoulders and chest. The pocket in his pants was very long, put in on the side. The man with the false beard they called Dick.[38]

While the gang was occupied with the express car, Lyons and A. N. Allen, the train's butcher, emerged onto the train tracks and were immediately ordered back aboard the train.[39] Allen told reporters that when he and Lyons emerged onto the tracks they were immediately confronted by two or three of the outlaws and "pistol muzzles were shoved in our faces." The men were ordered back into the car unless they wanted their "brains blown out." Both judiciously complied with the order. Lyons had the presence of mind to conceal his gold watch and most of his money. The robbers only gained six dollars from him. His foresight aided the passengers, whom he warned of the robbery, and a great amount of money was saved.[40]

> Presently two men came into the car with drawn pistols, which were pointed at the engineer, whom I only knew as Ben, and his fireman, these two being in front of the robbers. They were told to walk to the end of the car and keep in there and we were all ordered to do the same. Someone in a short time told the passengers to keep their heads in as, if they put them out of the windows, they would be shot. Then before the door of each car a man was placed as a guard when

> the others went through the cars and robbed every passenger there was in them. I saw seven men in all. The train consisted of one emigrant car, one second class car, a first class car and a sleeper, the number of passengers about fifty in all.[41]

Had it been a simple train robbery, the Flatonia holdup would have been newsworthy in itself. This was far more, however. The gang tortured and beat nearly every passenger on the train leaving three of them with pistols whose barrels were so badly bent they needed replace. Whitley's biographer names the men who robbed the passengers as Whitley and Powell, implying that the coaches were robbed at the same time as the express car was attacked. This was not the case.

Placing where the passengers and outlaws were on the train is difficult despite numerous accounts of the Flatonia train robbery. Having finished torturing Folger and looting the express car, the gang moved on to the day cars. Whitley's biographer states that John Barber entered the emigrant car where he robbed its single passenger, an old man traveling from California to New Orleans, of $12.[42] Three men entered the other passenger cars.

Forewarned by Jesse Lyons, most of the passengers had hidden their valuables.[43] In the day cars J. H. Mitchell, of Tombstone, Arizona, had the dubious honor of being the first man robbed. Mitchell had successfully hidden $300 from the outlaws under his seat and gave up only ten dollars.[44] A man from San Francisco variously identified as "Armaroux," "Pamaroux" and "P. A. Maroux" was the second victim. He lost ten dollars to the outlaws but saved $160 that he hid when the conductor gave the alarm.[45] Abraham Lasker, misidentified as L. Lasker, a sponge salesman, lost seven dollars "but saved over $100 by putting it in his shoe."[46] San Antonio native Walter Gregory gave them $20. The outlaws asked if that was all he had, then returned $2.50 to him when he told them it was. Whitley's biographer states that Bill Whitley returned the money, but the statement is speculative.[47] Dan Sweeney of Merced, California, contributed ten dollars to the robbers but saved twenty dollars.[48]

A. N. Allen was uncertain but believed that Mose Freiburg of Galveston was robbed of $1000, his gold watch and some diamond jewelry. Allen himself lost $10.[49] Conductor Lyons was also robbed of five dollars as he had "previously concealed his money."[50] Max Stokes, a drummer, lost $24 but saved $150 and a gold watch.[51] In short, the gang was efficient. "After going through the express and mail cars, the robbers turned their attention to the passengers, none of whom were overlooked or slighted, even the newsboy being robbed of his nickels," which amounted to three dollars.[52] The *Galveston Daily News* summed it up simply in a headline: "EVERYBODY FORCED TO PAY TRIBUTE."[53]

As noted, whatever good humor the outlaws originally expressed degenerated into violence at the express car where Folger was beaten and tortured. Robbing the passengers was no longer enough, and the gang promiscuously pistol whipped their way through the passengers. One young woman was struck on the head "for being slow."[54] One newspaper succinctly summed it up: "Nearly every man was given a blow with a revolver *after* [emphasis added] he gave up his money, and they even struck one lady.[55] These beatings had nothing to do with controlling the passengers. It was sadistic, gratuitous violence.

As the outlaws advanced on German-born William Newberger (or Neuberger) of New York, identified in newspapers as a "Jewish traveler for a New York house," Newburger became frightened and began to cry. One of the outlaws hit him over the head with his pistol then robbed him of his watch, $70, and diamonds, "valued at about $1,000."[56] Whitley's biographer makes the claim that Brack Cornett hit Newberger.[57] At least one contemporary account described it far differently, noting that Newberger "was severely beaten because he was slow in delivering his property.[58]

Another merchant on the train was R. L. Armistead from Nashville, Tennessee. Several sources reported that Armistead was robbed of $500.[59] The *New York Sun* reported a smaller loss. "R. L. Armistead of New York [*sic*: Nashville, Tennessee] gave up $20. He had a larger amount of money with him, but it was hidden in the sleeping car." Armistead brazenly told them "they had best give him back his silver, but they said they were not making change. He then asked them to take a drink with him, but they said it was not their night for drinking."[60] Perhaps it was due to Armistead's pluck in asking for his silver or his courtesy in offering them a drink, but the outlaws did not harm him.

While the gang terrorized the day coach passengers, Charles Johnson, the porter, busily turned out all of the lights in the sleeping coach in an effort to thwart the outlaws. The effort proved fruitless for three of the gang led by the "Captain" forced one of the brakemen to lead the way with a lantern.[61] The first man awakened by the gang was Lou Mayer from Cincinnati, the son of German immigrants and a dealer in wholesale clothing who occupied the first berth on the right side of the car. Mayer "did not take in the situation and proceeded to give his disturbers a blowing up, but a blow from the robbers pistol on the head and an emphatic request for 'Your money, and that d—n quick,' brought out all the money he had, $40." Mayer, who was employed L. H. Stroble Co. of Cincinnati, later stated, "The first thing 1 knew a rough fellow stuck a pistol in my face and told me to give him my money and that dam quick I saw at once that the train was in the hands of robbers and I put my hand under my pillow to pull out my vest and while doing this I slipped my watch out and left it under the pillow. I saved my watch but they got all the money I had."[62]

On the other side of the car was W. F. Beers, "an insurance man of Galveston," who handed the outlaws five dollars and told them it was all he had. "The robbers insisted that he had more and made him take an oath that this amount was all he had. He at first put up his left hand to take the oath but the robbers commanded him to put up the other hand."[63]

Another passenger they encountered in the sleeper was a young Englishman who refused to be robbed. The outlaws beat him "severely over the head and neck" until he yielded.[64] Another man was awakened and when he reached under his pillow for his money was beaten senseless by the outlaws who then secured the purse themselves.[65]

Realizing what was happening, Colonel Quintos of the Mexican army ordered his lieutenant, Citarino Cruz, to bring him his pistols. Close by, Sheriff James H. White's wife, Barbara, frantically begged him to stop, as they were overpowered.[66] Reluctantly Quintos desisted and handed over his money. The colonel was not molested, but Cruz was not so fortunate. The lieutenant was unable to understand English, and the outlaws pistol whipped him "remarking that they would as soon kill a Mexican as eat their breakfast." Reportedly the robbers gathered $400 from the men.[67] The colonel's attempt to thwart the robbers met with nearly universal approval. Almost defensively the *Austin Weekly Statesman* insisted "Unquestionably Mrs. White's coolness saved many lives."[68] Perhaps, but some of the lives saved were likely those of the outlaws.

It was at this point that conductor Lyons told the outlaws that a train from the west was about due there "and that it would be necessary for him to send back and flag unless they, the robbers, desired the train to be run into and everybody in the Pullman killed." The robbers responded quickly that they did not wish anybody killed and started to leave the car.[69] At the same time John Barber shouted, "We have been here long enough. Come on!"[70] There were only four people who were not robbed: Sheriff James H. White and his wife Barbara, A. J. Beach[71] of Palatka, Florida, and Lionel Hohenthal[72] of San Antonio.[73] Other stories mistakenly claimed that Hohenthal was robbed of $250.[74] Hohenthal's own statement to one reporter presents a more accurate picture.

> "I was quite lucky," said he, "for yesterday morning I went to the agent in San Antonio and told him I wanted a berth near the center of the car reserved. Somehow the agent forgot to have the berth reserved and I had to take a rear section just over the trucks. This is all that saved me from being robbed. I was in the section just in the rear of the one occupied by the Mexican officers. They were just getting ready to come to my berth when the conductor told them a train was then due and they were liable to be killed if a flagman was not sent back at once. You may imagine how much relieved when one of the robbers said "We don't want to see anybody killed, you can run your train along."[75]

Moments later the train pulled out with its terrorized load of brutalized and tortured passengers while the outlaws aimed for Newt Butler's pasture.

The Flatonia robbery leaves a number of unanswered questions. Which outlaw or outlaws pistol whipped their way through the passenger and Pullman cars? Who tortured Folger? How many men were involved in the holdup? How could five men successfully hold up a train carrying fifty passengers or more and at least ten train crew?

The identities of the three men who robbed the passengers is the least problematic of the questions. The first man to enter was called "Captain" by the others and "had no mask on." He was described as having a "heavy mustache, and his beard was about two week's growth and sandy." The man was "about 5 feet 8 inches high and weighed about 165 or 175 pounds."[76] The Wells Fargo circular later issued describes Cornett, Whitley, and Powell as the towheads, but the heavy mustache belongs to Cornett.[77] Whitley was described as having a "small, sandy mustache."[78] Powell's mustache was described as downy and boyish.[79]

The second outlaw had on a mask, beard, and mustache. The mustache was very large, the beard brown. He carried "a white handled revolver stuck in a belt in front."[80] Whitley carried such a weapon.[81] The third man, described as slight with a black cloth tied across his face was most likely Bud Powell.[82] It is also apparent that both Cornett and Whitley pistol whipped the passengers. Reeves claimed that he and John Barber remained outside the train.[83] Given the fact that Barber was left handed and not a single account mentions this detail, Reeves was undoubtedly correct as to Barber's location. Moreover, none of the outlaws aboard the train were described as having black hair, which very likely indicates that the trio was Cornett, Whitley, and Powell.

Concerning the men who tortured Folger, the evidence demonstrates that Cornett was one of the pair.[84] Whitley's granddaughter states that Ed Reeves was in the express car, insisting that he and Cornett tortured Folger.[85] Reeves stated that Cornett was in the car while Barber was on the outside. News stories of the day clearly state that more than one outlaw entered the car, possibly as many as three. The likeliest candidates are Whitley and Powell who accompanied Cornett in robbing the passengers. It is possible that Reeves also entered the car instead of Powell as he was one of three men who had to replace his pistol following the robbery due to the bent barrels from beating the passengers. The most likely candidates appear to be Cornett, Whitley, and possibly Reeves as the men who tortured Folger.

Reporters, many of the victims, and some modern historians since have questioned Reeves's account of the raid, insisting that there were far more men who robbed the train at Flatonia rather than the five Reeves testified to. The late historian Jeff Burton speculated that "deliberate suppression" by the authorities kept some of the facts from being known. He adds a host of other names such as Tom Jones (alias Montgomery), Henry Kelly, Milton Day, Will Jacobs, William Humphreys, John Creswell, and John (or George) Brown.[86] Whitley's biographer names John Kelly [*sic*: Henry Kelly], John Crowell [*sic*: Creswell], George Brown, William "Humpheries" (Humphreys), Tom Jones, C. H. West, and Milton Day.[87]

Wells Fargo & Co. disputed these claims, a ledger entry noting, "As the train drew up at Flatonia two me[n] with drawn revolvers mounted the engine and compelled the engineer to pull the train out into the open prairie 1½ miles where three confederates were in waiting by a fire lighted as a signal for the stopping place."[88] From a variety of sources, the evidence indicates that only five men held up the train at Flatonia.

How five men could brutalize, terrorize, and torture fifty-plus passengers and the train's crew is mind boggling on the surface. The simple truth is that the train was stopped on a trestle in the middle of the night with no escape route for the passengers. Only the Mexican officers and likely Sheriff White are known to have had weapons, creating what in today's terminology is a "gun free zone." The passengers, lacking any means to defend themselves, were simply victims that the outlaws could terrorize at will. The outlaws knew that the passengers were unarmed, allowing them to torture and terrorize their way through the train with impunity, a concept which many people find impossible to grasp even in the present day. It was not impossible for the *Fort Worth Gazette* to grasp, however. In a blistering editorial the *Gazette* concluded: "If the corporations are not liable and the state is powerless to give the needed protection, all railway travelers ought to take, to be authorized and even required to carry arms for their own defense. The Texas laws now disarm travelers and place them at the mercy of the robbers."[89]

Once again those in the public eye reacted in a predictable manner as their natures dictated. The gang had presented the challenge of raw primal power. The press, whose elastic ethics and questionable professionalism screamed for immediate arrests, castigated law enforcement, railroads, and the government itself for their failure to apprehend the outlaws without troubling themselves to gather the facts. In Austin, ever mindful of reelection, politicians promised swift action, action that they themselves could not provide, and conveniently overlooked the law that had permitted the atrocity. Only those who were charged with dealing with the gang, beleaguered and mocked from all directions, remained true to their mission, drawing together at all levels with private entities to further unite the brotherhood of the shield. For the moment none of them knew who they were dealing with, but the professional lawmen among them assuredly knew what they were.

The Flatonia train robbery told the world what the outlaws were. In European folklore there exist creatures known as the hellhounds (Scandinavia "hel hounds"). There are a wide variety of these creatures found in mythologies around the world but all of them are associated with ill fortune and death, even the Welsh *Cŵn Annwn,* which were regarded as benign. The press, politicians, and to some degree the law had overlooked, even disregarded, the early warnings at McNeil. At Flatonia they were impossible to ignore.

The hounds were out.

Chapter 6

Immunity from Unpleasant Consequences

The most succinct account of the Flatonia robbery appeared in distant Londonderry, Vermont, whose paper reported simply, "Robbers secured $75,000 by cleaning out an express train near Flatonia, Texas."[1] It was the exception. From coast to coast the majority of the media were far more lavish. One Texas newspaper termed it "the most successful train robbery that has been committed in Texas for years."[2] The theme echoed throughout the national news media. The *New York Sun* reported it as the "most daring train robbery that ever occurred in Texas."[3] Closer to home, the *Fort Worth Gazette* called it "a train robbery which for clearness of conception and boldness of execution is the counterpart of the most daring piece of highway work that has ever occurred in the west."[4] In Paw Paw, Michigan, the paper proclaimed that it had been accomplished in "Genuine Jesse James Style."[5]

Adding insult to injury, early estimates of the haul the outlaws made were vastly inflated. The highest reported amount was $100,000.[6] As the news spread throughout North America, other newspapers placed the amounts stolen far lower, ranging from $10,000 to $75,000.[7] More accurate sources placed the outlaws' haul at $10,000.[8] Ed Reeves placed the actual amount stolen at a little over $7,000.[9]

As humiliating as it was to state officials, the robbery itself paled in comparison to the atrocities that the outlaws committed. The *Daily Alta California* characterized the robbers as "very rough and ugly" and repeated the accounts of the outlaws beating women "who were slow in finding their pocketbooks."[10] Another newspaper heralded "FIENDISH ATROCITIES" and reinforced the claim that at McNeill's Station they had taken "between $20,000 and $50,000."[11] Yet another California news outlet chimed in about "brutal treatment."[12] In Montana the *Helena Weekly Herald* headlined their coverage as "BOLD TRAIN ROBBERY" followed by the fact that people had been "brutally beaten."[13] The *Butte Semi-Weekly Miner* castigated the outlaws for their "rough and ugly" treatment of the passengers but placed the number of women struck at one.[14] The *Indian Sentinel* in Oklahoma headlined its coverage "BRUTAL ROBBERS" followed by "A Texas Train Robbery Accompanied With Gross Brutality."[15] The *Iola Register* trumped this banner with one that heralded "Express Messenger Mutilated."[16] The *New North West* stated that their "deed was well planned and successfully, but brutally, executed. Nearly every man was given a blow with a revolver *after* [emphasis added] he gave up his money."[17] On June 25, 1887, the *Great Falls Tribune* stated the obvious: "TRAIN ROBBERS are becoming more audacious in Texas."

Criticism and castigation of both the railroad officials and civil servants by the media began immediately. The *Fort Worth Daily Gazette* published the sarcastic snippet "It is not recorded that the passengers on the Sunset train 'cheered' the robbers at

Flatonia." In a letter to the editor, which may have been written by the editor himself, the correspondent, TEXAN, offered, "The year 1886 will probably be remembered as the year of the great drouth; the year 1887 as the year of the train robberies." The letter continued that a "state that permits bandit robbery never will fully enjoy the word civilized." TEXAN then turned his wrath on Governor Ross:

> His friends claim that while he might be criticized for being slow he will yet be equal to the occasion. Yes, but we reply, our home is on fire and tardiness of movement, or the use of a sprinkling can, instead of a fire engine which is available, we cannot approve of. The protection of life and property is the duty of the state. . . . History tells us that Nero was fiddling or doing something unimportant while Rome was burning and for this his enemies unjustly accused him of being the incendiary.[18]

This was far from the worst of it. The train robbery at Flatonia and the accompanying atrocity spread on a global basis. Under the headline "Daring Robbery of a Train," Edinburgh, Scotland's *Falkirk Herald* provided an account of the heist, placing the amount stolen at $75,000.[19] Accounts appeared in Sydney, Australia, and Somerset, England, both of which considered the outlaws "daring."[20] In New Zealand the media took a far dimmer view of the outlaws, the *Auckland Star* among others considered them "very rough and ugly in their treatment, even striking lady passengers."[21] The Cornett-Whitley gang had achieved international recognition for their daring certainly, but their hallmark was their brutality, propensity for violence, and sadism. By extension, Texas had achieved international negative publicity. Nor is there much question that three men were involved in the brutal beatings and torture. Ed Reeves confessed: "When we got back from the Flatonia robbery, I staid about three days in Butler's pasture. The day before leaving the pasture we got three new 45 Colt pistols."[22]

As noted above, Reeves's confession of this fact helps validate the extreme violence the gang had unleashed on the passengers. One of the new pistols was for Reeves who had damaged his during the robbery, and while Reeves did not identify who the other two outlaws were one was very likely Brack Cornett."

June 1887 had begun inauspiciously in Texas when Rube Burrow and his gang held up a train at Benbrook Station on June 4.[23]At the time no one, except the outlaws themselves, were aware that two gangs existed. Officials of the railroad theorized that "the men engaged in the work here are the same that did a similar robbing near Austin, and also in north Texas."[24] So when the train that had been robbed at Flatonia halted at Shulenberg, the next station where the wounded could be cared for and the alarm sounded, Texas was in an uproar. From the station urgent telegrams were sent to the surrounding points.

In Flatonia word of the robbery arrived with the west-bound train at 3:20 a.m. Constables Sloan of Flatonia and Hall of Waelder led a small posse to the scene of the robbery.[25] The outlaws were long gone, as was expected, and some theorized that the gang had crossed the border into Mexico.[26] Undeterred by rumors perpetrated and perhaps originated by the media and spread in the same sources, the law did what it was supposed to do, cooperating at all levels.

Career lawman James Light Townsend, sheriff of Colorado County, left Columbus two hours after the robbery. The son of Asa Townsend and Rebecca Harper, Townsend was born November 12, 1845. Townsend was related to the Johnson family who were engaged in the Hoo Doo War in central Texas.[27] During the Civil War he served in the Fifth Texas Cavalry. Townsend was first elected sheriff of Colorado County in 1880 and was reelected for a number of terms.[28] At Flatonia

Townsend rendezvoused with Sheriff Brutus Lytt Zapp of Fayette County.

A son of Robert and Maria Johannah Hubertina Huepgen Zapp, and born August 15, 1854 at La Grange, Texas, Zapp served as marshal of Round Top, Texas, for a time. In 1882 he returned to La Grange where he became chief deputy under John T. Rankin. He was elected sheriff in 1886 and served consecutive terms proving himself both a popular and efficient lawman until he declined to run in 1894.[29]

In Fayette County Zapp had the authority, but there is no evidence of either of these professional lawmen head butting for jurisdiction. Once again the law pooled their resources. Newspapers reported that Zapp had arrived around 1:00 p. m. from La Grange and the pair were "making every effort in their power to get some clue to the perpetrators. Sheriffs and deputies are now out in all directions, in hopes of making a capture."[30]

Hall and Sloan's posse returned to Flatonia around 8 o'clock on the morning of June 18. They had located both where the gang had tied their horses and where the gang cut the fence on both sides of the railroad track. The lawmen reported that the outlaws appeared to have scattered. "The tracks seem to scatter in every direction so that it is impossible without the aid of bloodhounds to follow the trail."[31]

In San Francisco, Wells Fargo was not idle. On the morning of June 18, legendary detective James B. Hume received word that Southern Pacific train No. 19 had been attacked and Wells, Fargo & Co. "robbed of about $7500." Hume wired John Thacker who was in Arizona investigating another train holdup. Thacker was ordered to Flatonia. Nor did Hume leave the investigation to the highly capable Thacker. "I shall leave for the scene to-morrow morning," he informed reporters before heading for Flatonia.[32]

As the eighteenth drew on, more information developed concerning the robbery. The *Austin Weekly Statesman* reported that there were "seven men in the gang" all of them "old hands in the business."[33] In Houston J. W. Nichols, superintendent of the express company, refused to divulge how much had been taken from the safe. Robert B. Burns, postmaster in Houston, advised that there had been no registered mail on the train. At the same time the general agent of Southern Pacific, along with Jesse Lyons and M. E. "Frank" Folger, left for the scene of the robbery probably to help identify any outlaws captured. "Five well trained blood hounds of the Marshall breed were taken along to be sent out with the posse in trailing the robbers."[34]

Not surprisingly rumors that three of the outlaws had been captured began immediately but the report lacked confirmation. Undeterred by this niggling detail, the press declared in a heated trial by media that

> Two more of the Flatonia train robbers have been caught at San Antonio. Now let them be tried as speedily as they have been captured and as speedily punished. And let all the newspapers tell the tale of the capture and punishment of these men, that the world may see if we have train robbers in Texas, we also have men in Texas to capture them and punish them.[35]

In San Antonio lawmen received a tip that the gang was hiding in Karnes County. On June 19, 1887, Deputy U. S. Marshal W. J. Bell, Sheriff Nathaniel Lewis, Constable Ed Stevens, and deputy sheriffs Applewhite and Sandoval left San Antonio in pursuit of the outlaws.[36] Other newspapers provide the details that Sheriff W. L. "Will" Rudd of Karnes County telegraphed Lewis to come down and assist him in the arrest of parties believed to be implicated in the train robbery at Flatonia.[37]

Unlike the lawmen who came from San Antonio, William Rudd would not become a career lawman although he had good credentials. He was born in England on August 10, 1845, and parish registers indicate that he was a resident of Burnham-

Westgate in Norfolk when he was christened on September 6, 1845.[38] Around 1872 Rudd immigrated to the United States. Ranger muster rolls indicate that he served under Leander H. McNelly during 1874 and 1875.[39] On September 9, 1886, he was appointed sheriff of Karnes County and was subsequently re-elected in November of that year. He served through November 1888.[40] The "desperate characters" Rudd had located were not identified in the press. Moreover, the combined force of lawmen located the gang's camp but found none of the outlaws.[41]

At the state level, the Texas Rangers were not idle. Adjutant General King ordered Company F, William Scott commanding, to Cisco to break up "this infamous business."[42] Reports from various ranger companies are telling. Company B, commanded by Samuel McMurray, pursued suspect A. T. Barnes to Austin but was forced to release him when he could not be identified.[43] Company C under the command of George Schmitt had already been hunting the McNeil train robbers as of June 12.[44] In short, coming within two weeks of Rube Burrow's gang robbing a train at Benbrook Station on June 4, 1887, posses were everywhere, and still the outlaws eluded capture.[45]

Despite persistent rumors in the press that the gang had fled to Mexico, the law continued the pursuit.[46] Additional fuel was added to the outrage by the *Waco Daily Examiner* when a package was received at the Texas express office for a lady staying at the Pacific hotel "partially sprinkled" with blood spilled at Flatonia.[47]

Once again private and public entities coalesced. On June 20, 1887, the board of directors of the Merchants and Manufacturers Bureau of Fort Worth published a resolution expressing "perfect confidence in the wisdom and ability of Governor Ross" that promised to "heartily support" Governor Ross "in any energetic and extraordinary measures he may think proper to adopt for the prompt suppression of train robberies and punishment of the guilty."[48]

The same day it was announced that Wells Fargo was offering $1,000 for the capture of each of the robbers. The Southern Pacific added $200 and the state of Texas an additional $500.[49] San Antonio's *Daily Light* placed the reward at $1,750 per head.[50] The reward money proved a double-edged sword, however. While it was a huge incentive to pursue the outlaws, it also brought out the worst in some men.

As if in answer to the rewards, the first arrests came on June 20, 1887. Three men, John Otho, Ed Clark, and August Smith, were arrested and taken to Flatonia for identification.[51] The arrests added to the latest speculations made by the press.

> U.S. Marshal Rankin telegraphed yesterday to district clerk Duval that three of the train robbers had been arrested and identified but were being held at Flatonia for further identification. It is believed here that Ham White, the celebrated stage robber, is implicated in the robbery. The officers are still diligently at work.[52]

Credit for the arrests was given to Sheriff B. L. Zapp of Fayette County. Zapp had gone to Flatonia and ascertained that a well-known character of Fayette County named John Otho was "connected" with the train robbery through the testimony of local resident Leon Mansfield. In addition, a woman named Sarah Tevis (or Tivvis) informed Zapp that she knew three of the men involved in the robbery, but she refused to identify them for fear she would be killed. Still another woman, Laura Johnson of San Antonio, testified she saw Otho at Flatonia "where she then was, prior to accompanying some friends to Weimar to celebrate Emancipation day."[53] According to the account in the newspapers Laura Johnson and others identified Otho "by some lumps he has on his forehead" when the train was robbed. It was more than enough to establish probable cause.

Originally there were eight men Zapp suspected and wanted to interrogate. When they learned of his investigation, Otho,

Clark, and Smith surrendered themselves to Sheriff A. J. Smothers of Lavaca County.[54] Zapp and U. S. Marshal John Rankin led a posse composed of Constable H. Zork of Weimar, W. [*sic*: John R.] Rankin, and J. F. McClatchy "to Sweet Home, where all the men live, and arrested five more, who were afterwards turned loose for want of identification." An over-exuberant press categorized the trio as "hard characters," supposedly stockmen.[55]

The lawmen were immediately confronted by two issues. First, none of the witnesses were "able to see his [their] face, because he [they] had a blue handkerchief tied around it." The second problem was purely racist. All of the witnesses were identified as "colored" and the anger about black witnesses identifying and testifying against white men as train robbers boiled over. "Feeling ran very high in Flatonia and Marshal Rankin and assistants had to vigilantly guard the witnesses who were brought here, as many inhabitants threatened to make away with them."[56]

According to one report, one of the three men, identified as George Shoaf, "a noted San Antonio gambler," was believed to be one of the outlaws who participated in the Flatonia robbery.[57] Armed with this identification, on June 22 Sheriff George W. Ellis of Harris County and Captain A. Faulkner, general passenger agent for the Houston and Central Texas Railroad, chartered a special engine and rushed to San Antonio. They found Shoaf gambling in "Gus' cave" and coaxed him to the Maverick Hotel where Ellis arrested Shoaf and "bound him in irons" until the "proper officers" could be aroused so that the proper papers could be obtained to commit Shoaf to jail.[58] Later in the day John Hall was arrested by Sheriff Nathaniel Lewis. Hall was "said to be one of the men who wore a mask on his face and had in his pocket when arrested a woman's black lace vail [*sic*: veil]."[59] The following day, based upon the description given by Folger, a sixth man was arrested named Tillman Richardson.[60]

The arrests captured national attention, most particularly because of a report that Shoaf had been identified as Captain Dick.[61] Shoaf was not flattered by the identification and strongly denied his guilt stating that a number of witnesses could demonstrate that he was playing poker in San Antonio the night of the robbery.[52]

The sense of satisfaction from the news media was apparent. The *San Antonio Daily Light* proclaimed:

> Information was received in the city this morning that six men are already under arrest and the authorities are on the tract [*sic*: track] of others.
>
> This is well for Texas is getting a bad name abroad for infringing personal liberty and for desperadoism, three trains having been held up and robbed within one month. Texas must vindicate herself as a law and order state and is determined upon doing it, for the days of the desperado are past.[63]

In Fort Worth the *Gazette* added that "The brutes who knocked men and women over the head at Flatonia will, in all human probability, have a long life in the penitentiary to reflect—if they are capable of reflection."[64] California newspapers agreed: "As long as they can commit this species of crime with impunity, the breed will increase in number, and their robberies will become more frequent."[65] The suspects' trial by media was swiftly concluded. Justice in a court of law was far less speedy.

The first hearings were on June 23. Shoaf and Richardson, neither of whom the train men could identify, were released from custody. Smith, Otho, and Clark were held in the amount of $1000 each to appear before the federal grand jury on July 11. At the same time a warrant was issued for one Bud Woods of Flatonia, "who attempted to intimidate witnesses by threatening them with death if they identified any of the gang in jail here."[66]

By June 25 the rewards for the outlaws had risen to $1,950 each.[67] At the same time, the remaining train robbing cases were unravelling, and on June 27, 1887, a Fort Worth newspaper carried the telling headline, "Every One of the Supposed Train Robbers Discharged" due to the advice of the United States District Attorney who did not believe there was sufficient evidence to be had on which to warrant even a preliminary hearing. Sarah Tevis, who had been held in jail as an attached witness, was also released. The article concluded bitterly, "Bets are now offered without takers that the Flatonia crime will be repeated within the next two weeks."[68]

There was another brief flash concerning the gang during June's waning days. On June 28 a German who gave his name as Jim Jackson was staggering down the streets of Sherman under the influence of alcohol when he advised J. Long that he was one of the Flatonia train robbers and wanted to give himself up. Long duly incarcerated him. The officers quickly realized that Jackson was an assumed name as he spoke English "very brokenly." "Jackson" claimed that he was with Sam Bass when he was killed and wanted to surrender because one of the other robbers "struck the lady over the head with a pistol." Not surprisingly the case came to nothing. The motivation for the false confession remains unknown.[69]

What the press did not know was that another solid lead to the outlaws' identities had surfaced. John Barber was already suspected, and on June 20, only two days after the robbery, Vachel Weldon wrote to Adjutant General King from Cuero, Texas. Weldon was not the average informant, having served in the Texas state legislature. Born in Kentucky to Abram Brewer Weldon and his wife Sarah Eliza Ann Turner during 1833, Weldon and his wife Sophia Lodge settled in Texas by 1858. [70] Now Weldon informed King "that shortly before the McNeil robbery Reinhardt Schneider, Will Kelley, Will Jacobs and Bud Powell were in their old range near the line of this Karnes &

Gonzales Cos that horses were stolen from this neighborhood one of which is said to have been found near the place of the robbery." That in itself may have been coincidence, but Weldon continued that the men were "again in this country and immediately preceding this last robbery another lot of horses have disappeared." Weldon thought the matter curious as the men had left "the members of our stock association" alone.[71]

Establishing the location of the gang at this time is problematic. Secrest had fled the state and one account places him roaming through Montana, Wyoming, Colorado, and Arizona.[72] Ike Cloud likewise fled the state, possibly to Oklahoma. As to the others, following the robbery the gang fled southwest to Eli Harrell's home where they divided the loot. Reeves gave a butterfly scarf pin to Eli Harrell who also pocketed two or three diamond rings and a watch from Cornett. Will Harrell provided food for the gang. Newton Butler requested Newberger's stolen watch and some of the diamonds, which were provided. The gang moved on to Butler's pasture where they remained for three days. On the second day Eli and Will Harrell, Newton Butler, and surprisingly enough a deputy sheriff named Alfred Y. Allee joined the gang with three new pistols and scabbards that the outlaws paid for from the proceeds of the robbery.[73]

The presence of Alfred Young Allee, a deputy sheriff, at the rendezvous site has never been adequately explained.[74] Allee bore a checkered reputation littered with violence, and the *Saint Louis Republic* characterizes him as "a dangerous character."[75] As early as 1876 Allee was engaged in gunplay in Goliad, Texas. On December 13, 1876, he and Buck Lyons were riding around the town square. Lyons was drunk and flourishing his pistol following delivery of a herd of cattle from Karnes County. Sheriff John M. Yeary attempted to disarm them with the aid of Peter Miller. Lyons surrendered his weapon, but Allee fired at Miller who naturally returned the fire. Fortunately no one was killed.[76] In 1877 Allee was arrested by Texas Ranger Lee Hall and his detachment on charges from Karnes County.[77]

Despite the fact that Allee was a deputy sheriff, his presence apparently did not alarm the gang. One theory is that he was acting undercover and was assigned the job to locate the outlaws for U. S. Deputy Marshal W. J. Bell. He is supposed to have informed Bell of the outlaws' whereabouts, but this is unlikely since Bell had left for Karnes County two days before the outlaws met with Allee. Another possibility is that Allee, like the Harrell brothers and Newt Butler, was aiding them in some manner. It is possible but by no means certain that he was there to provide inside information to the outlaws. A third possibility is that the Harrell brothers and Butler found the rewards for the outlaws appealing and planned to betray them. Regardless, no one questioned his presence possibly because of his reputation and the fact that he and Cornett had known one another in their youth.

On the evening of June 24 John Barber entered Cuero. His first stop was the Southern Pacific depot where he inquired about fares and routes to various locations. He then bought a newspaper and headed to an ice cream parlor to cool off. His movements proved suspicious to someone who reported him to Sheriff Addison Kilgore. Kilgore and two other officers went to arrest or at least question him. Barber attempted to flee and the officers opened fire, wounding his mount. Barber abandoned the horse, stole another mount, and escaped.[78]

The other gang members were camped in Butler's pasture. Barber was forced to hide in the vicinity of Cuero until the evening of June 29. Someone learned or suspected that he planned on going to his brother Joe's home, but how much truth this has is undetermined. Barber might well have allowed his own loose lips to scuttle this ship or he may have realized that the lie would ring true and divert attention away from him. From available documents, it is apparent that the law had learned that the gang used Butler's pasture as a hideout. As the hunt for Barber intensified, the law came to believe that Barber would return to his four companions in the Butler pasture and provide himself with a horse.[79]

Barber got his new mount around the same time the gang acquired a new recruit, generally referred to as Milton Day in the newspapers of the day. Day was one of the men whom both Burton and Whitley's biorgrapher theorize took a role in the Flatonia train robbery.[80] Born Winnfield Martin Day to John Washington and Francis A. Lowe Day on December 29, 1865, in De Witt County, Texas, Day was a product of the Sutton-Taylor War, his family siding with the Taylors.[81] How Day linked up with the gang is uncertain. It appears most likely that he was recruited by Bud Powell, who may have known him. Day had recently been released, on April 22, 1887, from the Huntsville Penitentiary, having served four years for "burglary and robbery."[82]

According to Reeves, Day arrived in time to discuss several possible targets while they hid out. One was the bank at Cuero. Another was the bank at Fredericksburg. Reeves later informed investigators that "Whitley, Barbour, Milton Day and I agreed in Butler's pasture to rob a bank in Cuero or Fredericksburg. We went to Fredericksburg, but found people were on the watch. Thinking the Rangers were there, we changed our minds."[83] The idea of robbing the bank at Cuero came to an abrupt halt after Barber was nearly captured. In July the gang headed north.[84]

While the gang moved and manipulated, neither the government nor industry were idle. On July 4, 1887, J. Waldo, Commissioner of the Texas Traffic Association, met with Governor Lawrence Sullivan "Sul" Ross at the governor's request to discuss the protection of passenger trains within the state. Ross suggested "to commission train men as might be designated by each Road, as rangers to be members" of the

Frontier Battalion. These men were to be strictly "under the control of such persons as the Railroads might appoint, and not to be withdrawn from that service except as directed by the railroads employing them."

The plan was to commission 500 men employed by the railroads. All of these men needed to take the prescribed oath which could be done before any notary public in the state. A descriptive list of the officers was to be furnished to the state. The railroads would pay and arm the men, and their authority would be recognized throughout the state.[85]

The plan was proposed by the governor and accepted by the representatives of the railroads who were present.[86] It was not a perfect solution. The St. Louis & Santa Fe represented by Waldo with the authority of the general manager Mr. Morrill had "but a few miles in Texas at the present time, Mr. Morrill may not desire to enter the agreement now." The Southern Pacific representative needed to have the approval of his superior. Neither the Ft. Worth & Denver City nor the San Antonio & Aransas Pass railroad had representatives present, but Waldo was addressing their managing officers and hoped to hear from them soon.[87]

H. L. Morrill was not lax in accepting the proposal and promised cooperation "as soon as circumstances will permit" but pointed out the difficulties. "At present we only have 16 miles of road in the State and no trains running entirely within the State: the crews all run between Fort Smith, Talihina and Paris, so that it seems impossible to undertake to commission any of our men just yet. As soon as our mileage or arrangements will at all permit, you may count upon our fully cooperating in every way."[88]

C. L. Frost, Superintendent of the Fort Worth & Denver City, was also prompt in his response, seeking clarification on some points that demonstrate one of the difficulties of the plan. "What particular employees connected with passenger trains are meant in speaking of four men to each train? As you know it frequently becomes necessary to relieve train men for few days acct. sickness & c. In such cases would the new men be required to take out commissions or could these commissions be made transferable under such restrictions as might be deemed necessary?"[89]

Waldo forwarded the letters to Governor Ross on July 13.[90] Three days earlier Waldo was able to inform Adjutant General King that the San Antonio and Aransas Pass accepted the proposition while the Missouri Pacific promised prompt attention. A. C. Hutchinson, General Manager of the Southern Pacific, was "somewhat averse" to the plan. "He thinks that train men could not be utilized for the purpose of train guards in addition to their regular duties and suggests that the probabilities would be that they would be away from their arms in the event of an attack which, of course, would be sudden with much confusion incident."[91] There were other issues of course, but even before these were ironed out the governor and adjutant general were inundated with varying requests.[92]

One such letter recommended to Governor Ross that George W. Munden be appointed as a railroad guard. Munden was a former deputy sheriff and constable and owned a fine pack of bloodhounds.[93] Deputy U. S. Marshal Tom Bailes wrote directly to W. H. King offering his services as a private detective.[94] S. S. Johnston tried a different approach, getting Deputy Sheriff A. B. Coffee of Burnet County to approach Wilburn H. King. Johnston wished "to undertake the capture of Jno. Barber." According to Coffee, Johnston, was a reformed man who had changed his ways and wanted to be enlisted and only receive expense money, which seems odd except that he also wanted "all the rewards."[95]

What none of them knew was that the gang had no immediate intention of robbing another train. On the contrary, the Cornett-Whitley gang was under extreme pressure from the law. Like Cloud and Secrest before him, Bud Powell decided that he had had enough. Powell would later tell reporters that in July 1887 he, Reeves, and Cornett had gone to Burnet County.

> We traveled north together to Burnet county and there we met John Barber, Bill Whitley and another man [Martin Day]. I did not know his name; never saw him before. That was in the night. They wanted to rob another train or a bank, but I told them right there if they wanted to do anything of that kind they would have to get some one else to help them, for I was going to leave the country. They tried to persuade me to stay with them until we could make a raise, but I knew the whole country was after us, so I bade them goodbye and started.[96]

With Powell's departure went Ed Reeves. The pair headed east towards Arkansas.

July 1887 marks the end of the Cornett-Whitley gang. The outlaws had never had any common bond other than greed. Cloud and Secrest had recognized the growing violence and sadism that the gang embodied, wisely abandoning them prior to the Flatonia robbery. Quite likely they along with Reeves and Powell were afraid of Cornett and his irrational behavior. In Burnet the remainder of the dwindling gang resolved to separate. Cornett and Day were to have south Texas as their territory while Barber and Whitley took north Texas.[97] The Cornett-Whitley gang was dead, but like the cancer it was, the group metastasized into something worse.

Chapter 7

A Stream of Fire

George Schmitt and his company arrived in Karnes County on July 3. After selecting a camping spot one mile from Helena on the route to Kennedy Station, Schmitt wrote to Adjutant General King two days later. With characteristic sureness, Schmitt reported that Jacobs and Schneider had been seen the week previous. "Sheriff Rudd told me that there have been as many as eight together in Camp at Butler's Pasture." Always critical of others, Schmitt was unable to control his critique of fellow officers, noting that: "the San Antonio Officers came down here once but made it public before they did come and of course they found the camp but no robbers and done more harm than good."[1] In a separate report to L. P. Sieker, Texas Ranger quartermaster, Schmitt wrote that "the train robbers have all been in here about one week ago and they may be here yet. Jacobs & Schneider was seen at different places and we will have hard work on hand."[2] Schmitt's identification of Jacobs and Schneider incorrectly as two of the gang was an omen of things to come for Company C.

Schmitt continually bombarded both King and Sieker with updates. On July 8 he wrote that he had six men out "waylaying roads & suspicioned place." He also reported that Schneider, Jacobs, and Will Kelly had been seen two miles from Helena on July 5 trying to learn the number of Rangers present.[3] Three days later he confidently wrote that the gang of train robbers were in the area but not together. "We will soon catch up with them." Schmitt was excited because a telegram from Cuero from Vachel Weldon "will give me important information."[4]

What Schmitt did not know was that Weldon was providing the same information to Adjutant General King. Weldon reported from Cuero that on July 10 the gang had left, planning to meet near the line of Lavaca County and head from there to Flatonia to attempt another train robbery or, "if indications would not justify this" to go further north, possibly to McNeil Station. "Cornett, Hill (Whitley) and Barber started from a few miles below this place and some of the others from the south corner of Gonzales Co. Hill is riding a bay horse branded on the left thigh RAY stolen from John Y. Bell of this place. It will be much better if you can find any indication that your information comes from here as they will return in a few days and I think some of them can be caught. "[5]

Weldon then added, "I have a letter from Capt. Schmitt & will let him know if we can mature a plan with good prospect for making the capture but if he comes to this neighborhood it should be in such way as to avoid attracting attention." He also cautioned King that the information was provided by an "intimate of the parties and as reliable as such information ever is."[6]

On July 12, Weldon again contacted King. "I wrote you a hasty explanation on yesterday morning of the telegram I afterward sent." Weldon advised that Cornett, Barber, and Whitley intended to return to De Witt County and suggested that a guard at the crossing of the Colorado River between Flatonia and McNeil "would stand a good chance of bagging them as they returned."[7]

Schmitt's reports indicate that he had not been idle. Writing to the adjutant general, he reported that he returned from Cuero where he had consulted with both Weldon and "the parties who can work all the train Robbers in our hand." Schmitt confirmed Weldon's information that the gang planned to rob another train and would return. He had arranged to be notified at once and had everything "arranged to round them up and they will be taken or killed." Schmitt anticipated that they would return by July 17 "and we can be there in one night after receiving the telegram." Schmitt concluded "I am well posted of all the affair, and if they or any of them return alive, I will have them. I have the whole plan and all circumstances with it and I will do my duty and I think the whole gang will be killed or in Iron before long."[8]

Considering the information that Schmitt had at hand, his actions are curious. There is no indication that he notified local officials in Williamson County or elsewhere of the possible robbery, nor did he alert the railroad. He did not dispatch anyone to trail the outlaws, nor did he arrange for a guard at the Colorado River crossing for a possible intercept of the gang. Indeed, Schmitt did not even assign a part of his detachment to Cuero; his only deviation was to station a man at the local telegraph office so he could be there in a day after getting the telegram. Rather, he had already made his plans for a sweep that would round them all up in one swift encounter. Schmitt's weakness was that he could or would not deviate from the plan.

What Schmitt did do was to request aid from the San Antonio & Aransas Pass railroad. B. F. Yoakum, manager of the railway responded quickly:

> In compliance with your request of the 9th inst. I hand you herewith our time pass No. 72 which will

> be renewed if necessary when it expires. At anytime that you may be obliged to move your men over our line on short notice we will be pleased to extend to you free of charge the best facilities circumstances will permit.
>
> We have issued special covering half tariff rates on all shipments of Supplies & Co made or authorized by you.[9]

Characteristically Schmitt reported this to King on July 14.[10]

The real breakthrough in the cases came via Wells Fargo, the largely unsung heroes in unravelling the Cornett-Whitley gang's members. How they learned the identities of the men involved is unknown, but on July 2 Wells Fargo issued a circular providing the names and descriptions of the Flatonia train robbers. Topping the list was Brack Cornett, alias Bill McGinty or Bill Bradley. Cornett was "known among his fellows as Bill Bradley." Second was J. A. Powell, alias Bud Powell, followed by Ed "Pat" Reaves [*sic*: Reeves], Bill Whitley (alias John Hill), and John Barber.[11]

The obvious informants were the Harrell brothers or, far more likely, Newt Butler. The circular indicates that the information was obtained around the time of the Flatonia robbery. After identifying and describing the participants in the Flatonia robbery, the circular states that the "five men above named, with two others whose names and descriptions are known, robbed the train near McNeil's Station." In addition, in a note appended to this circular on Adjutant General's Office stationery and dated July 7, 1887, is a description of Frank Cline who was "engaged in train robbing in Arkansas."[12] None of the possible informants had ever met Cloud, and if Wells Fargo had had a description of Ross (Secrest) or Cloud more than their names, both men would surely have made the circular. This appears to indicate an informant or informants, quite possibly Will Jacobs.

Not surprisingly, the news media, always ready to criticize anyone but themselves, proved as sarcastic in July as they had in June. "Train robbing is becoming one of the most popular employments in our state, and those engaged in it seem to enjoy all immunity from unpleasant consequences."[13]

For Whitley and Barber, their return to Burnet County was nothing new. On July 17, James C. Martin, a local lawman of Manchaca, Texas, inquired of Governor Ross if Ross knew of any officers being on the lookout at Red Rock in Bastrop County for Whitley and Barber. Martin had been trailing an armed party who turned out to be hunters, but while he was in Burnet, a man from Red Rock informed him that "John Barber and a man who he introduced as Hill" had been there, staying about a week in early June. Whitley was sighted again on July 8 in a pasture near Marble Falls.[14]

Also, on July 27, William Safford wrote from Seguin that a horse had been stolen on July 12. Around 5:30 p.m. four men had been seen at the store of August G. Startz northwest of New Braunfels in Comal County. The men were both armed with Winchesters and two six shooters with a belt full of cartridges. The pair seemed watchful, and on their departure inquired for Blanco. From the descriptions of the four they appear to have been Cornett, Reeves, Day, and Powell. "1st (riding my horse) About 27 years of age, 5' & 10" high sandy chin whiskers a short moustache grey eyes [Brack Cornett]. 2nd Dark complected [*sic*] black moustache heavy dark hair [Ed Reeves]. 3rd Very dark black moustache & unshaven for two or three weeks [Martin Day]. 4th youthful light complexion & smooth faced [Bud Powell]."[15]

At Cuero Barber and Whitley were spotted on July 15. The informant, James E. Hollingsworth, send word to Governor Ross that he believed the pair had buried their part of the Flatonia proceeds, about $1500 each, in Joe Barber's field and were headed to Williamson County to get it back. On July 17

Barber and Whitley were again seen, this time along the San Antonio River near the property of someone named Brickford, who is so far unknown. Two of the Brickford boys and "the new man Day who joined on Sunday night a week ago" were with Barber and Whitley.[16]

In yet another letter Schmitt advised King that Joe Bennett, a friend of Barber, had given the gang away. Schmitt outlined his plan to ambush the outlaws when they returned to their hideout near Bennett's home in DeWitt County. Schmitt had been informed that Powell and the others were seen near Riddleville and immediately sent out a scout that failed to find them. As always Schmitt remained confident:

> I think I will succeed in Capturing some of the gang in a course of a short time if my plan[s] are not crossed by some fools, the high reward make some men mostly cracy [*sic*] and one Officer is trying to throw another off the track and run in ahead if they hear anything and do only harm and I hope that the leading men succeeded to get those Postal agts to go back and let my plan be carried out.[17]

Regardless of Schmitt's contention, no evidence has surfaced that any officer was attempting to throw another off the track of the gang. On the contrary, what emerges from the voluminous files is the fact that the only officer concerned about the "high reward" and competition from other officers was Schmitt himself.

As July moved toward August new excitement rocked Texas. On July 23 a man by the name of Ed Reeves was captured at Goliad, Texas. The press was again confident of Reeves's guilt. One news story predicted that Reeves might "have an immediate examination before United States Commissioner Stevenson, though he may possibly waive that preliminary and remain in jail until his trial," adding that the "description of Reeves in the circular corresponds exactly with the leader of the train robbers gang who was known as Captain Dick by his companions."[18] Other newspapers were more circumspect in the identification of Reeves as the bandit leader. "Reeves, the alleged train robber captured at Goliad a few days ago, is believed to be the 'Captain Dick' who bossed the Flatonia robbery."[19] Reeves was transferred to Austin on July 29.[20]

At the time it was reported that an attempt was made to rescue Reeves, supposedly by Whitley and Barber.[21] This appears to have been the product of some misunderstandings, a fevered imagination, or both. Within days of the announcement the truth was known: "Ed Reeves, who was arrested at Goliad last week on suspicion of being the leader of the Flatonia train robbers and was brought to this city last night, was taken before the United States Commissioner this morning and was immediately discharged without an examination, there being not a single circumstance to indicate his guilt."[22]

The Ed Reeves who had been captured was not the outlaw.

On the international front, stories about the horrific robbery at Flatonia were still being spread. In New Zealand newspapers told how two of the outlaws beat Folger mercilessly and cruelly split his ears with pocket knives.[23] Nor was the greed displayed by the outlaws ignored, and another newspaper told of how "the newsboy was robbed of his nickels."[24] In Australia the news summed up the robbery simply by referencing their savage treatment of the passengers, includeing the women.[25] All of it came back to Texas officials being maligned for not satisfying the media's unrealistic demands.

August began with Ranger movements as William Scott moved Company F south of Ballinger.[26] Schmitt reported that Company C had not succeeded in capturing the train robbers, but he was "mostly sure that I will capture some of them before long." In typical Schmitt manner, he laid the blame for his failure on the officers of Karnes and DeWitt Counties who "acted badly," but advised King that he was confident they would return.[27]

Company B was also on the move from their base at Quanah, but McMurry's efforts bore no fruit. He had theorized that the gang was in the vicinity of Butler's herd, but Butler had already sent his cattle to Kansas.[28]

Ira Aten reported that part of Barber's outfit was seen in Lampasas County on July 25 and in neighboring Williamson County the following day. They had been joined, at least temporarily, by Cordelia Whitley's brother Tom Cox who was, he believed, "more of a spy than anything else." Unlike Schmitt, Aten found that Sheriff N. O. Reynolds of Lampasas County, Sheriff Olive in Williamson County, and Sheriff John W. Wolf of Burnet County were cooperative. "The Shff. of the three named co's I can rely upon." Aten lost the trail of the outlaws and returned to keep an eye on Cordelia Whitley who was staying at her brother Tom Cox's home. Feeling that the outlaws had headed south, Aten "notified the officers in the lower country to be on the look-out for them."[29]

Aten had good reason for his confidence. N. O. Reynolds was a former Texas Ranger who had served during the infamous Hoo Doo War in Mason County and during the Horrell-Higgins War.[30] Another career lawman, John W. Wolf had been elected sheriff of Burnet County in 1884 and served until November 1888 when he became city marshal of Burnet.[31]

Aten did not have to wait long. On August 7, 1887, he received a rare telephone call from Deputy Sheriff William J. Stanley.

> We have just rec'd a telephone from Wm Stanley deputy Shff W[illi]mson that John Barber's outfit was making for Lampasas County. Perhaps in the co at this writing. Shff Reynolds a deputy & myself leave for Coxes ranch this morning. We didn't go out last

> night as the Anti Prohibitions had a big time here & trouble was expected. Every thing went off quietly.
>
> We will certainly search the ranch for Barber outfit. K knew they were below but now they are on their way back.[32]

The precise time that Aten got the call is unknown, but during the same evening Stanley was lured from his home with the news that the fence of his home pasture was down. As he headed for the spot, between eight and ten bullets hit him in the back, killing him instantly.[33]

To this day the reasons for Stanley's murder have never been adequately explained. The *Brenham Daily Banner* commented that Stanley "was a very efficient officer and a terror to law breakers."[34] Another newspaper stated that he was "very active in hunting up criminals."[35] Neither of these accounts provide a motive for the attack. Whitley's biographer, without naming the officer, implies that Stanley was killed in revenge for Jasper Whitley's death, but as demonstrated Stanley played no role in his death.[36]

Still another version, picked up by some of the exchanges, has it that Stanley was murdered "out of revenge for the prosecution in the McNeill train robbery."[37] This appears highly unlikely since none of the men arrested were taken to trial. All of them were discharged in the preliminary hearings. What is known is that Sheriff Olive swiftly identified Barber and Whitley as the suspects. Olive's suspicion has never been seriously doubted, and the real motive appeared under the headline "Foul Murder."

> GEORGETOWN, August 8. – Soon after dark on Saturday night, Deputy Sheriff W. J. Stanley was killed at his place a short distance south of Florence. He had gone out to put up a fence and restake a horse, and was fired upon by two persons in ambush,

> who shot Stanley ten times. Two men who were on the gallery of the dwelling, a short distance off, ran to where Stanley was, but he was dead when they reached him. Intelligence of the killing was received here about 12 o'clock Saturday night, and officers left in pursuit of the murderers, whom they trailed through Florence and in the direction of Lampasas. Stanley had taken an active part in efforts to bring horse thieves to justice, and it is supposed that this led to his assassination. No late news from the pursuing party.[38]

Stanley's pursuit of Barber's horse-stealing gang was noted in a number of newspapers.[39]

Also on August 7, Schmitt wrote to Adjutant General King that he had received King's letter of August 2 with a petition signed by a number of citizens. Schmitt hastily informed King that when he had received his orders to move to Brownwood he had to wait "nearly three weeks" because his men were on a scout to Cotulla. Schmitt not so subtly hinted that a great deal of good could be done "if I could be stationed somewhere down there for a while or at least to send about 3 or four men to be stationed there for a few Months."

Judging from his subsequent behavior and the fact that Cotulla, Texas, is half the distance from Helena that Brownwood is, it appears that Schmitt had become obsessed with the gang and, possibly, the huge rewards. Ignoring King's correspondence and without a hint of planning to move, Schmitt continued,

> I have worked up all the points necessary for the capture of the train robbers they have left here temporary but they will sure get back here in a short time then I am mostly sure I am able to capture & kill some of them. I received informations [*sic*] mostly every day of the whereabouts & movements of the

> gang they are divided up and commit depredations in different parts of the State the gang who robbed the Chinamen at Odessa Station near Midland are some of them, and I am satisfied that I can locate & capture some of them in a short time and if I should not be able to succeed in capturing some of them soon I will make a scout down there myself of send a sufficient number of men to be able to do good work.

King responded to Schmitt on August 10.[40] Two days earlier King had advised Schmitt of Stanley's murder.[41]

Schmitt's reluctance to abandon Karnes County is evident in a letter dated August 9 in which he stated his confidence that Stanley's murderers "will make their way to this Country, I will have men out to receive them, it [will] take hard work to catch them as they have to many friends in this Country to harbor & feed them, but we got things pin down and I will trap them yet."[42]

In defiance of his superior's orders, Schmitt remained in Karnes County. On August 17 he reported to King that "Martin Day an Ex Convict who went of[f] with three of the train robbers [Barber, Cornett and Whitley] some four weeks ago was seen the night before last and it is supposed that gang returned with him." He advised King that he had sent Sergeant Albert C. Grimes and four men to Cuero and was taking the train there to apprehend the train robbers.[43]

Schmitt was back in Helena on August 19, once again singing the same song about why he had not captured the outlaws. This time he charged that a special Ranger on his rolls named Cook "spoiled all of my plans." Cook allegedly told Joe Bennett, Schmitt's informant, "not to have anything to do with me that he was the ranking man to work things and that I work under him and I had to do what he says & co [*sic*: etc.] that I would deceive Bennett and that he would give him all the rewards & co." Rather curiously Schmitt concluded, "I am satisfied that said Bennett have seen the robbers that night and told them to get out as he know [*sic*: knew] that I was coming."[44]

Unsurprisingly Schmitt had still not moved to Brownwood when he wrote to King on August 26 from Helena. His stubborn determination is clearly evident in the letter. Declaring that he had a better chance than ever to capture the gang, Schmitt advised, "I have made up my mind not to let up until they are captured or killed, or be killed in the undertaking, it is for certainly not my fault that I have not yet succeeded." In a lengthy letter, Schmitt outlined plans and alliances he had formed to capture the train robbers, including one with Newton Butler. He concluded, in passive defiance of King after rationalizing why he should not obey orders, "but if you think proper I will send four or five men down there now, Gen. don't you take this for an disobeyance of orders I am to [*sic*] long in the Service to disobey orders and will go anywhere if it should cost my life."[45]

While the insubordinate Schmitt postured, procrastinated, and rationalized in Karnes County, Governor Ross continued to receive offers that backhandedly at the very least were insulting to law enforcement at all levels. One offer began, "As the officials throughout the state have utterly failed to trace up the perpetrators of the late train robberies, I write to offer my services as a detective."[46] Another one from Hall & Waller's Detective Agency noted "the numerous Gangs of Train Robbers, and Desperadoes now infesting our state."[47]

The criticism weighed heavily on some public officials, but all the signs were encouraging as they closed in on the gang. Existing records indicate that Barber and Whitley fled to Oklahoma where a requisition was sent to the Chickasaw Nation for their arrest.[48] The authorities may or may not have known that Cloud was there as well. Secrest appears to have been in New Mexico or Colorado. Reeves and Powell were aiming for Arkansas.

Even as Barber and Whitley were adding murder to their resumes, Brack Cornett was in the process of expanding the cancerous infestation the gang embodied by forming a new gang. Accompanied by Martin Day, Cornett recruited John W. Insall into his gang.[49] Insall, frequently misspelled "Ensall" in contemporary newspapers, was a likely candidate to Cornett's twisted mind. In 1882, while under sentence of two years for cattle theft in Kimble County, Insall broke jail in broad daylight.[50] He was recaptured on October 21, 1883, while sporting the alias John Campbell. The newspapers characterized him as "a fugitive from justice and a noted horse-thief."[51] One contemporary description of Insall described him as a "tall, rawboned, slender-built man, apparently twenty-five or six years old, dark brown hair and a beard of about three weeks' growth ornaments his face."[52] A more detailed description notes him as "5 feet 10 or 11 inches high, slender build, black hair, eyes and mustache, dark complexion, left arm has been broken and can't use it well, left leg shorter than right and walks with toe turned and heel not touching the ground, has several scars on back from gunshot wound."[53] It appears highly likely that Cornett knew Insall from his horse stealing days. Insall's family recalls that John Insall "was so mean that he would cut off his head and throw it at you."[54]

Cornett's final recruit was a chance selection. The gang needed at least one more man for what they planned, and Martin Day knew of an impressionable teenager who could fill the spot. Henry Peter Kelly Jr. was the son of Henry Peter Kelly Sr. and his wife Amanda Jane Taylor, and was born March 29, 1869, in DeWitt County. Like Cornett, he was a product of the Sutton-Taylor Feud, his father being murdered by agents of State Policeman Jack Helm on August 26, 1870. No one was ever legally punished for the murder.[55] During 1885 and 1886 he attended the Prime Cuero Institute.[56] Nothing in his record indicates that he was ever associated with anyone from the original gang except Brack Cornett, but that was more than enough.

The fledgling gang now headed east toward Houston with the intention of robbing the train at Gum Island.[57] The station received its name from railroad men of the Southern Pacific because of the gum trees that grew between White Oak Bayou and Willow Creek. Cornett was the gang's leader, but the operation proved that he was not "the brightest among them," as Burton notes.[58] En route to the robbery the men stole fresh horses when needed, heralding their impending arrival and route. On August 24 Cornett's gang arrived at Thompson Switch where they ordered dinner. Afterwards "they got drunk, fired off pistols and terrified the inhabitants and rode off in a northwesterly direction."[59] The following day the outlaws stole two horses from the farm of Tom Williford.[60]

Somehow Williford learned that the stolen horses and accompanying thieves were still in the neighborhood. On August 27 he arrived in Houston and notified Sheriff George W. Ellis. Ellis, a former Texas Ranger, gathered a posse and started in pursuit. The posse aimed for Navasota where the outlaws had last been seen.[61] In Houston Deputies Albert Erichson[62] and Ben Kegans[63] remained in charge, and it was Erichson who received word that men with "a striking resemblance to the alleged horse thieves" were camped near Eureka.[64] Accompanied by Tom Williford, the men left for Eureka to inspect the camp. Along the way they encountered a lone rider who tipped his hat and wished them a good morning as he passed, putting his horse into a lope as he did so.

The action was daring. Erichson and Williford reined in their mounts and turned them, Williford declaring to Erichson that the man was one of the gang and the horse was his. At the same time, Brack Cornett, the lone rider, turned in his saddle, gave them a cheerful wave and put spurs to his mount. The pair attempted to run him down, Williford firing once at the fugitive, but it was to no avail. Disgusted with their luck the men continued on to Eureka.

The remaining gang members were still camped near Eureka, and Erichson made haste to telegraph for help. Deputy sheriff Waites, Captain Dave Lubbock, and Charles Wichman, the jailer, headed for Eureka where they were met by "a Mr. Kniffe and two Germans."[65] The posse skirted Eureka and shortly came in sight of the men. At the same time the outlaws saw them and hastily saddled their horses. The first man mounted, probably Insall, opened fire with his Winchester, and as the second clambered into the saddle he opened fire with his six-shooter while the third was still saddling his mount as the posse charged them. When they got within range the posse began returning fire.

During the skirmish one of the outlaws' horses was hit, though not severely, and it was believed that one of the outlaws was shot in the left leg. On the posse's side Dave Lubbock's horse was killed outright and a Mr. "Kasaner" (*sic*: Kasiner) was shot in the arm with a rifle bullet. Some forty or fifty shots were exchanged during the shootout.[66]

The outlaws escaped across White Oak Bayou, and the posse broke off the pursuit. In the hastily abandoned camp they found "four slickers, two Hardin jackets for carrying six shooters (new), one jaunty white sombrero, one box of cartridges, one pair of riding gloves, one pocket knife and small file, one blanket, one belt and one paper sack with ammunition in it. The sack had on its side a printed card of Comminge [*sic*: Cummings] & Geisler of Houston."

The descriptions of the trio were vague except for the leader who was riding a roan and had a black plume in his hat and used his rifle so effectively "that almost a stream of fire came from its barrel." The remaining outlaws rode a bay mount and a black horse stolen from Williford.[67]

Once again men searched the area determined to capture the horse thieves. One posse headed out of Houston at noon with "Jim Grayson, John Burney, R. E. Lewis, Tom Lubbock and others" to scour the country around Eureka and Cypress. At the same time dispatches were sent to Sheriff Ellis so they could coordinate their efforts. The men were believed to be working their way toward Montgomery County's Big Thicket to the north.[68]

This time the law had the outlaws firmly in their sights. The hunt would be unrelenting.

Chapter 8

I Will Make Things Lively

Tips about the gang were developed as the pursuit heightened. Reportedly they had been seen the week ending August 20 at a store where they flashed a large roll of bills and claimed to be stockmen.[1] On the afternoon of August 31 a farmer named Levi Hargraves living near Westfield arrived in Houston and informed officers that the gang had eaten at his house on August 29 around four o'clock. Mrs. Hargraves recognized the man she thought was the leader as having sold her husband a stolen mule two years earlier. The outlaw immediately paid her thirty dollars, the same amount Hargraves had purchased the mule for.[2]

With the tips came the ever-present rumors. At least one report carried the tale that they were a part of the Sam Bass gang.[3] Sheriff Ellis was an old hand at the game, however. Unconcerned with rumor, he had a hot trail and wired Sheriff Thomas S. McDade of Waller County asking him to raise a posse and intercept the outlaws. At the same time Ben Kegans and Albert Erichson took a train to link up with Ellis.[4]

Ellis returned to Houston on the afternoon of August 31 having found four horses that had been stolen at Cypress and abandoned near Rose Hill. The authorities now knew that the leader of the gang was Cornett.

> The leader of the gang is a man about five feet ten inches tall light hair and mustache and weighs about 160 pounds. His name is Brackett Cornett alias Harrington alias Jones alias George Lacy, alias James W. Johnson, alias McGinty. He is the boldest and worst man in the gang. He has been an outlaw for five or six years and is wanted in several counties. He is wanted in Atascosa county for murder. It is said also that he killed a wealthy stockman named Brown, in Kansas, sometime ago, and that Browns relatives have made strenuous efforts to capture him, but to no avail. About two years ago Cornett stole fifty head of mules in one of the western counties, and Captain Lee Hall then in charge of the rangers, followed him to this county. Here Captain Hall was cajoled by Deputy Sheriff Ben Kegans, and together they pursued the outlaw to Reids prairie, where they lost the trail and had to abandon the pursuit. The course which the outlaw took then was identical with the one he took after having the skirmish with the officers at Eureka. It is thought that Cornett is slightly wounded as he had his head bandaged when he passed Hargraves house.

Cornett's identification is hardly surprising, but the names of the others "identified" are. Someone informed reporters that the balance of the gang was composed of Frank Hargraves and two men named Baker and Perkins. Very likely all of the gang were using aliases.[5]

Ellis had a much hotter trail than Lee Hall and Ben Kegans had followed. Between one and two o'clock in the morning of September 3 a report reached Houston that the outlaws were back in the neighborhood. A posse went out to the residence of a man living near Eureka who told them that two men had aroused him late that night. One of the pair was fully equipped but the other rode a barebacked horse. The pair forced him to provide a saddle "and generally conducted themselves like bad men." The posse finally returned to Houston without finding the pair and knowing only that one of them had ridden a gray horse and the other a black one.[6]

Deputy Sheriff Erichson had better luck of a sort. He and a posse tracked a band of four men, surprising them while they were eating. The men surrendered peacefully, but an investigation of the captives quickly determined that they were not the outlaws, whom none of them had heard of. "They said that on their route everybody they saw seemed to shun them. If they road [*sic*] to a house to make purchases or ask questions, the whole household generally fled. These mysterious movements on the part of the country people astonished them greatly, and when the posse pounced upon them from the brush they were doubly astonished." Erichson released them about half an hour after the capture.[7]

In Uvalde County, Sheriff Henry W. Baylor arrested a man named Baker for complicity in the McNeil Station train robbery.[8] Baker had "spoken of his connection with the robbery," and on September 3 U. S. Deputy Marshal Tom Bailes delivered him in San Antonio. The newspapers, apparently unable to grasp the concept of probable cause, sourly emphasized that Baker's arrest was another in the series "for which about a dozen wrong arrests have been made."[9]

The law did not give up on the outlaws. On September 10 rumors swept Austin that there had been a train robbery at Manchaca in Travis County. Another report had it that a posse had attacked the robbers and one of the officers had been killed.[10] These rumors led to more rumors of a bloody battle where three men, one officer, and two of the outlaws had been wounded. The truth was far less dramatic.

In Manchaca officer James C. Martin learned that three men were camped along a creek about a mile from the town. Early on the morning of September 10, John Insall came into town, "laying around until about 10:30 in the morning." Martin and George Bently arrested Insall then sent to Kyle for Martin's brother Tom and Tom's son Frank. It was a logical choice, for the Martins were all local lawmen. Tom Martin, the elder of the brothers by four years, arrived with his twenty-two-year-old son on the northbound train. After securing Insall, the Martins and Bently started for the outlaws' camp.

Day and Kelly saw the officers approaching and ran for their pistols, but before they could reach them the officers opened fire. The pair returned fire as they fled on foot. Jim Martin was hit in the right arm, the bullet breaking it. Day and Kelly escaped, leaving three horses, two pistols, and $115 in gold along with their hats and shoes. Martin telegraphed Austin for help, and City Marshal James Lucy and Sheriff Malcolm Hornsby rushed with a posse to their assistance.[11]

Day and Kelly were pursued to a pasture along Onion Creek, which was then surrounded by the posse in the belief that they were trapped. As it developed, neither Day nor Kelly were in the pasture. Near the scene of the fight the pair had stolen a horse from a black farmer and, mounted double, fled. At a wire fence the pair abandoned the mount. "About five miles down Onion creek they bought a horse and procured hats and shoes and a hatchet to cut wire fences in their route." The fugitives headed east.[12]

The outlaws had thoroughly aroused the country by this time. On the evening of September 10 Sheriff Hornsby led a posse consisting of several deputy sheriffs, City Marshal Lucy, and Constable Sharp to Lockhart. Here they were joined by Sheriff Albert Francis Field, who had gathered another posse in an attempt to intercept the fugitives.[13]

As the law closed in Day and Kelly fled to Gonzales County where Sheriff William E. Jones ensured it was a poor sanctuary.[14] Suspecting that a man named John "Brazel" [*sic*: Brassell] described as "a Bohemian" was sheltering the outlaws, Jones arrived at the man's home and arrested him on the night of September 10 or 11. John Morgan Brassell was not actually from Bohemia. Records indicate that he was the son of Dr. Phillip Haddox Brassell and his wife Mary Ann Gay and had been born in Georgia on July 16, 1868.[15] Brassell was nineteen at the time, and the arrival of the posse took him by surprise. Asking Jones if he was after Day, to which Jones replied in the affirmative, Brassell told him that Day was sleeping in the cotton patch and would be in for breakfast. Shortly after daybreak the fugitive approached the house and was confronted by Jones and a double barreled shotgun. At first he attempted to draw his pistol but gave up when he saw he was surrounded.[16]

Jones was not content with capturing only Day. Learning that Kelly had run off with a "sweetheart" in Lavaca County, he set off in pursuit. The following day Jones captured Kelly near Sweet Home in Lavaca County on suspicion of complicity in the Flatonia robbery.[17]

While Texas lawmen completed the destruction of Cornett's new gang, other lawmen were running down alleged train robbers. Near Meridian in Bosque County lawmen arrested Tom Jones and Bill Humphreys. Reports out of Texas stated that Humphreys was "a man who has been 'up' several times for stage robbery, but has been smart enough most of the time to prove an alibi. When this game would not work he turned State's evidence and got off in that way. He and Jones are noted pals."[18]

Armed with confessions from both Jones and Humphreys, Deputy U. S. Marshal Thomas Bailes and Constable Ed Stevens left San Antonio and headed for Bandera County to pursue one John Crisswell on September 9.[19] At Medina City they were met by Sheriff Henry "Buck" Hamilton who accompanied them.[20] Around daybreak on the morning of September 10 Sheriff Hamilton knocked on the door and called to Crisswell, who came out and shook his hand. Hamilton then informed him he was under arrest. The media, ever swift to add guilt, described him as having "a long, sandy moustache and thin beard. The face is one in which cunning predominates and his steel-blue eyes sparkle with shrewdness." The conclusive item, in the press's mind, was that Crisswell had "well-worn boots" with round heels as did one of the outlaws who robbed the train at McNeil Station.[21]

Another man charged around the same time was one George Brown. Like the others, Brown was arrested on charges of robbing the trains at McNeil Station and Flatonia. Humphreys turned state's evidence to implicate the others claiming that he kept their camp and had no part in the actual robberies.[22] All in all the authorities had netted seven men, all of whom were alleged to have participated in the McNeil Station and Flatonia train robberies. The only one who had escaped was Brack Cornett.

Henry Kelly turned state's evidence and told the authorities that Cornett had rendezvoused with the trio on Reid's Prairie but abandoned them. Somewhere along the line Cornett picked up yet another partner named Jim Herrin.[23] Intriguingly Kelly reported to the authorities that the man pursued by Erichson and Williford was named "Barbour" [*sic*: Barber], an indication that Cornett was using his former partner's name as his latest alias.[24]

Cornett was well aware that the country was alive with posses attempting to run him down. He and Herrin headed west through Caldwell County. On September 13 Reverend Ben Dixon[25] and local farmer Andrew Jackson Rife[26] had stopped to talk Near West Fork, a branch of Plum Creek roughly seven miles from Lockhart on the way to Luling when they were approached by a man with a drawn revolver who commanded, "Men, I have you; crawl off your buggy." The men complied and surrendered their money. Then the outlaw asked what their business was and returned their money with the comment, "I don't want money from your sort of men; it's drummers we are after."

From the exchange it appears likely Herrin was the man who stopped the men since Cornett never hesitated robbing anyone, including newsboys. Herrin let them go, but moments later they were confronted by Cornett who demanded to know when the stage would be along. They told him soon, and shortly the stage arrived. Both the driver and passenger, R, L. Young, a New Orleans drummer, were robbed. "The driver had no cash. Mr. Young gave them $1.25, telling them it was all the money he had, although he states that he had hid his pocketbook out of their sight, which contained considerable funds." The victims informed officers that one of the men was small and had gray eyes. The other was light or red complexioned, and was about six feet tall.[27]

While the dramatic roundup of alleged train robbers was taking place across Texas, another storm was brewing at the state level. From his longtime camp in Karnes County, Schmitt responded to an irate letter from Adjutant General King. Even as he finally moved to obey orders he threw out his veiled disapproval of King.

> I did not intend to disobey your orders and wrote you only the true facts of affairs here as I had better Prospect in Capturing these train robbers & outlaws then ever and your orders is to make the Scout as soon as practiceable [*sic*]. I have more Provisions & Corn on hand then I am able to carry and I will try

> to dispose of same and start at once I don't think that I done anything what could cause disappointment and dissatisfaction to you. I will get ready and start at once.[28]

Schmitt finally left Karnes County, but King's anger at the procrastinating officer leaked to the press as well. The *Galveston Daily News* floated a rumor that Schmitt would soon be replaced by Lieutenant Grimes.[29] On September 7, two days after the *Galveston News* published their article, Grimes wrote to Adjutant General King from Pearsall, Texas, that he was waiting for Alfred Y. Allee's return because the plans to capture the train robbers were in place once Allee showed up.[30]

By September 10 Schmitt was well aware of the *News* article. Schmitt wrote to Lamartine P. Sieker complaining that someone must have sullied his reputation, believing that it was the county attorney and Sheriff Rudd who "thought that they could command me." Schmitt charged that both men threatened to undermine him and have him discharged. "Rudd told them that Gen. King did not like no way and opposed me when I was appointed first but I had strong friends Hon. George Pfeuffer & Gov. Ireland, but as Pfeuffer is dead now and Ireland out of office it was an easy thing to put me out." Schmitt went on to say that he "consider[ed] myself one of the best officers in the Battalion." Then Schmitt wrote the not so veiled threat: "I have good friends yet with influence and if I am dealt wrongfully I will make things lively."[31]

It was an ill-advised threat, and in the end it did not bode well for Company C.

In his groundbreaking study of the Cornett-Whitley gang, historian Jeff Burton theorized that "Deliberate suppression by the authorities must account for Reeves' alleged statement that the Flatonia robbery had been carried out by five men—Cornett, Whitley, Barber, Powell and himself."[32]

Burton further postulated that others involved included Tom Montgomery (alias Jones), Milt Day, Henry Kelly, John Cresswell (*sic*: Crisswell), George Brown, Will Jacobs, and William Humphreys.[33] When he presented his theory in 1975 it was sound based upon the information available at that time. Forty years later new tools and sources are available on both the gang and these individuals.

As noted, Will Jacobs did intend to take part in the Flatonia train robbery but turned back when the gang encountered a swollen stream. This is not unreasonable given the fact that Jacobs was still recovering from the effects of gunshot wounds received when he killed Deputy Sheriff Lee Pool.[34] Moreover, the Wells Fargo Circular published on July 2, 1887, did not name Jacobs as one of the gang.[35] Finally, when Jacobs was brought to justice and sentenced in 1889, there is no hint in the existing documentation that he was wanted for train robbery. It is far more likely that he provided information to the authorities in hopes of some sort of clemency, possibly through his cousin, Alfred Y. Allee.[36]

It's not surprising that Burton would include Henry Kelly and Will Humphreys because both offered full confessions. Kelly admitted that he lost his hat in the fight at Eureka and described it. When the hat was handed to him he put it on and admitted that it was the one lost in the fight. Kelly also described the pocket knife that the posse had found in detail.[37] Humphreys claimed to have been on the Flatonia robbery, a confession later proven false. However, neither were involved with the gang's train robbing activities.

Even if Kelly had not admitted to being in the gunfight at Eureka there were witnesses who could identify both him and Day. After they had dodged the posse, Kelly and Day obtained a horse, saddle, bridle, hat, and pair of shoes from G. C. Yarbrough for $50. The men then rode southwest cutting fences as they went and encountered Tom Mercer whom they robbed of his horse, hat, shoes, and coat. Mercer later informed officers that one of the men had a three-inch gash in his head where a bullet had struck him a glancing blow.[38] Law enforcement also had the horses the outlaws had used and posted a full description of the stolen mounts in the newspapers.[39]

The media reveled in the captures. Still convinced that thirteen men had held up the train at Flatonia, the *Waco Daily Examiner* reported, "Eleven of the thirteen men who engaged in the Flatonia train robbery have been located."[40] The story was echoed throughout the state. "Through the vigilance of Bosque county's sheriff, J. M. Metcalf, eleven of the men who engaged in the Flatonia robbery have been located."[41] The *San Saba News* chimed in that "Officers along the Sunset and International railroads have been very busy recently endeavoring to locate, arrest and convict the desperadoes who sometime since robbed the train at McNeill station and soon afterwards robbed the train near Flatonia." The *News* added that "They have had some clues but not sufficient to warrant active operations until recently."[42] They would soon be disillusioned.

Kelly proved the weak link in the chain. According to reports of the day, Kelly talked, very likely to save himself. He was eighteen years old, and for the first time the grim reality of what Brack Cornett had lured him into dawned as the real possibility of prison loomed before him, but his admissions were seriously flawed. According to one account, Kelly not only admitted that he was in the fight at Eureka but attempted to implicate John Brassell as well. Brassell denied being in the robbery, but Kelly claimed that he was and that Brassell's home had been a rendezvous for the gang. "Ensall, Cornett, Whitley and Barbour ate supper at the Bohemian's one week ago with Kelley and returned Tuesday without Kelley. There is no doubt but these men were in the Flatonia and McNeill robberies."[43] There was doubt however, and the courts soon demonstrated it.

The first man brought before the court was John Insall. The news media reported that he was supposed to have been at the McNeil train robbery although the charge had yet to be investigated.[44] The truth emerged within days: John Insall was not at either the McNeil or Flatonia robbery.[45] Nor was Kelly involved. "It is a fact one of the Hughes brothers was in the robbery at Gordon, but it is not fact that Kelly and Brazell were in the Flatonia robbery."[46] In the end it was determined that none of the men were involved in either of the train robberies. On October 28, 1887, both Day and Kelly entered guilty pleas for horse theft and were sent to the Huntsville Penitentiary.[47] Insall was also sentenced to prison for horse theft.

Concerning the other arrests, William Humphreys turned state's evidence to implicate the others arrested on his word. So convincing was the testimony that officers were certain and announced that Jones and Humphreys knew "about the train robberies in the state. Jones was in the robberies at Gordon, Flatonia and McNeill. At Flatonia Jones got $800. In this robbery there were thirteen men."[48] Humphreys spun a convincing tale along the lines Charles Buckley had used earlier in the year.

According to Humphreys, he had met Crisswell in Bandera County and arranged to meet him and others along the Guadalupe River. Humphreys was to drive a wagon for them to Flatonia. Humphreys's story was that they camped ten miles from Flatonia, mounted their horses, having their saddles in the wagons, and rode off towards Flatonia declaring they were going to rob the train. "The wagon had a sheet over it, and his crowd kept themselves in the wagon under cover all the time he was with them, which was until the Monday following the robbery." Finally the witness offered the astounding fact that while "he had turned state's evidence in a former case" Crisswell and Brown knew this when Creswell (*sic*) engaged him to drive the wagon. Humphreys claimed that he had a bad reputation "having spent a large slice of his time for the past five or six years in jail, or else dodging jail doors." At the time of his arrest he was charged with horse theft in Bosque County. Northacker, the express messenger, believed Crisswell was one of the men who had entered the car.[49]

The similarities between Humphreys's testimony and that of Charles Buckley are significant. In the latter case, the Craft and Ussery brothers had a bad reputation resulting from the killing of Sam Brown. The same was true of George Brown. In September 1880 Brown shot Deputy Sheriff George Gleason of Bexar County in the chest. Brown was then sentenced to seven years for assault to murder and had the dubious distinction of serving time in both Huntsville and Rusk for the same crime prior to his pardon.[50]

Nor was Crisswell without blemish. One newspaper described him as a very powerful man, over six feet tall and stout. "His face is not a prepossessing one. He has a long and sharp nose, with nostrils curling upwards. The cartilage of the nose has been broken and this has not improved his appearance. Cresswell [*sic*] has been arrested several times before on charges of stage robbery but has always proved an alibi."[51]

The *Fort Worth Daily Gazette* provided insight as to how these cases would go. Humphreys, confined with Jones in the Bosque County jail on charges of horse theft, predictably squealed "in order to save himself."[52] On September 13, 1887, Tom Jones appeared in court and entered a guilty plea to "the theft of two horses." Jones was sentenced to ten years in the penitentiary.[53] A later report states that Jones plead guilty "to being one of the participants in the Flatonia robbery."[54] There is some obvious confusion here that is clarified in later reports. In November the *Waco Daily Examiner* reported that Jones had been brought to Waco as "an attached witness in what is known as the Flatonia train robbery. It is believed that he knows something of the occurrence, and hence his presence here."[55] In December the media clearly reported that Tom Jones, alias Tom Montgomery, had entered a guilty plea "to train robbery at Gordon and got five years at Albany."[56] No credible evidence has been located to date that Jones was at the Flatonia robbery.

The next man up was George Brown who proved an alibi for the time of the robbery and was discharged. John Crisswell also proved an alibi and was released, and Humphreys's testimony was repudiated.[57] Uncharitably one newspaper openly stated that "It is claimed and believed by many here that the arrest of Cresswell [*sic*] from West Texas, charged with train robbery, is a job put up by a detective in collusion with another party to get the reward."[58] If so it was similar to the case of Rube Boyce, an alleged stage robber, who was convicted after a Deputy U. S. Marshal tampered with the jury in 1882.[59]

Even as the cases proceeded, Cornett and Herrin were heading west. Burton theorizes that the outlaws robbed Startz's store fifteen miles west of New Braunfels on September 17. The men covered the clerk with their pistols. After the clerk surrendered the money, the pair made him "dance a highland fling one whistling while the other kept time with his quirt on a cracker box."[60] The robbery has the earmarks of Cornett's twisted idea of "fun" without the accompanying violence. If these men were indeed Cornett and Herrin, they soon split up. In the fall of 1887 Cornett made an appearance at the home of his cousin William Henry "Will" Cornett.[61]

According to William's daughter Matilda Malvina "Mallie" Cornett, Brack arrived at his house ten miles north of Llano. Will Henry knew of Brack's reputation "and told him to stay out in the brush and keep away from the house because he didn't want his boys to grow up being influenced by a fast gun nor did he want any trouble with the law." Descendants theorize that Will's objection to Brack's presence "was as much the law as anything because Will Henry only had two of his eight sons born at the time of Brack's death. They were one and two years old. It could also be that Will Henry wanted to stop Brack from coming around before the boys were old enough to be influenced." Will had grown up in the same area as Brack and reportedly knew man-killer John Wesley Hardin very well, yet the influence of the Sutton-Taylor War did not impact him as it had Brack.[62] Here Brack Cornett vanishes from sight as had the others.

It was a frustrating situation for the authorities. All of the proverbial chickens had vacated the Texas coop. Barber, Cloud, and Whitley appear to have been in Oklahoma. Ross (Secrest) very likely was in Colorado while Powell and Reeves were living it up in Arkansas. It is possible that Brack Cornett crossed the border into the sanctuary of Mexico although this is far from certain.

On September 29 another daring holdup occurred near Ballinger, Texas. Around eleven o'clock at night, a lone gunman halted the stage, robbed the coach and passengers, then held them hostage until the stage from Ballinger to San Angelo came into view. The outlaw halted this stage as well and robbed it before making his escape.[63] On October 3, 1887, the same outlaw struck the stage again at the same spot.[64] Once again the press reacted with predictable outrage, heralding stage and train robbery as "The New Industry."

> There seems to be little more danger in it than eating one's supper. And it is much easier for a young man to get a start in life by drawing his six-shooter, ordering the train to stop and leisurely walking off with $10,000 or so than in sweating and working himself to death in the corn field. . . . From present appearances it looks like train and stage robbing is going to be a regular trade in Texas. As in the olden time, people may eventually have to purchase protection by paying blackmail to wandering brigand chiefs.[65]

That this editorial appeared in Austin, the seat of power, was calculated and inflammatory. The state had been humiliated by the rash of robberies, and the news media fanned the fires to stir up public outrage. Things would soon change, however. In Hot Springs, Arkansas, Powell and Reeves's celebration had been short lived.[66] According to Reeves's account the men were arrested for carrying pistols, made bail, and hustled back to Texas before their true identities could be discovered by local authorities.[67] Powell's account was substantially different. According to Powell, during their first night in Hot Springs, Reeves got drunk and was arrested. Powell was sick when the law arrested him but made bond.[68] Following misadventures of his own, Powell skipped town and fled to Arizona. Reeves also jumped bail and headed back for Texas.

Finally, hard work would pay dividends. In Johnson County, Texas Sheriff John H. Boyd learned that Reeves was on his way back to Texas and would stop at his sister's home. In company with J. E. Walker, S. J. Lancaster, and others they surprised Reeves at the home of Kinch Hamilton on October 6, 1887.[69] Reeves had gone outside to feed his mount, and hearing the officers, fled on foot into a field where he took cover. Boyd left five men to watch the house, and about 8:00 Reeves abruptly rose from the field as the small posse approached the house and opened fire, which was returned in kind, the posse chasing him until they ran out of ammunition. The outlaw was not found until October 7. The posse located him sleeping one mile north of the Hamilton home. Reeves had been shot once in the head, once in the thigh and twice in the calf.[70] Within hours the news broke conclusively. "Ed Reeves, who was captured in Johnson County, is regarded beyond a doubt as one of the McNeil robbers."[71]

While Boyd was running Ed Reeves to ground, elsewhere, authorities working in conjunction with private enterprises continued their efforts to protect the railroads. On October 1, J. Waldo had submitted lists that described new railroad guards.[72] In Austin the train robbery trials progressed as noted earlier. The trials could not have come at a worse time for those accused.

On October 14 an attempt was made to rob the Missouri Pacific train at Spring Station, some twenty-eight miles from Houston. Two men rushed the train, one boarding the engine and the other the baggage car. The robbers covered the engineer, but fireman George Linn jumped from the train and caught onto the rear car as it passed. Panicked that the fireman had notified the crew and passengers, the outlaws ordered the engineer to slack his speed and leaped from the engine and gave up their robbery attempt.[73] Jeff Burton cautiously extended the possibility that the robbers included Cornett. "This might have been one of the several hold-ups attempted in Texas by imitators of the Cornett and Burrow gangs; but it is equally possible that Cornett himself had again slipped into Harris County and was directing matters."[74] This appears unlikely as Cornett never proved himself as a train robber when away from John Barber. Regardless, none of those involved in the aborted Spring Station robbery were ever identified.

Into this George Schmitt once again rose to prominence.

Chapter 9

Wild, Woolly and Hard to Curry

The stench of the Flatonia outrage lingered throughout Texas and clung to everyone and everything involved, both the good and the bad. In early October, rumors that Schmitt's company of rangers was going to return to Helena prompted Attorney F. R. Graves to pen a blunt letter from Karnes County to Adjutant General King about Schmitt. Noting that he had been requested to contact King by "some of the prominent citizens of this county" he stated that if troops were absolutely necessary "we ask that you send us someone in whom we feel that we can place more confidence than in Captain George Schmidt—our past experience with that officer has caused almost every good citizen of this county to lose confidence in the entire ranger force." Graves related that during the two months Schmitt had been there the company had made one "accident arrest" of a Mexican horse thief.

> He the captain was out of his camp on business only twice and during his stay here his individual conduct

> was displeasing our good citizens & brought a poor widow into scandal and disgrace by his attentions to her. And whether or not he really does belong to the lawless element in our county his conduct in office has been such that *all* the law abiding ones look upon him with distrust & we can show that in two instances he refused to attempt to arrest parties because there was no reward for them—he told parties here that he knew where a criminal was & would bring him in if we would offer a reward for him.

Graves went on to state that if anyone wanted Schmitt there it was "the lawless element." Graves admitted that he and Schmitt were not on friendly terms and noted that he preferred "that you investigate the matter further if you consider that it deserves attention—but if a petition signed by our citizens will be more effective in securing the object herein requested please signify the same & I shall forward to you a well signed petition."[1] The revelation that Schmitt had concentrated strictly on train robbers, not to mention his less than professional conduct, reflected not only upon Schmitt but the rangers as well.

On October 25, 1887, news of the conviction of Kelly and Day was spread in the press. Kelly received five years for theft of a horse and two years for "conspiracy to rob the Central train." Day's sentence was tougher. He was convicted for three cases of horse theft at five years each and conspiracy to rob the train, which netted him an additional two years. The state opted not to prosecute the men for several other cases of horse theft.[2] On November 1, 1887, Kelly and Day entered Huntsville Penitentiary as convicts 4755 and 4756 respectively.[3] It was not enough to satisfy the press. Flatonia had been a crime so heinous that no one could forget it. The *Atlanta Constitution,* after noting that "the average Texan resented with a snort of indignation any insinuation that his lone star home of the brave was not less lawless than any part of the globe" went on to add:

> This dream of security was shattered three months back by the McNeill train robbery, which took place at night ten miles north of Austin. Some fourteen men were engaged, who struck a very light run, and were badly paid for their pains. The risk, of course, was infinitesimal.
>
> The Flatonia affair on the Sunset line followed. There were eight men concerned and they got a good deal of money, outside of the pleasure derived from splitting the express messenger's ears . . .[4]

On October 25 the Central train was derailed at Ledbetter. The facts of the event, according to the press, "leave no doubt the purpose was robbery," adding, "there is every reason to believe they belonged to the same gang who took part in the McNeill and other robberies." While there is no hint that any of the Cornett-Whitley gang was involved, the paper suggested that "No doubt had not the fate of the two El Paso robbers stared the thugs in the face, the passengers would have been subjected to the same treatment as at Flatonia."[5]

One bright spot for the rangers came from Ira Aten who was also hunting the train robbers, but in stark contrast to George Schmitt continued with his other duties. Reporting to L. P. Sieker, Aten offered, "Nothing very new in the Barber & Whitley case. I am satisfied that they are still about."[6] Perhaps this was fueled by a report that an attempt was made to free Reeves from the jail. Reportedly Whitley, Barber, and two others attempted to free Reeves by posing as friends of John Boyd and entering his home, which was in the front part of the jail. Mrs. Boyd refused admittance and the men rode off.[7] That such an attempt may have been made is possible, although highly unlikely. The only members of the gang who exhibited any semblance of loyalty to one another were Barber and Whitley, and that proved tenuous. Reeves had both family and friends in the area, and they may have made what appears to have been a half-hearted attempt. It is also possible that the incident actually involved men who were friends of Boyd's and that the entire incident was over blown.

The pressure on Adjutant General King mounted as the year progressed. From Helena, F. R. Graves advised that he was coming to Austin and would "make a personal explanation" concerning Schmitt's conduct in addition to bringing "expressions of the desire of some of our citizens in the matter."[8] The evidence appears to have been both irrefutable and damning, and Schmitt did not return to Helena. Added to this, the criticism intensified with the *Ballinger Leader*'s sarcastic quip, "How would it do to organize a train robbers bureau; all other permanent professions are organized, and why not one for the robbers' protection?"[9]

In November Sheriff John Olive received information as to the whereabouts of Whitley and Barber in the Indian Territory. Accompanied by Sheriff James W. Evans of Fannin County, W. C. Bailey, special agent for the International & Great Northern branch of the Southern Pacific, and Texas Ranger Ira Aten, Olive led the small posse into Oklahoma where they narrowly missed capturing the outlaws. The pair abruptly left camp at midnight and headed south. Their pursuers managed to catch sight of them, but the outlaws had fresh mounts and avoided the lawmen.[10]

Another outlaw attempting to avoid punishment was John Insall, who had appealed his conviction. The Texas court of appeals found no error in the judgment.

> John Ensall vs. the State; appeal from Travis. When a party relies on the opposite party to have certain witnesses present, and they fail to attend, this will not constitute sufficient ground for continuance. It is not necessary that the evidence of an accomplice be corroborated. It is sufficient that it tends to connect

> the defendant with the offense committed. No error. Affirmed. Wilson, J.[11]

Nor did the outlaws who struck the train at Genoa Station make any errors when they robbed the train eight miles east of Texarkana. Under the banner "At It Again" the *Fort Worth Daily* Gazette stated that the robbery for "successful daring rivals any incident of the kind that has occurred in the southwest." As the train pulled into Genoa Station between seven and eight o'clock in the evening, two men boarded the train. One clambered aboard the engine and covered engineer Bob Roe and the fireman with his pistol while the other mounted the platform in front of the express car and held the bell rope so that no signal could be given by the conductor, named Kinement. Roe was forced to increase his speed "to a frightful rate until a point was reached that had been selected to complete the robbery." A third man was waiting for them.[12] When the train came to a stop, the conductor climbed down from the train and made his way forward with his lamp when a bullet whipped past his head, followed by a volley from the outlaws. The conductor jumped to the protection of the cars, suffering only a bullet hole in his coat, passing under his right arm.[13]

The outlaws first attempted to force the express messenger to open the doors by firing a number of shots through the windows, but the express messenger, named Cohen, refused to open the doors.[14] The outlaws then made use of the engineer to batter in a portion of the door and had the fireman place a lantern inside. The express messenger was forced to open the door and the safe. Estimates of the haul varied between $10,000 and $40,000 but were actually around $3500.

Writing to L. P. Sieker concerning the crime, Ira Aten expressed the opinion that the outlaws were Barber, Whitley, and Mark Jones, "the same three parties that I was telling you about" who robbed the train on December 9.[15] In this case Aten's theory was mistaken, for the outlaws were later identified as the Burrow brothers Rube and Jim and Leonard Brock.[16]

As 1887 wound down the outlaws again made news. On December 19 John Insall and another prisoner made their escape from the Travis County jail.[17] A week later an unsuccessful attempt to rob another train was made five miles north of Denison, Texas.[18] There is nothing to tie Barber and Whitley to this attempt, but on Christmas Day 1887 still another attempt was made on a train near Atoka, Oklahoma. Burton theorizes that the robbers on this occasion may have been Whitley, Barber, Kep Queen, and Jim Stephens.[19] None of them were identified with certainty.

At 4:00 Christmas morning, Train No. 507 on the Missouri, Kansas and Texas Railway was stopped at North Boggy, four miles from Stringtown. The train was behind schedule nearly two hours, because they had stopped at Stringtown to let off a passenger. While they were stopped, two men clambered onto the engine. When engineer W. T. Ragland ordered them off, the pair drew their pistols. Four miles from Stringtown the men ordered him to stop with the coaches on an iron bridge over the North Boggy.

One of the robbers first climbed up the stairs to the postal / baggage car and knocked. Route agent Armstrong opened the door, swiftly took in who it was and slammed it in the outlaw's face, locking it at once. The outlaws then moved to the express car where John Grimshaw had already blown out the lights and was prepared to shoot it out with the outlaws. After failing to break in the door, the gang began firing into the express car. When that failed to get the door opened to them, the outlaws abandoned the attempt to rob the train.[20]

The year continued with additional casualties, of a sort, for the law. The legislature had decided that the Texas Rangers needed once more to be reduced in staff to three companies. Charitably one ranger historian writes that George Schmitt's

Company C being disbanded was "an indirect tribute to Schmitt for cleaning up his territory."[21] Perhaps, but it appears that the decision had been an easy one. Schmitt had boasted once "that he could run the Frontier Battalion better than King."[22] During the year his obstinate insubordination, crowned by the vaguely veiled threats he had made, made Company C the obvious choice for reduction. It was disbanded at the end of November 1887.

The year 1887 had proven dismal for Texas. The Cornett-Whitley gang had fractured to the point that it was unrecognizable as the same group that had swarmed together earlier in the year. Despite this, most of the gang had eluded capture. A deputy sheriff had been murdered. The gang had humiliated the state government, committed a heinous atrocity at Flatonia, and generally ran roughshod across the state. Their actions had captured not only the country's unfavorable attention but the attention of the world. As one newspaper had predicted, it was the year of the train robber. Beyond this, Schmitt's obsession with the gang and the lucrative rewards offered for them contributed to the destruction of Company C. It was a bitter dose to swallow. Things would get worse before they improved.

The next year, 1888, began with an innocuous letter to Governor Ross requesting commissions from the state for Van Hall and J. M. Waller to continue their operations pursuing train robbers, citing their role in the capture of Leonard Brock, a member of the Rube Burrow gang.[23] Hall and Waller provided a supporting letter asking for commissions as special rangers on January 13, 1888, as did the law firm of Clark and Dyer on January 18, 1888.[24]

January also saw George Schmitt live up to his reputation. The *Brenham Banner* published a piece in support of Schmitt, probably written by him but in the third person, saying,

> CAPT. GEO. SCHMITT, whose company of state rangers was disbanded some time ago, promises to

> make it lively for certain parties when the legislature meets. Mr. Schmitt was the oldest and one of the best and most faithful ranger captains that were ever in the state's service, and his dismissal was an unjust piece of doing.[25]

Schmitt charged that the management of the Ranger service was in need "of a change of the commander-in-chief." Schmitt claimed that there was "great dissatisfaction with the officers and men of the different companies on account of the palpable partiality bestowed on some." The newspaper article continued, "The captain makes numerous charges and complaints against the administration of the service. Some of these charges are of a criminal nature, which Captain Schmitt promises to bring before the proper committees of the next legislature."[26] Schmitt proved unsuccessful in damaging the Rangers, and here he vanishes into the murky mists of history. His ultimate fate remains unknown.

During 1888, the tide turned in favor of the law so far as the Cornett-Whitley gang was concerned, and the first signs appeared in January. In Johnson County, Sheriff John Boyd, concerned that friends of Ed Reeves would attempt his release, decided to move the outlaw to San Antonio. Rumors reached the sheriff "that a large party of Reeves' friends would attack and rob the train" conveying Reeves to San Antonio, and Boyd took precautions. The sheriff deputized forty men, armed them with pistols and Winchesters and chartered a special car to move the outlaw. No attack materialized, and at his preliminary hearing on January 30 Reeves entered a guilty plea for participating in both the McNeil Station and Flatonia train robberies. Bond was set at $5,000. Reeves bragged that he would escape or be killed before going to the penitentiary.[27]

Bigger news broke during February 1888, heralded by a telegram from Sheriff W. C. Daugherty of Frio County.[28]

> Pearsall, Texas, February 13, 1888.
>
> Have got Brack Cornett, alias Captain Dick. He fought to the last. Had to kill him in making the arrest. Have you any instructions. If not will bury him here to-day.
>
> W. C. DAUGHERTY
> Sheriff Frio county.[29]

Governor Ross took no chances, wiring back instructions that he wanted to have the body positively identified and an inquest held on the outlaw. The reply was positive, coming from Sheriff John Olive who happened to be at Pearsall hunting the outlaw, that Cornett was fully identified.[30]

There are contradictory accounts of Cornett's whereabouts prior to his death. According to several newspapers, Cornett had been hiding out in San Antonio at the St. Leonard Hotel.[31] One paper stated that Cornett was "making his habitat in the pastures of Capt. Millett, Mr. Allee and other ranchmen of that vicinity."[32] Another stated that he had been hiding in Frio County for about six weeks, roughly from the end of 1887.[33]

Every account of Cornett's death on February 12, 1888, emanates from a single source, his killer Alfred Y. Allee. According to Allee, Cornett had abruptly appeared at Allee's home on February 11 asking for supper. Allee recognized Cornett of course, having grown up in the same region with him. Allee had also been with the outlaw following the Flatonia robbery. After supper was over Cornett went to the woods for the night. The following morning Cornett appeared for breakfast. Allee told reporters that the cooking and eating were done outside. By Allee's account, Cornett had finished breakfast. "After breakfast he was preparing to leave. I stood on one side of the fire and he was sitting down on the other, when I threw my pistol down on him and told him to throw up his hands and consider himself my prisoner."[34]

"The hell you say," Cornett snarled as he came erect and drew. Both men fired at the same time, Allee's bullet hitting Cornett in the chest as Cornett's shot tore through Allee's hat brim. "As he fired I jumped across the fire to him. We were about eight feet apart. As I jumped I shot him again and he fired another shot and fell, when I fired two more shots. The last shot broke his neck."[35]

This was not how one member of the Cornett family saw it, however. Mattie White wrote "The True Story of Brack Cornett's Death."

> Brack was stealing horses. Then Alfred Alee was seling them in Mexico. One morning Brack had stooped over to light a cigarette from his camp fire and was shot in the back of his head by Alfred Alee in order to collect the $3000 reward for Brack. A partner turned traitor.[36]

Not surprisingly Allee was cleared of any wrongdoing, yet the available accounts do leave unanswered questions. Why did Cornett feel comfortable coming to the home of a Frio County deputy sheriff in the first place? Was Allee truly a partner of Brack Cornett? At the time, lacking modern forensics, Allee's story was taken at face value, but it was and remains only half a story.

One Cornett descendant writes, "I have not heard any family stories or found any newspaper accounts of any family member trying to claim Brack's body for burial. His mother and sister were both living in the Mason County area at the time as far as I can determine. It most likely would have cost too much for them to make the trip or to have the body brought back to Mason for burial. I figure also that they didn't want people to know that Brack was any kin to them since he was in all the newspapers at the time with his misdeeds."[37]

Cornett was buried quietly at Pearsall.[38] As noted above, no one ever attempted to claim his body. "Not only did Brack's sister not claim the body but other relatives that were as far as I know living in the area made no attempt to claim the body. This would include his uncles John Cornett, Joseph Cornett, James Cornett, and aunt Agnes Whaley."[39]

Information and misinformation concerning Cornett and the gang spread rapidly. One erroneous conclusion was that "John Barber and one other of the gang are still at large; three have been captured and one killed."[40] This view was echoed by the *San Francisco Bulletin,* which reported that Cornett "was about the last member of the band to be taken."[41] In Austin one journal correctly pointed out that "Bud Powell, Bill Whitley, alias John Hill, and John Barber, his confederates and assistants in the robbery, are still at large."[42] Another newspaper claimed that, in addition to being considered "the most dangerous and desperate man in the southwest" he was "said to have been a member of the famous James and Younger gangs in Missouri.[43] In Florida at least one story claimed that the gang "were as successful in their career as the renowned Frank and Jesse James gang, which excited such terror in Missouri."[44] Still another newspaper, characterizing Cornett as "wild, woolly and hard to curry" noted incorrectly that his mother lived in Burnet County when in truth she lived in Mason County.[45] The press was not wrong about Cornett's nature, however. "'Captain Dick' may have had some good traits of character, and possibly he did have, but his bad qualities outweighed them, and society is infinitely better off now that he is dead."[46]

From the media's coverage it is evident that the press was either ignoring or had forgotten the McNeil Station robbery along with both Cloud and Secrest. Their lack of notoriety worked in their favor. Unlike the fickle press however, the law had not forgotten, and only two days after Cornett's death others of the former gang provided ample evidence that they were still in business.

At 3:30 p.m. on February 13, a man entered the Cisco bank and asked cashier F. C. Leveaux for some change. As Leveaux stepped to the cage, three more men entered, one of them pointing a pistol at Leveaux's head. Two other men in the bank, T. R. Blake and M. B. Owens, attempted to leave but were forced into one corner while the outlaws ransacked the bank. Owens did not move quickly enough and was struck on the head by one of the robbers and knocked to the floor. While in the bank the outlaws scaled a seven- or eight-foot iron railing to access the teller's cage and forced Blake to do it "for their amusement."[47] When the bandits had taken everything in the bank they forced Leveaux to open two rear doors, which led to a fenced yard behind the building. The men were forced to climb the plank fence into an alley where the outlaws climbed a second fence into a wagon yard where their horses were hitched.

Leveaux was slow crossing the fence, and when the others dropped into the alley he ran back through the bank and sounded the alarm. In the meanwhile the outlaws rode some 200 yards from the bank, then drew their pistols and fired four or five shots to announce their departure. Only minutes later Marshal J. T. Thomas and a small posse were riding in pursuit northwest out of town.[48]

Once again the gang seized national headlines. The *New York Times* called it "a cool and daring bank robbery."[49] In Texas it was referred to as "one of the boldest and most daring robberies" ever committed in the state.

Once again the outlaws did not use masks. Contemporary reports described them as "big, rough-looking fellows, one of them is cross-eyed, all had mustaches, three light and the other black. The cross-eyed man had dark mustache, dark complexion and is about forty years old." All of them were riding fine horses.[50] While no one knew who the outlaws were at the time, the dark haired man is easily identifiable as John Barber, who was aging poorly and looking ten years older than he was. Another of the outlaws was Bill Whitley, but the others were new recruits to Barber's gang although not to a criminal life.

The best known of the other two outlaws is Samuel DeKalb Queen, a cousin of John Barber who was recruited in Oklahoma and is best recalled by the nickname Kep. He was born March 27, 1860, to Samuel David Queen and his wife Jane Ann Petty, a sister of Barber's mother in Lampasas County, Texas, Records indicate that he was raised in Williamson County where he married Nancy Adeen Smith on April 1, 1881. Their lives were not the stuff dreams were made of.[51] By 1882 Queen was in trouble for cattle theft in Bell County, but the charge was later dismissed on the motion of the county attorney.[52] Family tradition has it that while in San Saba, Texas, he and a number of others were arrested by the law for gambling.

> Before being called to appear before the grand jury they all agreed to lie and say they were not gambling. The last one questioned, however, broke down and confessed, naming all the others.
>
> To gamble was to be fined, but to lie under oath was prison. That is when Kep turned bad. He swore he would not go to jail. So he and a cousin, John Barber, and a friend named Will Whitley lit out. They got in a lot of trouble doing what had to be done hiding out in Oklahoma and Missouri.

Family members recalled that Queen was kind, gentle, and caring.[53] Unlike the others, Queen achieved a minor level of attention as the villain of a story published by *McClure's Magazine* in 1908.[54] Federal records describe Queen as thirty-two to thirty-six, about six-feet tall with dark hair and eyes, adding the comment "Injured in one eye by hook spot or cataract."[55]

Whitley's biographer concurs with the identification although she mistakenly identified Queen as a man named Green.[56]

The final man went by the name of Jim Stephens. While his numerous aliases make identification difficult, one theory from the available records is that the name Stephens was an alias for William J. Jones, a son of Elisha Jones and Malinda Emeline Kendrick, who was born in Mississippi during 1857.[57] Like Queen, Jones got into trouble in Bell County. In 1881 he was charged with theft of oxen. On October 26, 1881, he entered a plea of guilty and was sentenced to three years in the penitentiary.[58] Jones did not go meekly. Prison records indicate that he escaped en route to Huntsville Penitentiary and was recaptured on December 10. Jones was transferred to Rusk Penitentiary in Cherokee County on January 1, 1883.[59] He was released at the expiration of his sentence.[60] Contemporary records describe Stephens as 5 feet 8 or 10 inches in height, light hair with a coarse beard and heavy moustache, gray eyes, and red complexion.[61]

By all accounts, the robbery netted the outlaws somewhere between $4000 and $6000.[62] The chase was a hot one, the posse following the gang closely until they overtook them four miles south of Putnam, Texas. Ultimately the lawmen could not close with the gang because their armaments consisted of pistols and shotguns while the outlaws all had the longer-range Winchester rifles. It had snowed, and the snow made it easy to track the men. On the morning of February 16 one of the gang's pursuers, Perry Paschell, returned to Cisco where he rendezvoused with Sheriff James K Schmick.[63] The sheriff went out with Winchesters and ammunition.[64] Lawmen from "Albany, Breckenridge, Baird, Brownwood, Coleman, Comanche, Eastland, Ranger and the rangers at Ballinger" were notified and it was believed that escape was "almost impossible."[65]

On the same day Thomas and part of his posse arrived back in town reporting that the gang had circled Cisco and was fifteen miles south heading east. The posse had found where the gang made camp and divided the money. The same day a report reached Baird, Texas, that the outlaws had been surrounded "on Battle Creek between Putnam and Cottonwood." At least 150 men were reportedly surrounding them, but the weather now took a turn for the worse as the "recent heavy sleet is melting and creating a heavy fog."[66] Schmick's exhausted posse returned to Cisco on February 17. Due to the rapid snow melt they had lost the trail. The outlaws were aiming toward Brownwood and were reportedly still together.[67]

The deteriorating weather affected the outlaws as well as the posse. Sometime after Schmick's posse returned, a rider from Rising Star arrived in Cisco with the news that two of D. P. Sayle's horses had been stolen the previous night. Another posse set out after the stolen mounts, and four miles south of Cisco they found an iron grey horse still saddled with two Winchester rifles on it. Further on they found "a fine white ivory handled six shooter and a white Stetson hat" where the horse had fallen and thrown its rider. The prevailing theory was that in the dark the outlaw could not find his property and had slipped into Rising Star and stolen a horse. This corresponded with the discovery of one of Sayle's stolen horses. The posses hunting the outlaws were soon augmented by reinforcements from Weatherford led by Sheriff Henry S. Sisk of Parker County. Sisk was only in his first term as sheriff but his determination to catch the outlaws is unquestionable.[68]

Whitley's biographer expressed her belief that the thrown rider was Bill Whitley. The account states that after resting and feeding their mounts, Whitley "gave his horse his head and was loosely holding the reins." In the darkness his mount ran into a barbed wire fence and threw him. Whitley crawled to some "deep underbrush" where he found that the stock of his pistol had broken "and the sharp end had punctured his side." According to this account Whitley then carved a new stock for his pistol, stole a horse from D. D. Daniel, and rode for Lampasas.[69]

While the family story has merit, there are some issues. A description of the outlaws notes "The iron gray horse, white hat, pistol and Winchester suit exactly for one of the bank robbers. One of them was riding an iron gray horse and two of them wore white hats, and all of their pistols had white handles."[70] Moreover, forensic evidence indicates that Whitley's rifle stock, not his pistol's grip, was hand made. One Whitley descendent writes that the current owner of Whitley's rifle "sent me pics of the Winchester and it definitely has a homemade stock fashioned to it."[71] This was confirmed by the rifle's present owner.[72]

Regardless of who was thrown from their mount, the outlaws managed to escape. From existing documentation it appears that the group divided their spoils before splitting up. Stephens and Queen headed for the Indian Territory while Barber and Whitley angled for Lampasas. The law did not emerge empty-handed, however. On February 23, 1888, one Tom Price was arrested in Comanche County "on suspicion" of being one of the outlaws. Price was considered "a notorious horse thief," a fact apparently confirmed since he was riding a horse stolen from James Irby of Rising Star several weeks earlier.[73]

One, possibly apocryphal story growing out of the Cisco bank robbery was that the outlaws threatened to return and rob the entire town. Panicked, a local politician wired Governor Ross with the ridiculous inquiry "What can be done?" According to the story the response was terse: "If not men enough in town to protect it, burn and evacuate."[74]

Chapter 10

Prefer Them Dead

Aside from an amusing anecdote, one thing the gang accomplished was further unification of the banking industry, which offered additional rewards for Barber and Whitley. In Cisco the *Fort Worth Daily Gazette* was informed that a large reward for the outlaws would be offered, "probably $5000 or $10,000." There was good reason to believe this. On February 15 George T. Reynolds, president of the First National Bank in Albany, Texas, expressed his condolences for the Cisco bank's loss and posted a $500 reward for the capture of the robbers "dead or alive. Prefer them dead."[1]

Nor were other towns idle. A. F. Stair, president of the First National Bank and Mr. H. P. Hilliare, cashier of the Citizens National Bank, both in Weatherford, offered large rewards for the capture of the outlaws. The Gainesville National Bank offered a $100 reward "for the capture and conviction" of any or all of the bank robbers. The *Gazette* summed it up simply: "The banks throughout the country have responded nobly, and the reward now runs up into the thousands. Several banks have wired Mr. Leveaux to call on them if he runs out of money."

In Austin Governor Ross added an additional $250 for each of the outlaws.[2]

In addition to the new rewards, older rewards were paid out in February. On February 21 the governor ordered the reward of $500 paid for Cornett.[3] Nearly unheralded was the reward paid out for an important arrest in New Mexico. Around the time of the Cisco bank robbery, a man going by the name Frank Benson was arrested in Magdalena, New Mexico, for carrying concealed weapons. Benson was sentenced to three months in jail, and during that time it developed that he was far more than he appeared. How the Magdalena law made the connection is unknown, but weeks following the arrest it was reported that Benson was an alias adopted when he left Texas "for his health his real name being Searcy Secrest." According to the reporter, Benson "had only been in this vicinity for a short time, but had been roaming about Montana, Wyoming, Colorado and Arizona since he left Texas. Magdalena's efficient marshal will secure $200 for the important capture."[4] It remained for the *Galveston Daily News* to put a name to the face. "He fled to Arizona, where he assumed the name of Charles Ross, and for the past year he had lived in the territory of New Mexico under the name of Frank Benson."[5]

Sheriff B. L. Zapp and Tom Bailes, acting in his capacity as deputy sheriff, went to Magdalena with the proper requisition papers. Secrest was still in jail, and it was necessary for the pair to obtain his release. Once the legal work was dispensed with, the officers started back to Texas.[6] On April 5 Zapp, Bailes, and Secrest, "alias Charley Ross," breakfasted in San Antonio en route to LaGrange.[7]

The press justifiably hailed Zapp for Ross'sarrest for the murder of Bob Ragsdale, "one of the bloodiest killings ever perpetrated in this county."[8] Even more credit was due Zapp because he had put an additional $50 bounty on Secrest out of his own pocket.[9] Indeed, Zapp had known who his prisoner was from the time he returned to Texas. "Sheriff Zapp informs the Journal that at the time he arrived at El Paso, he met an old detective, who had been working up the McNeil and Flatonia train robberies; that he claims Secrest participated in the McNeil robbery and very probably in the Flatonia. His trial will probably be had in May."[10] Considering the amount of press generated by the gang, it appears surprising that Secrest's capture was not seized upon by the press to identify Secrest as one of the McNeil Station train robbers. On the contrary the media did very little to cover the story. The question is why.

There are several factors involved in the lack of interest in Ross's capture. The McNeil Station train robbery, unlike the one at Flatonia, had faded in the public's mind, and while the authorities had Ed Reeves's confession, it was uncorroborated. As such it could not convince a jury beyond a reasonable doubt. Moreover, the evidence against Ross was poor. The Wells Fargo circular dated July 2, 1887, notes simply, "The five men above named, with two others whose names and descriptions are known, robbed the train near McNeil's Station."[11] There was no reason not to publish Ross and Cloud's names considering the wealth of detail Wells Fargo provided on the balance of the gang, which appears to indicate that the information on Cloud and Ross was not as well developed.

Still another factor may have been the presence of Bailes himself, who had made two sensational arrests that turned out to be nothing and the subsequent tarnishing of his reputation by the media. The deciding factor probably came down to simple logic. Even with Reeves's confession the evidence against Ross at McNeil Station was scant. Unless Secrest himself entered a guilty plea, the likelihood of a conviction was not good. On the other hand Secrest faced a capital murder charge where twelve witnesses had seen the killing of Bob Ragsdale. In short, as the *Magdalena Mountain Mail* put it, "The fellow stands a good chance to stretch hemp."[12]

Nor was Sion Secrest the only person affiliated with the gang rounded up during February. The chief detective for the Missouri Pacific system "lodged William Harrold [*sic*: Harrell] of Karnes county" in jail on February 17. The paper explained that Harrell "belongs to the clique of ranchmen in Karnes, Bee and Wilson counties who have been harboring a majority of the gang of Flatonia train robbers since the date of the robbery." T. K.Furlong advised the newspapers that the law was "determined to arrest and bitterly prosecute all parties who have been instrumental in keeping the bandits out of the clutches of the law." The detective reportedly worked up several cases and expected to lodge a "number of well-known and wealthy cattlemen of the southwest behind the bars."[13] Presumably that included Will's brother Eli and Newt Butler.

Elsewhere Constable Lee Jenkins of Waco arrested a man who gave his name as John Ghio. Ghio was nabbed in a gambling hall where he was losing heavily and arrested on suspicion.[14] On February 23 one J. L. Alexander was arrested at Rising Star by several officers and brought to Cisco for positive identification. Alexander had the misfortune of resembling one of the outlaws who had robbed the bank. He was not identified and proved an alibi.[15]

There is no indication that Barber and Whitley ever knew Ross had been captured, or that either of them cared if they did. What is known is that the pair made their way to Lampasas County where they hid out with the Cox family.[16]

During March further evidence of the original gang's destructive collateral damage rose when Sheriff A. J. Lewis of Milam County addressed a letter to Adjutant General King concerning Will Jacobs, who had backed out of the Flatonia train robbery. Lewis had sent one of his deputies, Jonathan H. Bickett, to Austin with a request for assistance in capturing Jacobs who had killed his deputy the previous year. Bickett conferred with Governor Ross and King and returned empty handed.

> Jacobs without provocation cruelly murdered one of my deputies a most estimable young man who at the time was faithfully performing his duty to the law. The atrocity of the murder aroused the whole people of this country since its occurrence citizens and officers have spared no efforts to arrest Jacobs. Liberal rewards have been offered by people and officers. I have expended of my individual means several hundred dollars until at last when I all but have my hands on the man I am confronted with the startling announcement that the law has declared a truce with Jacobs and will not aid in his apprehension.

Lewis went on to point out that "you knew all the while what efforts I was making to effect this arrest and yet no suggestions that you were using Jacobs as an instrument to arrest grave offenders." Lewis concluded that he understood from Bickett's information that "Jacobs in not to be arrested and brought to trial" for Pool's murder.[17]

Two days later Adjutant General King responded to Lewis in a six-page letter protesting that Lewis and Bickett "totally misapprehend the circumstances connected with the continued freedom from arrest of one Will Jacobs." King spent half of the six-page letter reassuring Lewis that "the Governor has no desire to place any obstruction nor to interpose any authority between you and Jacobs." From the tone of the letter, King had used information provided by Jacobs, possibly through his cousin Allee, but had made no special arrangements. King further claimed that Jacobs was not under the authority of the state, concluding that "The Governor and I will both take pleasure in doing all we lawfully can to assist you."[18]

Collateral damage also touched the Cox family. On March 21, 1888, Tom Cox, one of Cordelia Whitley's brothers, was released following an examining trial for participation in the Flatonia train robbery.[19] Family lore states that Cordelia's brother Samuel was also charged and that the men were held in jail for thirty days.[20] As March closed an erroneous report reached Adjutant General King that Whitley and Barber were in Oldham County in the Panhandle.[21] At the same time, Powell was working in a store some eleven miles from Camden, Arkansas, on the road to Texarkana.[22] Cloud was in Oklahoma while both Reeves and Secrest were cooling their heels in various jails.

Barber and Whitley were too high profile to remain in hiding long, but for some time they remained elusive, until April 26. Knowing Barber's penchant for involving his family in trouble, deputy sheriffs John Jamison and William Patton from Burnet County staked out the home of Brice M. Smart who was married to Barber's sister Ailcy Jane.[23] The men had barely hidden when around one o'clock in the morning Barber and Whitley emerged from the house. The pair moved into a thicket near the house where their horses were hidden, mounted and began riding toward where the officers were hidden.

There is good reason why Ed Reeves informed lawmen that Barber was the best runner in the gang. As the pair approached, Barber suddenly balked, shouting, "There is something wrong here." He spurred his horse into a gallop "and disappeared like a flash." Whitley drew his pistol as he dropped himself on the side of his mount and fired under his horse's neck at the officers. Jamison and Patton returned the fire with their double-barreled shotguns. Whitley's horse was killed instantly, but the outlaw successfully vanished into the night. Somewhere in Smart's pasture he stole a horse and escaped into the timber.[24]

According to some sources for Whitley this was the final straw in his partnership with Barber—or was it? "Bill told me the reason he quit Barber was on account of Barber's cowardice. He said Barber deserted him several times in a moment of peril," Joe Whitley told a reporter several months later.[25] Whitley's biographer states that the reason for the breakup was that Barber allowed "Aunt Hulda" to help him, which appears unlikely given the known chronology of the pair.[26] This may have been an incident described by Ernest Langford. According to Langford, Barber was in hiding at a house when a posse surprised the occupants. The man who owned the home asked that he first let his daughter or sister out as she was expecting a baby and did not feel too well. After the officers agreed, Barber left the home disguised in a dress.[27] If this incident caused the division between Barber and Whitley, it was nothing Whitley should not have anticipated. From the beginning the gang's members had been loyal only to themselves. In any event, contemporary evidence suggests that Barber and Whitley did not split at this time.

The claim that the outlaws split up originated with Bill's brother Joe in October 1888. "Bill came to my house about the first of June last, and went from there to San Francisco; thence by steamer to England, where he remained until about three weeks ago."[28] Whitley's biographer places his departure around the last day of May 1888.[29] It is not a story that has been accepted by all of Whitley's descendants, however. "I have researched steamers that left SF in 1888 and they only went as far as China. Then another steamboat would take you to England. It wasn't possible and no steamers even left SF during that time frame. . . . the timeline is impossible."[30]

There is more than a little credence to family suspicions that Whitley never departed for England. On May 30, 1888, a man named T. B. Dillingham, giving his address as Chicago, checked into Galveston's Washington Hotel.[31] Under ordinary circumstances this hotel arrival might have gone unnoticed, but Dillingham's did not. According to press releases Dillingham was Bill Whitley. "He was a high roller and blowed in something like $150 a day in an effort to have a good time. Wine, women and hacks were his diversion and he was reckless of expense. He stayed about a week, but during that time he succeeded in giving it away that he was from the wild and woolly west Texas instead of the overgrown village at the foot of lake Michigan."[32] When Whitley realized that he was being shadowed by the police, he left Galveston but was arrested in Houston on suspicion sometime around mid-June. The police did not have enough evidence for probable cause to hold him on and released him.[33]

What is certain is that on April 28, 1888, federal authorities, unconvinced of Joe Barber's innocence, issued a writ for him, charging him with conspiracy to rob the United States mail.[34] His brother John headed back to Oklahoma already considering his next heist.[35] On May 8 Sheriff John Boyd and a couple of deputies transported a recovered Ed Reeves to San Antonio.[36] All in all the gang's remnants were quiet during May 1888. It would not last of course. In June their minds would once again turn to train robbery, and to murder.

Wending its way through Oklahoma, in the 1880s the Verdigris River was bordered by dense forest and underbrush where visibility was limited to twenty feet or less. Taking its name from the Spanish words *verde* (green) and *gris* (grey) it was mentioned as early as 1806 in the writings of Zebulon Pike. It is a serene area, perfect for quiet contemplation, and for train robbers. In June 1888 this thickly wooded area was "a perfect wilderness of tangled vines and creepers, and as the country contains a wild and lawless element that has given the authorities much trouble, and where human life is not held as particularly valuable." On June 15, 1888, this place was visited by what the *Galveston Daily News* termed "Train Robbery Terror."[37]

All accounts state that Missouri, Kansas and Texas train 507 stopped at Gibson Station, roughly eight miles north of Muskogee, to take on a tank repairman named J. N. Bishop. Bishop had work to do at the water tank located at the Verdigris Bridge. What none of them knew at the time was that they had also picked up unwanted and undesirable cargo.

Around 10:30 p.m. the train halted at the tank so Bishop could disembark. With him was one of the brakemen or the pumper (accounts vary) named Harrison who helped Bishop to unload his tools. It is at this point that witness accounts as provided by the media of the day diverge, fraught with internal inconsistencies and contradictions. Fortunately the testimony of those most directly involved has survived.

According to the media's accounts, as the train started to back up, the engineer was abruptly confronted by one or two outlaws with drawn pistols.[38] The number of outlaws boarding the engine proved important in the subsequent court case. The *Indian Chieftain* states that "the engineer was covered by a revolver," implying, but not definitively stating, that only one man boarded the engine.[39] This appears to be confirmed by the *Galveston Daily News,* which reported that "a man climbed over the engine tender and shoved a six-shooter under the engineer's nose."[40] This corroborates the testimony of one of the outlaws as well and would seem to resolve the question.[41] However, the *Galveston Daily News* contradicted itself in the same article stating that "two men immediately sprang on the tender."[42] This report was echoed by other newspapers across the country.[43] Wallace H. Rasback, the train's engineer, later stated under oath that "We left Gibson Station and passed along about a quarter of a mile, and in the meantime there was a man stepped up behind me."[44]

According to Rasback, the outlaw ordered him to stop just beyond the bridge with the express car over the trestle. Ironically, the repairman Bishop had given him almost the same instruction. Rasback described the outlaw as "a medium size man, dark complexion—that is dark hair and dark complexion" with a moustache and unshaven. He was later identified as Kep Queen although Queen identified himself as Captain Buck. Rasback drove the train across the bridge until the passenger cars were all trapped on the span.[45]

Contemporary interviews of the passengers are sparse. Bertie Colter of Dallas was riding in the sleeper car at the end of the train and saw none of the outlaws. While having no first-hand knowledge of the raid, she believed that the outlaws had boarded the train at Fort Gibson "and secreted themselves in the baggage car." While her theory was incorrect, she astutely realized that the train crew had done part of the outlaws' work for them. "It seems that the robbers had returned to stop the train at that point, but stopping itself for that purpose. I stated that they were not put to the trouble of stopping it."[46] This was the view of Sterling Clark as well. Clark stated that "several men, who are now believed to be members of the robber gang" boarded the train at Gibson Station.[47]

Queen ordered the fireman to take the coal pick and forced both men out of the engine where Rasback observed a second man by the mail car armed with a pistol. The outlaw was "of a light complexion, looked to have sandy mustache and chin whiskers."[48] This varies from media coverage, which stated that "four armed men appeared."[49] No sooner had the engineer and fireman been herded off the train then everything went to hell.

Mail clerk Willis P. Colton leaned out of the doorway of the mail car asking why they had stopped. Colton recalled that Queen snapped, "Get back you son of a bitch, or I will blow your head off."[50] Rasback recalled Queen's words somewhat differently: "Take your head in there, or I will put a hole through it." Both men were in agreement as to the result however. "And he hadn't any more told what he would do than he shoved his revolver up and fired," Rasback testified.[51] Colton confirmed this. "Before they fairly got the words out of their mouth, before I had a chance to move, they shot." The bullet hit him in the left arm.[52] He was fortunate, for the shot was close enough to powder burn his face. Colton stated that his "eyebrows all singed off; and my eyelashes; and my face filled full of powder.[53]

Queen then forced the men out of the car, marching Colton's companion Jenks to the express car intending to use him as a human shield if they "found the expressman in a belligerent mood."[54] In the express car A. B. Codding heard the shot and went to the door and shouted. When there was no response he returned briefly to his work. Then he heard someone demand, "Where in Hell is that express car?"

Codding again went to the east door. He started to look out when one of the outlaws "threw a gun up in my face" and demanded, "Get back you damned son-of-a-bitch, or I will blow your head off." Codding jumped back and blew out one of the lamps as he went to retrieve his pistol. Moments later Jenks was forced into the car with one of the outlaws behind him covering Codding. The outlaw announced unnecessarily that he "was a damned bad man" giving his name either as Captain Jack or Captain Buck, Codding was unsure which. He further testified that he saw a third man run from the brush carrying three Winchesters, two of which he gave to Queen and the other outlaw.[55] The remaining gang members now clambered into the express car demanding that Codding open the safe or they would kill him. Codding's reply was simple. "I am a dead man then, for I know no more how to open the safe than you do." The gang then demanded the loose cash, which Codding gave up.

From Codding's testimony it appears that Queen had smeared mud on his face to disguise himself. The sandy-haired man seen by Colton had pulled his bandana up over his face before entering the express car. Codding put the loss at $8.75. He also stated that he could not have recognized anyone other than Queen.[56]

Codding's testimony is corroborated by a number of witnesses. One of the passengers, N. C. Blanchard, believed that the outlaws only secured around $8.50.[57] Another passenger, Sterling Clark, also placed the loss at $8.75.[58] This was further corroborated by one of the outlaws.[59] At least one newspaper placed the amount at $850, but this may well have been a printer's error.[60]

Codding added that the three outlaws who accosted him were on the east side of the south-bound train. Attracted by the shot that wounded Colton, newsboy Henry Ryan emerged onto the platform of the smoking car just behind the express.[61] According to his testimony he had his right hand leaning on the car and his left on the brake wheel when he saw something the size of a man about half way down the express car on the west side. "It was carrying something looked like a stick or Winchester, or gun of some kind. About the time I saw it he raised it, I saw a flas[h], and the next thing I felt my arm was shot." The following dialogue occurred during Ryan's testimony:

> Q. Did he say anything before he shot?
> A. I never heard him say anything.[62]

Ryan's account agrees with newspaper reports to a point. While Ryan reported only one shot, the *Indian Chieftain* reported two shots, one of which hit Ryan in the right forearm.[63] The *Galveston Daily News* also reported multiple shots, one of which "lodged in the shoulder of Frank Ryan."[64] Another newspaper carrying a report from Texas stated that Ryan had been shot in the leg.[65] Still more misinformation had it that "Ryan's arm was so badly shattered by the highwayman's bullet that amputation was necessary."[66] In court Ryan demonstrated that the arm had not been amputated:

> Q. Can you show that place where you were shot?
> A. Yes sir. (Witness does as requested, showing that it entered under forearm and went through the flesh of the forearm.

Ryan further offered that he had returned to Muskogee to have the arm treated and spent the night there, not days, convalescing.[67]

The shooting drew attention, and a number of people looked out windows and emerged onto the platforms at the train's abrupt second stop and the subsequent gunfire. When Ryan emerged onto the platform he was followed by cattleman Ben Tarver who was returning from Chicago.[68] Hearing no further shots, Tarver returned to the car where he was talking with his friend William P. White, a cattleman from Milam County.[69] White was sitting in the second seat on the west side of the train and Tarver was standing on the end of the first seat when the bullet that struck Ryan hit him in the head. Tarver was wiping sweat from his forehead when the bullet hit him in the left hand and passed through his head, killing him instantly. Another shot followed but did no damage.[70]

White's account of the murder coincides in part with press coverage of the time.

> The train boy, named Ryan, ran out on the steps of the first second-class carriage and the same man that shot Codding fired at Ryan, the ball crashing through his left arm, shattered the bone into fragments, passed through the open door and struck a cowman named B. F. Tarvin [*sic*] of Marlin, Texas, under [illegible] and came out over the right eye. Tarvin [*sic*] fell forward on the seats in front of him dead, and the fellow on the ground fired two more shots without doing any damage.[71]

This account would appear to name Queen as the shooter but Queen was on the east side of the train at the express car. It was following the shot that killed Tarver that the belated command to stay inside the coaches came.

The interview of passenger N. C. Blanchard, a resident of Emmetsburg, Iowa, took place at the Ellis Hotel in Fort Worth where Blanchard was staying when reporters found him.[72] Like the other witnesses, he testified to the passengers being trapped on the trestle with the only exit through the front door of the smoking car. Blanchard believed that the command to get back in the train was given by the outlaws before the promiscuous gunfire, possibly basing his thought on the commands given at the express car, which were not heard at the smoker. "The baggage man looked out and was ordered back, an order he promptly obeyed without the emphasis of a shot from the rifle that closely followed the command." Blanchard lay down on the floor of the smoker with other passengers including "one very portly man complaining that he was so large he could not flatten out enough."

Blanchard also related that he had been talking with Tarver for some time before he moved to a coach further back. He saw none of the shooting, but heard a revolver shot followed by the heavier Winchester blast. Moments later conductor Hugh Hogan came through the cars and advised passengers of the train robbery and to hide their valuables.[73] Blanchard believed that seven men were involved in the robbery of whom "two had handkerchiefs tied over the upper [*sic*: lower?] part of their faces and one or more were disguised by smearing their faces with mud."[74]

As noted, the media's accounts of the Verdigris Bridge robbery are filled with inconsistency and contradictions. For example, according to Sterling Clark both Ryan and Tarver received the command "go back into that car, damn you" as they stepped onto the platform.[75] Bertie Colter misheard the express agent say that they had gotten $850, and one paper reported that the outlaws had rifled the mail car.[76]

While all this was transpiring, further excitement in the form of a freight train was racing toward them from behind. Accounts disagree, but either a brakeman or one of the outlaws, most likely the former, ran back and flagged the freight before it plowed into the back of the passenger train. At this point the outlaws withdrew and vanished into the night.[77]

Given the confusion and fear attending the robbery, it is understandable that there was disagreement about how many men were involved in the heist and the murder. The *Indian Chieftain* placed the number of outlaws at seven.[78] The train's crew stated that they saw only five men, but some of them believed that as many as eight were involved. According to other accounts, the crew further stated that only one man armed with a Winchester did any shooting although this was clearly not the case.[79] This is a distinct variance with Clark's statement that there was a volley of pistol shots.[80]

The train robbery at the Verdigris Bridge added more infamy to the gang's remnants. For more than a year they had tortured, maimed, terrorized, and killed across two states. The law had not forgotten and never let up. It was the law's turn now, and in the weeks to come the gang would fall on even harder times. They would receive the same mercy they had shown others.

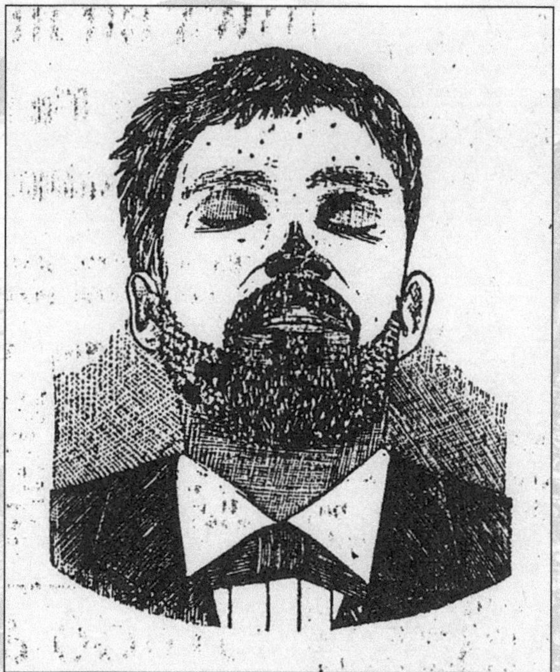

Bill Whitley.

Sketch from the *San Antonio Express* of September 27, 1888.

Brack Cornett.

Courtesy M. Lynn Cornett.

City Marshal James E. Lucy.

Courtesy Richard Lucy.

Map of Cornett-Whitley Gang region of operations.

Author's photo from a map in the Texas State Archives.

John William Cornett. Half-brother of Brack Cornett. He may never have known of his younger, infamous sibling.

Courtesy M. Lynn Cornett.

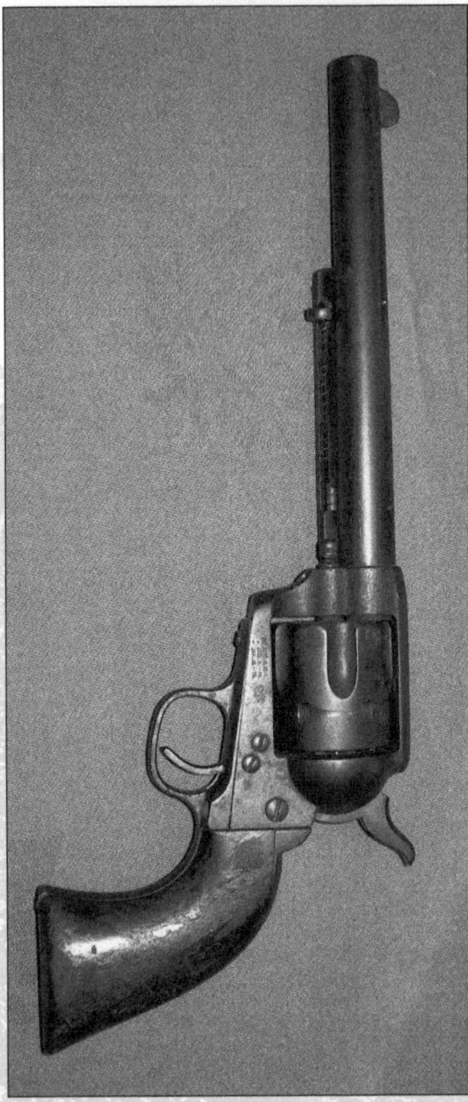

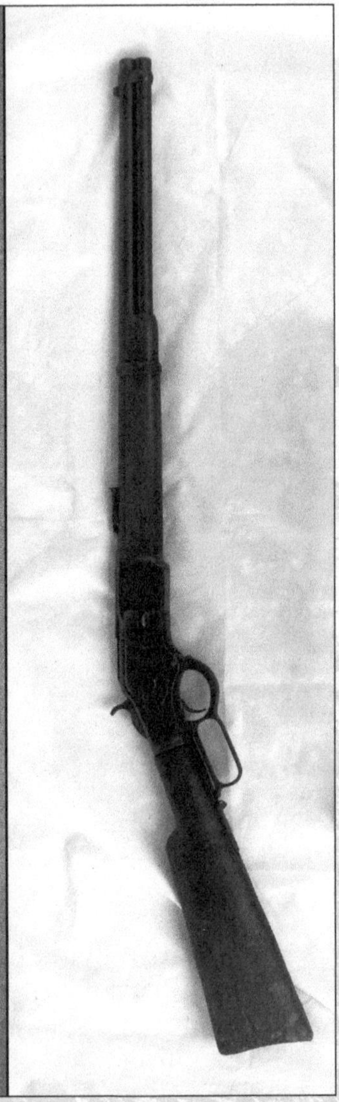

Bill Whitley's pistol. The pistol Whitley carried when he was killed is now in the possession of two great-grandsons, Steve and Mike Buck.

Courtesy Mike Buck.

Bill Whitley's rifle.

Courtesy Doug Dukes.

Henry J. Labatt. Noted attorney and worthy citizen.

Courtesy Chris Butterworth.

Ben Pickren, engineer on the Flatonia train.

Courtesy John Henry Pickren, Jr.

Reinhardt Schneider and wife Elveree Powell. Schneider was an early criminal associate of Bud Powell.

Author's collection.

William Henry Cornett and wife Etta Lewis.

Courtesy Roger Cornett.

William Henry Cornett (*left*).

Courtesy Roger Cornett.

Thomas O. Bailes.

From *A Twentieth Century History of Texas,* Volume 1, Chicago, IL, 1907.

Legendary Texas Ranger Ira Aten.

Courtesy Bob Alexander.

Bill Whitley.

Courtesy Keith Reed.

Sheriff Brutus L. Zapp.

From Frank Lotto, *Fayette County: Her History and Her People*, privately published, Schulenburg, Texas, 1902.

William Martin Walton. He defended some of those accused of train robbery.

Author's collection.

Duval West, deputy U.S. Marshal.

Author's collection.

Vachel Weldon.

From L. E. Daniell, *Personnel of the Texas State Government,* Austin: Press of the City printing company, 1887.

Chapter 11

Lawless and Violent

As noted, both contradictions and internal discrepancies mark the accounts concerning the Verdigris River bridge train robbery. One report has it that the express messenger claimed he could identify "the four who were about his car, and says that one of them was a black man."[1] This latter was a mistake due to some of the outlaws smearing their faces with mud as a disguise. The report led to the first arrests on June 19 when a posse captured three men at the home of Harry Sisson.

Why Sisson was targeted by lawmen is unknown. According to newspaper accounts, not always accurate, Sisson was known as a bad man and did carry a bad reputation. Other than this, what the probable cause lawmen had for making the arrests remains a mystery. Years earlier Sisson had been sentenced to hang for murder but was saved by the intervention of Judge Isaac Parker. He had served two years in the penitentiary in Detroit.

One possible reason for the arrests may have been the presence of "One-eyed" Rogers Columbus, a black man. Sisson escaped capture, but Columbus and two brothers named Phipps were captured. All of them were released for lack of identification by the train's crew.[2]

Not unnaturally, news of the train robbery blazed across the country, but it never achieved the notoriety of the Flatonia robbery despite Tarver's murder.[3] Why the media chose to ignore the pursuit of the criminals and follow up of the holdup remains unknown. Perhaps train robberies had become too *passé* for the jaded media, but whatever the reason the train robbery at Verdigris River Bridge never achieved the infamy Flatonia did and the identities of the outlaws remain controversial, at least in some minds.

One group whose minds were not confused was the federal officials who apparently had no doubt as to who the culprits were. On June 22 arrest warrants were issued for Kep Queen, William Whitley, Joe Foster (J. H. Holloman), Sam Holloway (Bob Rogers), John Barber, Jim Stephens (AKA Johnson), A. S. Lewis, William R. Dawson,[4] Oscar Coulter,[5] Tobe Dustin, and John Dustin on a charge of murder.[6] It was a comprehensive list made up from probable cause, and in time some of the suspects would drop away. One historian writes, for example, that Whitley "probably has nothing to do with that robbery."[7] Regardless, on the same day Heck Thomas arrested Dawson eight miles west of Tulsa.[8]

Like Ira Aten, Henry Andrew "Heck" Thomas was and remains one of the great lawmen and folk figures of the nineteenth century. Thomas was born January 3, 1850, in Newton County, Georgia, to Lovick Pierce and Martha Ann Fullwood Bedell Thomas. Thomas served in the Confederate Army after which he became a policeman in Atlanta. When the family moved to Texas, Thomas went with them, first serving as a railroad guard. He later became a Deputy U. S. Marshal in the Oklahoma Territory.[9]

Following the Verdigris River Bridge fiasco, elements of the gang scuttled back into Texas. Rogers and Holloman aimed for their home in Leon County. If Burton's theory is correct, Barber and Whitley returned to the Hill Country although it is by no means certain that either of the outlaws were at the Verdigris River Bridge holdup. As to the others, no trace has been found of either Tobe or John Dustin, and their involvement in the Verdigris River Bridge train robbery appears speculative at best. By June 22, 1888, their names had vanished from the list of wanted men.[10] Dawson and Lewis were both captured. Queen and Stephens dropped from sight, possibly fleeing to Arkansas. Coulter was not captured until the following year for a murder in Arkansas.[11]

On July 2, 1888, there was a bank robbery at Fredericksburg. Burton theorizes that Whitley may have been one of the men who robbed the bank and if federal authorities were correct in their allegations concerning Verdigris River Bridge, Barber might well have been the other. The outlaws netted $300 and escaped, although one was believed to have been wounded. The identities of the outlaws remain unknown with certainty.[12]

As July closed, Texas Ranger Frank Jones wrote to Adjutant General King that he was starting a scout to Frio County in an attempt to capture Will Jacobs, briefly associated with the gang.[13] In strong contrast to Schmitt's self-aggrandizing correspondence of the year before, Jones added that "I have notified Lieut. Brooks so that he can look out for him in Edwards Co. where he usually goes when he leaves Frio."[14]

August 1888 was relatively quiet for the gang. Ed Reeves and Sion Secrest remained in jail. Powell was in Arizona living under an assumed name.[15] Cloud remained in Oklahoma keeping a low profile. Barber and Whitley may have split up for a final time. According to his biographer, Whitley was even then returning from a trip to England although it is highly unlikely that such a trip ever occurred.[16] What is certain is that in September Whitley resurfaced in Texas. It was not a wise decision. Luck had abandoned what remained of the Cornett-

Whitley gang, and the world had already seen enough and more of them.

Writs were issued for Kep Queen et al. on September 10, 1888, for the Verdigris River Bridge holdup and Tarver's murder.[17] Less than two weeks later, on September 22, Whitley again attempted a train holdup, this time near Harwood, Texas. What he did not know was that his former cohorts had already betrayed him. In February 1888 Will Harrell had been arrested for harboring the gang, and very likely Eli Harrell and Newt Butler traded the charges against them for their cooperation with federal authorities.[18] It is likely that when Whitley returned to his old haunts he contacted one or both of the Harrell brothers who in turn contacted U. S. Marshal John T. Rankin.

Aware of Whitley's plans, Rankin had provided a nasty surprise for the train robbers. The first car behind the coal tender was the mail car in which Deputy U. S. Marshals Duval "Bud" West[19] and J. S. McNeil[20] were stationed, both of them armed with double barreled shotguns. The next car back was the express car where Rankin, Deputy U. S. Marshal William Van Riper,[21] and Southern Pacific detective J. J. Kelly were concealed.[22]

Two or three miles east of Harwood, engineer Dan Toomey was flagged to halt passenger train 19 around 7:20 in the evening.[23] No sooner had the train halted than "a broad shouldered man with chin whiskers and moustache" boarded the engine with a drawn pistol. A second man, described as having a "smooth face and apparently not over twenty-two or twenty-three covered the fireman and ordered him to go back and uncouple the express car from the rest of the train.[24] As the fireman, one Mr. Greeser (or Grosser), and the outlaw moved down the train they met the conductor, E. E. Shackford, who demanded to know what was going on.[25] Shackford was greeted by the outlaw who demanded that the car behind the tender be detached.[26]

While the fireman did as commanded Shackford returned to the passenger cars. His first action was to walk through the cars with the admonition to "Keep still and hide your valuables."[27] Having warned the passengers, Shackford dispatched brakeman J. T. Bentley to flag a freight train that was following them. Milton Everett, the ticket agent from San Antonio, was sent back to send a telegram to San Antonio.[28]

One of the passengers on the train was Louisiana-born attorney Henry J. Labatt who was returning from a business trip to Mexico.[29] Labatt recalled that as the train approached Seguin a friend of his who worked for the railroad cautioned him to secrecy and told him the train would soon be attacked by train robbers. "He told me that if I had any valuables I had better secure them, and do it as privately as possible, as it was not known but that the robbers might have some confederates on the train among the passengers to note the secreting of any valuables." Labatt hid $1600, $1500 of which was a draft, in a basket of grapes. When he asked why his informant thought it would be attacked, the railroad employee told him that Rankin and the others had been on the train the night before as well.

Near Harwood the train had stopped to pick up a pump repairman named Bishop, and shortly after the actual Harwood stop Labatt's informant told him that robbers were on the engine and "we would have h-ll in a few minutes." As other accounts note, about a mile and a half from Harwood the train came to a dead halt. Labatt apparently confused the two stops, but the result remained unchanged. The conductor returned to the passenger cars and "passed through them hastily." The warning was obvious: secrete your valuables. "The compliance with this injunction was but the work of a moment, each passenger holding out $5, $10 or $15 as a sort of a contribution to the robber fund, in order to prevent being seriously dealt with."[30]

Inside the express car Rankin and the others waited expectantly for the door to be opened. They were startled when the train began pulling forward leaving them behind. In the mail car West and McNeil and mail agent Ed Saran might have been initially puzzled when the train started back up, but the realization that the outlaws had cut part of the train loose would not have taken long. Labatt was confused as well when he heard the engine pull away with the mail car.

Labatt recalled that the officers' plan had been simple. "United States Marshal Rankin, having been apprised of the intent to rob the train, had boarded it with nine deputies just before reaching Harwood, the point where the robbers were expected to take charge of the train. Marshal Rankin, with six deputies [*sic*: two], took a position in the express car, the other three being placed in the mail car and well armed. The engineer, conductor and balance of the crew had all been instructed that when the robbers boarded the train they were to obey their orders explicitly and without resistance, the defense of the train being left exclusively to the marshal and his deputies."[31]

Toomey was forced to stop the train at what the *Gonzales Inquirer* referred to as "a dark and dreary spot. It is just at the foot of a little hill. Tall live oaks and thick underbrush cut off any light which might struggle to pierce the darkness, but on this occasion the stars were not even shining. Heavy clouds hung in the heavens and the rendezvous of the bandits was a cave of black gloom."[32]

Whatever confusion may or may not have existed, it was abruptly dispelled when the train again came to a dead stop. Whitley and the other outlaw herded the engineer and fireman back to the mail car. Here Whitley ordered Toomey into the car. Dan Toomey recalled somewhat bitterly, "If the men on the inside of the car had faced the music at the door they could have killed the entire trio—there were but three robbers—without especially endangering their own lives, for they stood thirty feet from the car door conversing with me right in the full glare of my kerosene torch, which made our immediate surroundings light as day."[33] Rankin's plan did not include suicide. The bandits told Toomey to enter the mail car, but he protested earnestly. One of the outlaws took his side, "telling them that the men in the car would surely kill me." Whitley's response was simple. "By God, you will go in that car or I'll kill you here." Between the proverbial rock and hard place, Toomey entered the car with the lantern above his head, his lantern that made the car "light as day." Toomey entered the car announcing as he did so that he was the engineer. "This I repeated, and it seemed to me as if the man who fired ought to have distinguished my overalls. I saw he was going to shoot anyhow and I squatted suddenly. That is all that saved my life, for the load aimed at my breast partially struck my right jaw and shoulder by the dodge. It knocked me out of the car, or I got down on the opposite side in some manner."

Whitley was less than sympathetic, demanding at first that Toomey reenter the car until he realized Toomey had been shot. Toomey believed that this evoked Whitley's better feelings. "He placed his hand on the side of my face, and discovering the wound, sympathetically said: 'Well, well; that's too bad. I didn't think they were cowardly enough to shoot you after you told them you was the engineer.'" Whatever sympathy he might have had was of short duration, however. Moments later the outlaws forced the fireman into the car. "He appealed to the men on the inside of the car time and again not to shoot, but they did all the same, but he was not hurt. One shot struck the tip of his finger, and several shots passed through his overalls. He bore a torch as I did."[34]

Labatt stated that about twenty minutes after the train was separated, gunfire was heard from in front of them.[35] The outlaws opened fire into the mail car, but Whitley realized that the attack was useless and they abandoned the train.[36] Whitley's biographer writes that "One of the gang got shot, and two other members carried him behind a car. Bill didn't want anyone else to get hurt, so he called the whole thing off."[37] Considering the fact that Whitley had ordered the fireman into the car after Toomey had been shot, this appears doubtful.

Information and misinformation about the attempted train robbery was broadcast by both the media and some of the witnesses themselves. Distance from the crime added to the distortion. In New England it was reported that the attempt had failed and that Toomey "was shot by the robbers and will probably die."[38] Local reports were no better. Duval West stated to reporters his belief that "two of the robbers were wounded."[39] At least one paper added flair claiming that two or three of the outlaws were limping off "beseeching their fleeing companions not to desert them," further stating it was not until after the outlaws fled that they realized Toomey had been shot.[40] Factually none of the outlaws had been shot. West may well have believed that two of them had been hit, but the only men struck were the engineer and the fireman.

Historian Jeff Burton theorized that several men who had been members of the Cornett-Whitley gang were at the Harwood robbery. "Will Harrell was undoubtedly at Harwood with Whitley, as in all probability was Eli Harrell. Also in the party were Sam H. Neff and some two or three others whose names are not known."[41] Contemporary sources likewise overestimated the number of outlaws in the range of six to ten.[42] Keeping in mind that only two men, Toomey and Greeser, saw any of the outlaws, Toomey's testimony is of value: "I am positively sure there were but three robbers, only one of whom seemed to be experienced. He wore a bandana handkerchief over his face, and gave orders to the other two."[43] Very likely these were Whitley, Neff, and Will Harrell. Also, contrary to the claims of the lawmen, the only men shot were the engineer and fireman, both by the marshals themselves.

The trio was hotly pursued by Sheriff William E. Jones of Gonzales County accompanied by bloodhounds.[44] Sheriff Addison Kilgore from DeWitt County also joined in the pursuit.[45] Rankin had one advantage that Jones lacked. Eli Harrell had betrayed Whitley, first by informing him of the attempt on the train and then by directing Rankin to the home of his brother, Will, in Floresville.

Accompanied by Deputy U. S. Marshals Eugene Yglesias, Duval West, and William Van Riper, John T. Rankin went to Will Harrell's home in Floresville, arriving a little before dark where they found a black child in charge of the home. The child was held by the officers and ordered to remain quiet.[46]

Harrell's house was a two-roomed building "facing south, with no front gallery. The front room is sixteen by sixteen feet and is used as a bedroom. The one behind is eight by sixteen feet. A door midway in the partition connects the two."[47] A more detailed description was provided by a San Antonio paper.

> The building was a common one-story lumber affair of two rooms, one in front and one behind, connected by a door midway in the partition. The front room, evidently the best bed room, sitting room, nursery, parlor and conservatory of the family, was some 16x16 feet in size. It had two beds, a couple of chairs, an affair that did duty as a bureau and a shelf in the corner that held a lamp. It was lighted by three windows and the front door. It had a fireplace and no carpet, and gave at first glance the condition and hard lives led by its owners. The rear room, little more than a shed, was about 8x16 feet was used as a kitchen and lodging place for the Negro. It had a rear door and no windows. The whole place was worth no more than $500, but if it had been shot down, would have mounted in value to the $1000's.[48]

The officers waited in the back room of the small frame house. They did not have to wait long. Shortly after the men had concealed themselves Will Harrell and Whitley arrived. After securing their mounts, the men entered the house. Will Harrell lit a lamp while Whitley took a seat between the two beds in the front room. As Harrell lowered the glass chimney Rankin burst through the door and demanded Whitley's surrender.

It should have been an easy arrest, but Whitley was not an easy man. Rankin was five feet from him with a double barreled shotgun leveled, but Whitley came erect as he drew and fired. As his bullet flattened itself into the wall above Rankin's head, Rankin returned the fire, the shotgun blast taking Whitley in the head. One sensational report stated "Whitley fired one or more shots after receiving his first wound, and was literally riddled with bullets and died on the spot. None of the officers were hurt. All the officers got in their work."[49]

Whitley's death made national news.[50] One New York newspaper summed up his career succinctly.

> Floresville, Tex., Sept. 26.—Captain J. T. Rankin, United States Marshal, and Deputies West, Van Riper and Yglesias killed Bill Whiteley [*sic*] here last night. Whiteley [*sic*] was one of the men who attempted to rob a train near Harwood on September 22. He was also in the McNeil and Flatonia train robberies, and was concerned in the robbery of the bank at Cisco. He and Barber killed Deputy Sheriff Stanley, of Williamson County.[51]

While the articles appearing across the country were generally brief, the most detailed accounts appeared in Texas newspapers.

On the afternoon of September 25, Rankin, West, and Van Riper, all of San Antonio, and U. S. Deputy Marshal Eugene Yglesias of Laredo left San Antonio on the 2:20 passenger train bound for Flatonia. It was now that the misinformation appeared in several journals that the Harrell brothers were Whitley's cousins. Possibly the information was given out to protect Rankin's informant, Eli Harrell.[52] Whatever the case,

Rankin had been pursuing "this wandering Ishmael of the Brush" for some time.[53]

All contemporary sources agree that Rankin surprised Whitley and ordered him to surrender, a response answered by Whitley's swift draw and a shot that could easily have killed Rankin. His granddaughter, however, presents a far different view, many years after the fact.

> My Grandpa Will Whitley was framed by his cousins Will Harrell and Eli Harrell. They made a deal with Sheriff John Rankin to kill Grandpa. Will Harrell took him to his house at Floresville. Rankin and four others hid in the kitchen. When Grandpa came in and sat on the bed they shot him in the back of the head. His body was carried to San Antonio, and for more than a day crowds came by to view the body. His fancy yellow legging boots hung at the foot of his bier.[54]

All of the officers fired on Whitley, newspapers noting that "the beds and bedding were absolutely ruined."[55] Leah Harrell, Will's wife, was horrified as she rushed into the house, but Rankin paid her a liberal amount for the furniture and bedding.[56]

Whitley's body was transferred to San Antonio on September 26 to conduct the official inquest, which amounted to a formality, the judge ruling on September 28 that Whitley was killed while resisting arrest.[57] Whitley's granddaughter asserts, "A request was made of Cordelia Lucinda 'Cord' Cox Whitley and Jehu Thomas Cox to come to San Antonio to identify the body before the reward was paid. Upon their arrival in San Antonio they 'could not positively identify the body'—thus the killers were denied the reward."[58]

This may well have been what she was told, but historical records indicate that a number of witnesses were summoned to the inquest to identify Whitley. On September 26 one of the first to identify him was the fireman from the aborted Harwood train robbery. After viewing the body, Greeser told Rankin, "Yes, this is the fellow who made Engineer Toomey go into the car; I recognize him."[59]

Rankin was thorough in identifying Whitley. He had Ed Reeves and Joe Bennett, who were both in custody, view the body. Bennett had been charged with harboring train robbers.[60] The men spoke highly of Whitley, particularly Ed Reeves, who lacked "a good deal of being a lamb himself."

> "I knew him well," he said, "He couldn't be scared. We all considered him the nerviest man among us. He would look straight into the muzzle of a six-shooter, expecting it to go off every minute, and never blink his eye. Even Buck Cornett, who was known as Captain Dick, and who was killed by Allee in Frio county, for downright sand wasn't a patch to Whitley. This fellow Barber, who run with him, has got a reputation as a bad man, but he ain't. He was the best traveler in the crowd, and that was about all we expected him to do when things came to a pinch."[61]

Telegrams were also sent to Newt Butler, who had harbored the gang for a time, Sheriff Addison Kilgore. and others at Cuero.[62] Still another telegram was sent to city marshal J. J. Thomas at Cisco asking Thomas to send someone who could identify him as one of the Cisco bank robbers.[63] Among those who ultimately identified Whitley were Sheriff John Olive of Williamson County, Sheriff Addison Kilgore, Newt Butler, John T. Pleasants, W. E. Bennet, and S. F. Flens of Cuero.[64]

Cordelia Whitley was telegraphed, but the family tradition that it was to identify Whitley has become garbled over the years.

> The body of Bill Whitley, the dead train robber, continues to attract large crowds and is still well preserved. His wife, who lives near Lampasas, has been

> telegraphed, and if she wants the corpse it will be shipped to her; if not, will be buried here. Officers are still at work, trying to identify the other members of the gang, which endeavored to rob the train at Harwood.[65]

By September 28 Cordelia and her brother had still not arrived in San Antonio

> Mrs. Whitley who is now living near Lampasas, has been notified of her husband's death, and the body has been offered to her who has the most right to it. In the event of it not being claimed by her or other relatives, it will be buried by the federal officers in the Potter's field.[66]

When no instructions were received from Whitley's wife, the embalmed remains were buried.[67] Cordelia did not arrive in San Antonio until after the burial. On October 2, 1888, the *San Antonio Daily Light* reported:

> Mrs. Whitley, wife of the train robber recently killed, is in the city accompanied by her brother. The object of their visit is to have the body of Whitley exhumed and shipped to Bertram, Burnet county, Texas, forty miles from Austin. The undertaker has charge of the transshipment and is executing his orders today.

Regardless of Cordelia Whitley's grief, the press descended on her when she arrived in San Antonio. The *Dallas Morning News* reported in part that she was in town to supervise the removal of Whitley's body. "She is a small, pale woman with a scared look in her eyes. She says that she never had any idea that 'Bill' was engaged in train robbing, does not believe that he would do such a thing and believes that he was murdered. He was kind to her and the children, gave them money enough to keep them decently and always showed a desire to see that they were comfortable. He was rather a quiet sort of man, would take a great deal before he resented it and seemed anxious to have things pleasant around the house."[68]

For Cordelia Whitley it must have been a humiliating ordeal in addition to her grief over the loss of her husband. The media however was concerned only with the story, sensationalizing it as they wished. One paper reported untruthfully that "Up to the train robbing, though, he had no particular occupation beyond stealing all the stock he lay his hands on and shooting anyone that objected. When he met a kindred spirit in John Barber, however, he began to realize that there was some money in rifling passenger trains."[69] Another stated that Whitley "is supposed to be one of the men who robbed the bank at this place on the 15th of February. He is a desperado, and a relative of John Barber; is said to be Barber's lieutenant, and was perhaps one of the worst men in Texas."[70]

On top of this were stories that Whitley had spent time in south Texas drinking, fraternizing with women, and generally having a good time. Perhaps the worst humiliation came when the family attempted to bury him at the Mahomet Cemetery. Here they encountered a large group of citizens who would not permit them to bury Bill Whitley's body in the cemetery. The family was forced to move the body through the woods at night and tear down a section of the fence to bury the outlaw. His tombstone reads in part "He was an affectionate husband, a fond father and a friend to all." Perhaps, but today he is best remembered by the epitaph the *Galveston Daily News* provided: "lawless and violent."[71]

Rumors floated that John Barber had been captured, and confidence in the law again soared.

> Barber, it may be added, is reported to have been arrested at Konntze [*sic*: Kountze] the night of the Harwood robbery, though officers here have received

> no confirmation. If he has been caught train robbing will be pretty dead until a new race of heroes arises. With Whitley and Captain Dick dead and Barber and Reeves in jail, the heart has been cut out of the gang.[72]

The rumor proved false, but the heart had been cut from the Flatonia robbers. In the days to come those who had hitched their wagons to these "heroes" would face justice, both legal and otherwise.

On October 2, 1888, Bob Rogers, who was involved in the holdup at Verdigris River Bridge, was killed by his cousin John T. Bell.[73] It was not known at the time that Rogers was one of the Harwood bandits or more would have been made of the killing. As it was, the news was confined to Texas.

> JEWETT, Tex., Oct. 4. – Another horrible homicide was committed in this county on Oct. 2, this time near Rogers prairie. John R. Bell shot and killed Bob Rogers. Particulars not learned.
>
> Bell and Rogers are cousins, and the killing arose from some former trouble. Bell is still at large with officers in pursuit.
>
> Some believe the killing justifiable, and that Bell will soon come in and give up.[74]

Another gang associate did make national news. Will Jacobs, who had intended to participate in the Flatonia affair, was arrested ten miles south of Pearsall, Texas, by sheriffs W. C. Dougherty[75] of Frio County, Dan Lewis[76] of Bexar County, and Giles Everett[77] of Milam County. The outlaw was taken by surprise and hauled to Austin where newspapers erroneously reported that Jacobs was the man "who planned and engineered the McNeil railroad robbery."[78]

Another of the gang who resurfaced during 1888 was Ike Cloud. In Oklahoma, on September 6, a white mare belonging to Chad Owens was stolen. "One" Cloud and Seven Star (alias

Jim Stop) were charged with the crime.[79] While this was not the first encounter with federal justice in the Oklahoma Territory for Seven Star, it was the first for "One" Cloud.

The identification of the man known as One Cloud as Ike Cloud is based on a number of facts. In 1892 another One Cloud was indicted by the court in Fort Smith. In a letter Deputy U. S. Marshals requested writs for James Norman and Cloud, noting in part "this man Cloud we can't find out his given name." Hence the writ was issued for One Cloud.[80]

Family researchers know little of Ike Cloud. One relates that "Little is known of Ike other then he left home in his early 20's. He is found on a Deed sale in Williamson Co. TX in 1884 and it says he is a resident of Williamson Co. TX. I do not have this deed record. It is rumored by family he may have gone off to start his life elsewhere (this makes no sense, the family was to[o] closely knitted together) or he may have been killed on a cattle drive."[81] Still another researcher writes "Issac [*sic*] left home as a young man. Rumors placed him as having gone to New Mexico or California. The family has steadily held to his innocence of any law violations, but he had been in the wrong association of company, otherwise his absence is unexplained."[82]

In general there are three family traditions concerning Ike Cloud. One is that he was killed on a cattle drive between Texas and Oklahoma by cattle thieves. The second was that he moved to Oklahoma and lived to an old age. Rumors also placed him in New Mexico and California.[83] All of the traditions indicate that Cloud was indeed in Oklahoma at some point. Like the others he had not abandoned his chosen vocation: stealing horses.

On November 5, Sheriff N. O. Reynolds of Lampasas County telegraphed U. S. Marshal Rankin that he had captured Sam Neff, charged with horse theft in Lampasas County and the attempted robbery of the train at Harwood.[84] Like other members of the gangs, Samuel Herbert Neff had come from a good family. Born September 25, 1858, to Noah Neff and Isabella Eleanor

Shepherd in Coryell County, he enjoyed the advantages of a good family and having a mother who was a teacher.[85] He and his brother Charles were running a horse ranch in Lampasas County, and following his brother's death Neff bought out his brother's interest on January 13, 1887. On September 18, 1888, Neff married Margaret "Maggie" Hamilton in Lampasas County.[86] Neff's biggest claim to fame was that he was an older brother of Pat Morris Neff, a future governor of Texas.[87]

The most sensational news came out of Oklahoma, however, where John Barber was hiding out with the remnants of his scattered group, Jim Stephens and Kep Queen. Ever watchful, the law responded to reports that Queen, who was noted in some newspapers as the gang's leader, and the gang had been seen in Claremore, Oklahoma. On November 16 Sheriff Ed Sanders gathered a posse and surrounded a cabin about a mile from "the Dog Creek Court House." One of the posse politely knocked on the door and asked if he could warm his feet.[88]

Inside the cabin two men were lying in the bed with a blanket drawn up over their heads while a third eyed the newcomer. After a short time, the posse man thanked the residents and left the cabin. Moments later the two women in the house emerged, saddled three horses and led them to the doorway. As Ed Reeves had told lawmen at another time, John Barber was the best traveler in the gang, and he had sensed that now was the time to travel.

As the men rode out they were suddenly confronted by the posse with a demand to surrender. The outlaws drew and fired at them. The posse returned a hail of gunfire. Queen was shot from his horse, and the mounts of both Stephens and Barber were killed. Stephens, by his own account, was pinned under his horse when it fell. The women dragged Queen into the house. A bullet had cut the femoral artery in the thigh and he bled out in around ten minutes. John Barber fled in a different direction and ran into more of the posse who opened fire on the fleeing outlaw. Barber's horse was killed, but the wounded outlaw escaped into the woods.[89]

News reports of the time stated that the two women in the cabin were Queen's wife, Nancy, and "Barber's sister" although the latter identification is not likely, since his sisters had their own homes elsewhere. According to some researchers, Barber married one B. Palmer in January 1889 which, if true, appears to indicate that the other woman could have been Barber's betrothed. No record of Barber's marriage has been located to date, however. The matter is unresolved.[90]

Queen's body was taken to Vinita and embalmed for the purpose of identification. The *Fort Smith Elevator* reported in part:

> Queen, Barber, Stevens [*sic:* Stephens] and a man named Whitley are charged with a bank robbery at Cisco, Texas, and Whitley was killed a short time since by Texas officers. The same four men are the ones who robbed the passenger train on the M. K., & T road above Muskogee this June last and killed a passenger. They were all from Texas, but have been in the Territory off and on for a year or more.

The outlaws had apparently not planned on remaining long. Queen's wife informed the officers that she had only been there about two weeks "for the purpose of collecting a note of $350 which the father of Barber had given to her husband in a cattle trade."[91]

Queen's death created a minor tempest in a teapot. The *Indian Chieftain* reported in part that Queen "spent his last moments in praying, cursing and talking with the women."[92] On November 19 Nancy Queen and her three young children arrived in Vinita where it was believed that she would probably take her husband's body to Texas for burial.[93] In response to the *Cheiftain's* report of Queen's final moments, Nancy Queen wrote.

> EDITOR CHIEFTAIN:—Permit me to reply to the article in your issue of the 22nd, in regard to my husband cursing in his last moments. It is a mistake for he was in my arms from the time he called me until he was gone, and I know every word he said. Great things are laid to Queen's door, but there is no proof of his guilt.
>
> NANNIE QUEEN[94]

Queen was buried in Vinita on November 24. There remained only one final act to close the accounts of Queen's death. Jim Stephens was angry over Queen's death and wrote a bitter letter, which he entrusted to Belle Starr.[95]

Starr was notorious during her time. Born Myra Maybelle Shirley near Carthage, Missouri, on February 5, 1848, to John Shirley and his third wife Elizabeth Hatfield, Starr was well educated for her time, graduating from Carthage's Female Academy. The Shirleys were southern sympathizers, and following a Union attack on Carthage, moved to Texas. She was married twice and became involved in a number of illegal enterprises and had served time in the Detroit House of Corrections.

According to the written report, Starr pronounced the official story false and delivered Stephens's letter, which claimed in part that "A braver man than Queen never fell, and although we mourn his untimely fate, yet we had rather that he was in his cold and silent tomb than to have fallen alive into the hands of parties who under no circumstances would have met us man to man."[96]

It was the final word from the fugitives. Both Stephens and Barber eluded the law during the balance of 1888. It was not the last word from the law, who had neither forgotten nor forgiven any of the Cornett-Whitley gang, however. The year 1889 would bring their final destruction.

Chapter 12

The Wages of Sin

On November 30, 1888, Sam Neff was released by the court on a $4000 bond following his indictment for attempted train robbery. A deputy sheriff from Lampasas County promptly rearrested him on charges of horse theft based upon testimony brought against him by Eli Harrell.[1] The confrontation between Harrell and Neff was heated, according to the *San Antonio Daily Express*:

"Who made this affidavit?" demanded Neff, in curt tones.

"I'm the man," Harrell drawled lazily in answer.

"Well," remarked Neff, after a pause, "you'd better make another one."

"I will before night," was the response.

Neff waived examination and was placed under a $300 bond, which he set out to get.[2] His abrupt second arrest created a legal dilemma. Both the state and federal governments wanted him on diverse charges, but while he was on bond in federal court Lampasas County now had legal custody of him and expected him to be taken to Lampasas for trial. Federal attorneys objected as he was then involved in the proceedings of the federal court.[3] Neff's attorney filed a writ claiming that he was under the jurisdiction of the United States court and could not be taken by the state. On December 2 Neff filed a habeas corpus petition.[4] A clash of jurisdictions was avoided on December 5 when N. O. Reynolds agreed to surrender the prisoner to the federal court on the condition that Neff was brought to trial immediately by federal authorities. It was a stipulation the federal authorities readily agreed to.[5] It was an amicable decision, more palatable by the fact that if Neff came clean on the train robbery charges he would be taken to Lampasas to face the horse theft allegations.[6] Neff's trial went forward, but it was not resolved until 1889 when he was convicted and sentenced to five years in the penitentiary.[7]

Eli Harrell was an important figure in insuring that Neff remained behind bars and in Whitley's death. One newspaper reported that Harrell was the man who betrayed the gang at Harwood and provided the information leading to Whitley's death. "There is nothing against him save the charge of harboring the highway men, and this is said to have been forced upon him. He had relatives in the gang and they and companions called upon him repeatedly, demanding food for themselves and corn for their horses. He kept his mouth shut and so got into trouble."[8] None of the gang were related to Harrell, but it may have been Eli Harrell's story that convinced some that he was related to Bill Whitley.

Elsewhere other legal issues dominated both the gang and the lawmen who pursued them. On December 10, 1888, Deputy John Carroll, accompanied by Joe Alford, John Ward, Bob Hendrix, George Russ, and Jack Ross, arrived in Fort Smith. All of them had been members of the posse that killed Kep Queen, but now they found themselves charged with murder. Sheriff Ed Sanders joined them. On December 12 all of them returned home under bond. "The case will be investigated by the next grand jury, and in all likelihood no bill will be found against them."[9]

Another man who arrived in Fort Smith was Ike Cloud, arrested on December 16 by Barney Connelly.[10] Cloud was convicted of larceny on February 15 and sentenced to three years in the Arkansas State Penitentiary.[11] Unlike that of his former comrade Ed Reeves, Cloud's conviction drew little or no attention. On February 20 Reeves once again drew national attention when he was convicted of the train robberies at McNeil Station and Flatonia. On February 21 he was sentenced to life in prison.[12] Following his conviction Reeves complained bitterly that the officers had not "toted fair" with him as to his trial and conviction. "After his arrest, on promises made him, he says that he divulged secrets connoted with the operations of the gang, believing that he would be dealt with lightly if not set scot free."[13] Reeves appealed his conviction, but ultimately it was to no avail. His life sentence was upheld and he was shipped off to the penitentiary.

Another of the gang's associates, the man who came close to participating in the Flatonia atrocity, received justice on May 14, 1889. Will Jacobs was convicted at Cameron, Texas, for the murder of Lee Pool. The jury sentenced him to prison for ten years on a charge of murder in the second degree.[14]

In Arkansas, Cloud entered the penitentiary on March 19. Five months later, on August 12, Cloud was admitted to the prison hospital suffering with "pernicious malorial anemia ulceration of the bowels," a condition caused by a lack of vitamin B12 that could well have evolved into stomach cancer. He died in the penitentiary on September 22.[15]

Of the original gang, John Barber was now the proverbial last man standing. According to some family sources, Barber married B. Palmer on January 4, 1889, in Logan County, Arkansas, and the couple had a son also named John.[16] While the contemporary records of this marriage have not been located, it may well have been the brightest spot for any of the original gang during 1889.

While Cloud was dying in Arkansas, Will Harrell was arrested at Floresville on a charge of train robbery.[16] In Oklahoma arrests warrants were issued for Kep Queen, William Whitley, Joe Foster (J. H. Holloman), Sam Holloway (Bob Rogers), John Barber, Jim Stephens alias Johnson, A. S. Lewis, William R. Dawson, Oscar Coulter, Tobe Dustin, and John Dustin. The return shows Oscar Coulter had already been arrested on another warrant. The court may not have known that Whitley and Rogers were dead, but they certainly knew of Queen's death.[17]

Contemporary documents indicate that Barber was now using the alias William Snow.[18] He would ultimately abandon this alias to reinvent himself as George Wright, hoping to find sanctuary in yet another assumed name.[19] It was an old ploy, one that could be used successfully with a modicum of intelligence. The operative words are "could be," and for Jim Stephens the penchant for aliases was his undoing. The headline screamed "Too Many Aliases" on September 5, 1889.

On September 4 Sheriffs I. G. Coombs of Washington County and Sheriff F. P. Galbraith of Benton County arrested Jim Stephens on suspicion due to the fact that he had too many aliases. "In this county he is known as Wm. Hall and in Benton as Bill Horton." Stephens was tentatively identified as one of the Cisco bank robbers, and the paper noted that he had arrived in Fayetteville during December 1888.[20] On September 10 Heck Thomas left for Fayetteville in company with Deputy Isbell "for the purpose of identifying John Barber and a man named Stevens [*sic*]."[21] By September 25, officers were herding Stephens to Texas to stand trial. Three people positively identified him, and this less than happy reunion was amplified by the fact that he was also identified as an escaped convict who owed the state of Texas ten years in the penitentiary.[23]

John Barber had now lost the muscle that he had relied upon. Cornett, Whitley, and Queen were dead. Both Reeves and Stephens were in jail. There are any number of things he could have done, from surrendering to the law to leaving the area as Bud Powell had. Instead he remained, tenaciously clinging to the very life he should never have embraced. The law doggedly pursued him, and he had crafted a steel breastplate which had been captured.[24] Life on the run had aged him years so his age was mistaken for thirty-seven, although he was only twenty-nine.[25]

From available accounts, Barber was hiding at the home of his Palmer brother-in-law. As the fall advanced, authorities believed that he teamed up with Eugene and Hamp Standley, cousins of one another, to rob a farmer named Marion Horn. Eugene Standley was a like-minded individual, having already served two terms in the penitentiary. Horn later testified that on the evening of November 25 Eugene Standley had arrived at his home and asked for a job picking cotton.

Horn obligingly gave Standley lodging and supper. As soon as the family had retired, Standley stepped out of the house and summoned "two companions who wore masks made of handkerchiefs." Then the terror began. The outlaws confronted Horn with drawn pistols and demanded his money. Horn gave them what money he had in his pocket, but it was not enough for the outlaws. They forced Horn out of bed and "hobbled him with a trace chain, and made such vicious threats that Mrs. Horn got up and took from a drawer $600, which she gave them."

This was still not satisfactory to the rapacious thieves. The outlaws hauled Horn to the smoke house where they "burned his feet with matches and hung him twice, swinging him up so long the last time that he became unconscious." The outlaws waited until Horn had recovered before dragging him back to the house where "they swore if he did not give up the rest of his wealth they would pour coal oil on his wife and set her on fire." Not unnaturally Mrs. Horn fainted, and the outlaws finally left.[26] It was a vicious and sadistic crime, and John Barber was later linked to it although other than the obvious sadistic brutality, echoing the Flatonia raid, the matter is speculative.

Another matter of historic speculation involves the Missouri, Kansas & Texas train robbery of November 24.[27] At 9:30 p.m. the train stopped at Pryor Creek near Perry Station in the Indian Territory. Almost immediately a man "boarded the engine and covered the engineer and fireman with his two revolvers" demanding "Do as I tell you and do it quick." At the same time a second man uncoupled the mail and express cars from the rest of the train. The second outlaw then signaled the train to move forward before he "jumped into the express car" and covered the express agent.[28] The engineer drove the engine about a mile from the rest of the train.

According to the expressman, O. H. Johnson, who was taken totally by surprise, he emptied the safe for the outlaw who placed the money packages "in a bag which he had brought into the car with him." That done the outlaw exited the train, ordered the man in the engine to join him and the pair escaped into the dark. "The two men did not appear in the least excited and evidently did not want to harm anyone. The whole transaction was gone through with in such a methodical way that the train hands could hardly realize what was going on."[29] Allowing for the possibility, based purely on circumstantial evidence, it does not appear likely that Barber was involved in this train robbery. None of the train robberies the gang had been involved in demonstrated this level of sophistication. Whitley, as an example, had to have the train's crew uncouple the train at Harwood. Nor was the robbery accompanied by the promiscuous violence that characterized the gang's other holdups.

Whatever the case, Barber was never positively linked to either crime. Flatonia had faded from the pages of the media in favor of more sensational news, and the incident had faded in the minds of the general public, and while Barber's involvement in these crimes remains speculative, what is not speculation is that the law had doggedly tracked John Barber for two years. The world had had enough and more of John Barber.

On December 7, 1889, Deputy U. S. Marshals Barney Connelly and S. C. White, aware that Barber was hiding near Tahlequah, started for his hideout. The men arrived before dawn and had barely concealed themselves when Barber came riding toward them. The deputies ordered him to halt, and for once his fight or flight reflex failed him. Barber wheeled his mount and opened fire. According to most accounts, Connelly shot him in the chest and killed him.[30] Details of the shooting were provided by the local news: "Barber was riding when discovered. He immediately began firing his Winchester, Indian fashion crouching behind his pony after each shot, but was shot through the heart after fifty shots had been exchanged."

The same newspaper provided more accurate details, likely received from Connelly himself. "The officer was standing behind a sapling and when the man had advanced to within fifteen steps he gave the command to 'throw up.' A Winchester cracked in a second and then Connolly leveled his gun and fired. As he did so the horse turned and ran, and its rider poured a streak of fire after him from his weapon. When he had covered some 230 yards Connolly fired again and the man fell, but it was the first shot that had done the work."[31]

Barber's death was the fourth of the primary suspects in the Verdigris River Bridge holdup. Others had rapidly been eliminated as suspects, leaving only J. H. Holloman and Alexander Lewis. Of the original Cornett-Whitley gang, only Reeves, Secrest, and Powell remained.

The remaining trio endured vastly different fates. Reeves's appeal fell through and he was shipped off to an eastern penitentiary with a life sentence. Reeves may have made the news during 1897 in connection with the execution of William Haas in Ohio. Haas had raped the wife of his employer, then cut her throat and set the home on fire to conceal the crime. Haas was convicted and sentenced to death. On April 8 while testing the machine the coil failed.

> The final test had been made at 3:30. Electrician Green and one of the prisoners who assists in the dynamo room, John Crevisson, were at the cabinet in the electrocution chamber and Ed Reeves, a prisoner, and Martin, the wiper, were in the dynamo room. The machine was making about 1680 revolutions and had been at a voltage of 1700 to 1800, and an amperage of 12 to 14. The signal had been given from the annex to stop the machine, and Reeves was just starting, according to his statement, to stop the engine, when a blue flash as big as a man's two hands shot out from each side of the dynamo and it was known the apparatus was disabled.[32]

Investigation of the incident determined that the failure was caused by an accumulation of copper dust that caused a short circuit. Haas's execution was delayed until April 21 when he had the dubious distinction of being the first man to be electrocuted in the Ohio Penitentiary.

The remainder of Reeves's life was anticlimactic. In the 1920s he was released from the penitentiary and returned to Texas. The census taken in 1930 found Reeves living in the home of his grandson. His years in the penitentiary had aged him. From available records it does not appear that Reeves enjoyed anything like a close relationship with his family. He died in Dallas on December 9, 1942, of natural causes.

Secrest, alias Charley Ross, on the other hand skated out of both his participation in the train robbery at McNeill Station and the murder charges that loomed against him. The witnesses who would have testified against him had moved on.

One account states that Secrest was to be tried in 1912 in La Grange although this is far too late. They could not find the key witnesses, and as a result the case was dropped. The date seems very late for a trial since Secrest had been in custody since 1888. Nor is the romanticized story that Secrest later teamed up with Pancho Villa likely. News accounts of the day place his trial in the spring of 1889.

Doubtless Secrest considered himself fortunate, returning to his old ways. But while he escaped the law, he did not escape justice. While crossing a swollen river near Llano, he fell from his mount and drowned. According to family tradition, he was carrying several bandoleers of ammunition that pulled him under.[33]

For Bud Powell, fate proved kinder. He had prudently abandoned the gang and distanced himself from their promiscuous violence. In 1892 he was in Montana using the alias John Thompson. While he was on the run his father had died on December 7, 1890, and Powell had seriously reevaluated his life. In Montana he had settled down, and when he was arrested on July 6, 1892, he made no resistance although officers had clearly expected a fight.[34]

The news made headlines both in Montana and Texas where the name Flatonia once again surfaced. In Galveston it was reported as:

> Bud Powell, the notorious desperado of southwest Texas, who was the leader of the band that held up and robbed the Atlantic express train of the Southern Pacific road near Flatonia, Tex., on June 18, 1887, was arrested in Helena, Mont., yesterday by United States Marshall Paul Fricke of this city. Mr. Fricke is now on his way to Austin with his prisoner.[35]

The sentiment was echoed in San Antonio which reported that "Bud Powell, the notorious Texan, wanted for the robbery of the Southern Pacific train at Flatonia some years ago" had been arrested.[36]

In Montana the press detailed the capture of Powell in full. Marshal Fricke informed reporters that John Thompson's real name was "'Bud' Powell, and the gang which committed the robbery, and of which Powell was a member, consisted of seven men, of whom three have been killed in resisting arrest, two are in the penitentiary and one is still at large."[37] The dead men were obviously Cornett, Whitley, and Barber. Reeves was in the penitentiary, but Cloud had died in prison although Fricke likely did not know of his death. The man still at large was likely Secrest who may also have been dead at this time.

While many in the news industry persisted in "trial by media," most Montana newspapers reported the facts. "Thompson has been living in this vicinity for two or three years, generally farming and caring for horses. Last winter he attended the Helena business college, and it is supposed someone passing through Helena recognized him and afterward put the officers on his trail."

"While here Thompson behaved very well, joined the church and Good Templars and was paying his respects to the daughter of a wealthy ranchman near town, who is a lady high in social and religious circles." Powell was unarmed when he was captured, and the officers' belief that "they would have had a hard fight had he been given an opportunity" was only their own belief.[38] Even Red Lodge's newspaper, which quoted Marshal Fricke as having told Sheriff Halford that Powell "was one of the most desperate that ever invaded Texas. His brothers are all outlaws, and in fact the whole family are considered a tough lot" stated that Powell had been living in Montana for some time "and has recently been attending the business college at Helena. It is said he repented of his crimes some time since."[39]

These statements were echoed by other Montana papers. "He came to Montana several years ago and went by the name of Thompson. Last winter he attended a business college in this city and was well liked by his companions. Previous to and since that time he lived near Boulder and worked on a ranch. He repented of his criminal career, joined the church and was well thought of by all who knew him. . . . No one who knows the young man doubts that he is truly repentant, but that will not save him."[40]

Powell had indeed changed his ways, attending the Englehorn Business School for about four months, but the work bored him and he returned to ranching.[41] In the end, Powell's poor decision to turn to outlawry betrayed him. In Montana he was safe, but Powell missed his family. Sometime during 1892 Powell wrote a letter that was intercepted by law enforcement and traced back to him.[42]

Powell's arrest created great interest in Texas, and the newspapers that were so swift to castigate both him and his family proved fickle, soon singing a much different tune. Now they castigated their own citizens. "His story of reformation is firmly believed by those who know his traits of character, but so far the spirit of charity and generosity that is supposed to exist among church members and ministers of the gospel toward the reclaimed Christian has not been extended to him here, and beyond the words of consolation from Rev. Wickes, his friend and pastor, of Boulder, Mont., he has received no kind attention or religious ministration since his confinement in jail here."[43]

Unlike Reeves, Powell was reluctant to speak of his life. It was only after some persuasion that he recounted his escape and life following the Flatonia train robbery.[44] Attempts were made to post bond for him, but despite this Powell remained in jail.[45] On February 21, 1893, he entered a plea of guilty in the federal court at Austin. The media liked Powell, and even the *New York Times* picked up the story from San Antonio. "Arriving at Helena, Mon., he determined to better his ways. He entered a business college there from which he was graduated with honors. He then joined the Church and became an active religious worker."[46] It was expected that Powell would get off easy, and he did in some respects. Powell got five years in the penitentiary and returned to Texas. He died in Medina County, Texas, on April 26, 1936.[47]

The gang had begun with a feral ferocity that stunned not only the nation but the world. In the end they were simply men running the gamut of viciousness from sadistic psychopaths to mean-spirited ruffians. It had not gone well for them. When the Cornett-Whitley gang first gathered in 1887 they were confident, optimistic that nothing could or would touch them. They were the wrong men, in the wrong place at the wrong time. The gang itself lasted less than half a year, but for three years the members proved a plague upon society. Their notoriety was already dying in 1888 as other stories replaced them. It was the year of the great blizzard of 1888 that began as a heavy rain storm on March 11. By 4 a.m. the following day it had changed to snow. The blizzard lasted for three days, severing telegraph wires and causing numerous fatalities.

In England serial killer Jack the Ripper rose to prominence, and while he is generally credited with only five victims, during 1888 numerous other victims, some of whom may have been Ripper kills, occurred during the year. The case was never solved and remains a continual source of books, movies, and television programs.

In America H. H. Holmes, real name Herman Webster Mudgett, was a wanted conman and bigamist. It would be a number of years before he began his own career of murder, but the idea had bloomed in 1886 when he began constructing the "murder castle" in Chicago. He was apprehended and hanged on May 7, 1896. So by the time the last of the gang met justice, interest had faded concerning the atrocity at Flatonia. The interest of the press had faded that is. The law had never given up hunting the outlaws. The *Telephone* of Tahlequah in the Indian

Territory had once called it correctly. It was "the wages of sin."[48] In his classic play *Julius Caesar*, Shakespeare insightfully writes "The evil that men do lives after them; the good is oft interred with their bones."[49] There are no truer words that describe the gang. They were a primal force of destruction—destruction that lived after them. While most of them were dead within two years of their formation, the darkness they brought with them destroyed not only themselves but much of what they touched. The men who had hunted them proved no exception as if the evil they embodied sought revenge for their deaths.

Fate caught up with Barney Connelly first.[49] Connelly had captured Cloud and killed John Barber. In 1891 he was sent to arrest former deputy U. S. Marshal Shepherd Busby on a charge of adultery.[50] As Connelly approached Busby's home on August 19, Busby opened fire, killing Connelly.[51] Pursued by lawmen, Busby finally surrendered and was brought to trial. He was found guilty and hanged at Fort Smith, Arkansas, on April 27, 1892.[52]

Sheriff John Olive, who was instrumental in the pursuit of the outlaws, came to a violent end in 1892. Olive and John Rankin were on their way home and standing on a railroad platform when Olive was shot from ambush.[53] In time two brothers named Armstrong were indicted for the murder. The apparent motive was revenge, Olive having killed two of their brothers twelve years earlier.

Alfred Y. Allee did not substantially reform following the killing of Brack Cornett. By 1896 he had killed another man and escaped the hangman's noose. Allee was on the downhill slope, however. Through a haze of alcohol Allee admitted, if the story is more than a reporter's fabrication, that he saw ghosts. According to the story "a San Antonio man" asked him why he had killed so many people. "Because I like to change ghosts," was the reply.[54]

According to this very likely apocryphal embellishment, Allee had killed a newspaper editor who had offended him because he was haunted by the ghost of Brack Cornett.[55] Whatever the case, Allee was haunted by more than the ghosts of those he killed. One of them was the city marshal of Laredo, Joseph Barthelow.[56]

According to the news accounts, Sheriff W. W. Shely of Starr County had arrested Allee with Barthelow's assistance. Once out on bond, Allee unwisely began making threats. On the evening of August 21, 1896, Allee was in Reiwald's Saloon in Laredo when Barthelow stepped in and announced, "I want you old man." Allee came erect from his chair and in the next few moments Barthelow knifed Allee. The killer of Brack Cornett died within moments.[57] Barthelow was brought to trial in January 1897 for Allee's killing.[58] Barthelow was exonerated, living on until September 2, 1915.

> A. J. Barthelow, one of Laredo's most prominent citizens, died suddenly at his home tonight at 10:30 o'clock of a complication of heart failure and acute indigestion. Deceased was one of the best known peace officers in Texas, was formerly a State Ranger at Brownsville, later City Marshal, and up to a few months ago for ten years was Deputy United States Marshal at Laredo, under Marshal Brewster. Mr. Barthelow was also a County Commissioner and member of the City School Board.
>
> As an officer Barthelow handled some of the most notorious crooks on the Rio Grande border. He is survived by a widow, two sons and other relatives.[59]

Nor was John Rankin immune to the ill fate that fell upon those who had destroyed the gang. On November 27, 1897, Rankin was walking along the streets of Austin when policeman Jim Grizzard opened fire on him. Rankin was shot four times and, like Allee had been, was unarmed.

According to some sources, U. S. Marshal John Rankin's death was due to a "political difference over the coming municipal election."[60] Other sources disputed the claim, stating it was a personal matter.[61] Grizzard was indicted on December 8, 1897, for Rankin's murder and came to trial in June 1898.[62] Grizzard was released on a $1000 bond following his habeas corpus hearing the same month.

The media railed against Grizzard, the town council, and Austin's mayor who had refused to even suspend Grizzard.[63] In the end it was to no avail. Grizzard was brought to trial in June and ultimately acquitted.[64] Grizzard died of a stroke on February 21, 1951, in San Antonio.[65]

The gang's evil legacy was not confined to the original seven members. In 1891 the *Dallas Morning News* reported that Richard Whitley (no relation to Bill Whitley) was acquitted on a charge of being a train robber on March 26. According to the report Whitley was arrested on March 17 at Amarillo. The unfortunate Whitley was hauled to Dallas where it was found that while he met the description of John Insall, the authorities "ascertained that Ensall had been recaptured" and was serving time at Rusk penitentiary.[66]

Another man who apparently suffered from the Cornett Whitley "curse" was Albert Erichson. Erichson had played a significant role in running down Brack Cornett's gang in 1887. He was elected sheriff of Harris County in 1894 and again in 1896. On April 24, 1898, while sitting in his office in full view of two of his deputies he suddenly drew his pistol and shot himself through the heart. The reasons for his suicide were unknown at the time and remain so. "The cause of the deed is a mystery and not even his closest friends knew that there was any trouble rounding him to cause him to commit the deed."[67]

Ben Kegans, also instrumental in running Cornett's gang to earth, was another who came to a violent end. On October 8, 1901, he and Judge Walter Malsch were in a saloon in Houston having a friendly drink and talking of how long they had been friends. Suddenly both men drew their pistols and fired at each other. Both men died. The cause of the sudden argument and violent confrontation has never been determined.[68]

No mystery exists in the tragic death of Eugene Yglesis, however. One newspaper reported that Yglesias "has been suffering greatly for many months with a dreadful cancer of the face and that he had undergone several operations, and was finally told not long ago that there was no hope for his recovery."[69] He died on March 30, 1911.[70] The *Laredo Times* eulogized:

> It is with deep sorrow that we chronicle the death of Eugene Yglesias, which occurred in San Antonio at 5:30 o'clock yesterday afternoon from the effects of the gun shot wound inflicted upon himself last Tuesday night. The burial occurred in that city, this afternoon.
>
> Eugene Yglesias was raised in Laredo and made this city his home continuously up to a few years ago, when he moved to Mexico, then later to Galveston and then a few months ago moved to San Antonio and had been residing with his half brother, Mr. M. R. Perron. He was City Marshal of Laredo for a great many years, and was chief deputy sheriff of Webb County and Deputy United States Marshal for a number of years. He was fifty-two years of age and was one of the best known peace officers of the state.[71]

For the others engaged in the killing of Bill Whitley, fate was somewhat kinder. According to his obituary, Bill Van Riper became involved in spiritualism and eventually moved to California around 1904 where he became "devoted to spiritualism, later engaging in healing practices." He died of a stroke on May 9, 1924.[72] The last of those involved in Whitley's killing, Duval West, proved an able jurist, serving as a federal judge. West died of in San Antonio of natural causes on May 13, 1949.[73]

Over the years there was an attempt to glamorize the gang, or at least Brack Cornett, by the news media whose inability to separate fact from fancy is evident. The *New York Sun* first published the article later reprinted by the *Omaha Bee*.

> One of the most celebrated of them was Brack Cornett, also of Texas, better known as "Captain Dick." The Southern Pacific railway was his special prey. He robbed its trains five times in a year, always obtaining a respectable booty. On one occasion he cut off the ears of an express messenger who had resisted him, and subsequently mailed them to his victim. After holding up a train east of Del Rio, he kept in duress for an hour an aged maiden school teacher and compelled her to dance upon the prairie to lewd cowboy ditties, accompanying himself on a guitar. "Captain Dick" was killed across a camp fire by Alfred Allee, who shot him through the heart for a reward of $2,500.[74]

In Texas journalists and the general population knew both Cornett and what he was. No copy of this article has been located in any Texas newspaper. Most of the families to this day refuse to discuss the outlaws comprising the original Cornett-Whitley gang.

The collateral damage that the gang caused is extensive. George Schmitt's lust for the glory and money that the outlaws could have gotten for him led to his downfall as his weakness of character was exposed, and in his downfall he took his company of Texas Rangers with him. Schmitt himself died in obscurity far from the fame and wealth that he craved. In addition, men were crippled, disfigured, and killed by the gang.

Two groups emerged from the gang's wake stronger than they had been before. The first was the victims who went on to live prosperous, meaningful lives. For the lawmen who had diligently tracked the outlaws, despite the attempted tarnishing of their reputations by the media of the times and their elastic ethics, the gang represents yet another step in forming the brotherhood of the shield, and from the chaos that the gang left in its wake the law rose stronger and more professional than before. The media remained unchanged, quick to criticize and working to develop narratives that were often untrue and that remain to this day.

For those who believe that the gang was cursed, there is some basis in fact. Under the headline "Ill-Fated No. 19," the *Fort Worth Gazette* reported that on September 9, 1890, the track was "saggy and springy from the hard rains of the past few days." Concerned with the safety of the train, the engineer halted near Johnson's Bridge some ten miles west of Del Rio to send men to inspect the structure. The train had hardly stopped moving when "a tremendous waterspout rushed down from the mountains on the north. The huge column of water in a jiffy lifted engine and mail and baggage cars from the rails and turned them over on their sides and washed out 400 or 500 feet of the track. The passenger coaches stood firm and none of the occupants of the wreaked portion of the train were hurt." The washout delayed all traffic along the line. "Another curious feature of the mishap was that the train involved is the ill-fated No 19 which has been the victim of nearly every accident on the Southern Pacific road for the past two years starting with the famous train robbery at Harwood."[75]

With this final act the Cornett-Whitley gang faded from the public memory leaving as their legacy shamed families, murdered men, and a haunting legacy of terror and misspent lives.

Appendix 1

The following editorial was reprinted in the *Fort Worth Daily Gazette*, of May 24, 1887. Mild by modern standards, this editorial ignored a number of facts. It did however serve to galvanize the pursuit of the Cornett-Whitley gang.

The Texas Train Robberies.

New Orleans Picayune.

Train robberies in Texas and Missouri occur almost as often as did the stage coach robberies in the days of the "gentlemen of the road." But a train robbery in 1887 is a much more serious matter than were the stage robberies on the old-time turnpikes. Then there were from six to nine passengers who were to be relieved of their valuables. There was no such thing as a money express, and robbing the mail was a tedious business. Now a train will carry hundred of passengers, whom one or two men have no trouble in plundering. The express car will contain tens of thousands in treasure arranged for the convenience of the highwaymen while in the mail car the registered packages containing money are specially marked and placed by themselves in a particular receptacle, so that the robbers may not have the slightest difficulty in finding them. Thus nothing is simpler than plundering a railway train, and apparently no enterprise is attended with less danger to the robbers, while they are sure of a rich harvest to pay them for their trouble.

The strangest part of the entire affair is that no efficient and systematic effort is made by either the state or by the railways to crush out this evil or to protect passengers and shippers and their property. It is a question whether or not a transportation corporation would be liable to its passengers for loss in these robberies, but at any rate the state ought to take steps to protect the thousands of people whose business requires them daily to risk their lives and property among the highway men who infest the railways in its limits. If the corporations are not liable and the state is powerless to give the needed protection, all railway travelers ought to take to be authorized and even required to carry arms for their own defense. The Texas laws now disarm travelers and place them at the mercy of the robbers.

Appendix 2

One of the more galling mockeries heaped upon the law was the "Song of the Train Robbers" by George Chase. Historian Rick Miller discovered this song while preparing his notable biography of Rube Burrow and brought it to the author's attention. It appeared in the *Fort Worth Daily Gazette* of June 9, 1887.

SONG OF THE TRAIN ROBBERS

BY GEORGE CHASE

A jolly set of boys we train robbers are.
We live upon the best, we scorn coarse prison fare,
We spend our money freely until it is all quite run out,
Then pull up another train without the slightest doubt.

After we take a train we go right into town,
Upon a soft spring mattress lay us gently down.
We hear about the officers and how they run all night
Without a single train robber being in their sight.

We have heard about the Governor of the Lone Star state,
And the reward he offered in hope to seal our fate;
It is best we keep quiet, and therefore write this letter –
We will see your 500, Governor, and go you 500 better.

We have gone into the business, and we intend to stay.
The work is very easy; we are delighted with the pay,
We are not exposed to danger, as they are in many trades,
The work is just as easy as a soldier's dress parade

We have read the Austin dispatch dated the sixth,
Which intimates quite plainly you will put us in a fix.
It is just the same dispatch we have read two times before.
What are you goint to do about it? We would very much like to know.

The song concluded with the sarcastic note "No; there isn't any news from the train robbers."

Appendix 3

The robbery of the Flatonia train prompted a swift letter or an editorial disguised as one to appear in the *Fort Worth Daily Gazette* on June 20, 1887, taking both the government and the railroads to task. It was typical of the outrage stirred up by the Cornett-Whitley gang.

Train Robbing in Texas.
Fort Worth, Tex., June 19, 1887

To the Editor of the Gazette

Another train robbery at Flatonia Tex., better organized more determined and brutal. Success gives confidence. The year 1886 will probably be remembered as the year of the great drouth; the year 1887 as the year of the train robberies. Ordinary theft is not only punishable by law but can be provided against by prudence and carefulness, but for protection against bandit robbery or train robbery, the citizen has to rely upon the state. A state that permits bandit robbery never will fully enjoy the word civilized. You may rely upon it, Mr. Editor, that until train robberies are done away with, travel and capital will avoid our state. The falling off in travel is already quite evident, while bankers in the larger towns report that eastern capital is not coming into the state as it was sixty days ago. In conversation with our citizens, we find much confidence expressed in the courage and ability of Governor Ross. His friends claim that while he might be criticized for being slow he will yet be equal to the occasion. Yes, but we reply, our home is on fire and tardiness of movement, or the use of a sprinkling can, instead of a fire engine which is available, we cannot approve of. The protection of life and property is the duty of the state. If the state does not give this protection it does not fulfil its mission; it is a huge organization of delegated power without a purpose. In addition to other energetic measures a reward of $5,000 per head should be offered at once for train robbers. If they are not caught the state will not have it to pay. For every dollar so paid out hundreds will be returned in that prosperity that follows the full protection of life and property. History tells us that Nero was fiddling or doing something unimportant while Rome was burning and for this his enemies unjustly accused him of being the incendiary.

TEXAN

Appendix 4

Jim Stephens's letter to the press was published in the *Fort Worth Daily Gazette*, December 12, 1888, and describes the fight from the outlaw's point of view. His bitterness is evident:

Please be so kind as to publish this in answer to an article published in the Indian Journal regarding the death of my comrade, Kelp [*sic*: Kep] Queen. The house we were in was surrounded after night by a party numbering nearly sixty men. Never were men more surprised as we when the shooting began, and as for our horses being led around by our women folks, that is false as can be, as they were saddled before sundown and tied to the fence near the house. My horse was shot from under me the first three shots that were fired, which was our first intimation of danger. As he fell my right leg was pinioned under him, and there I lay imprisoned, in expectant dread of the crowd advancing on me. I was pleasantly surprised when I found they had no such intentions. When I succeeded in extricating myself I fired two shots at them, being protected by my horse, which they returned with compound interest, which my horse showed afterward being almost riddled with bullets. I managed to back to a tree and opened fire again. My Winchester being on my saddle, I had nothing to fight with but my six-shooter. I remained near the house until 10 o'clock the next day, and witnessed the removal of my unfortunate friend. A braver man than Queen never fell, and although we mourn his untimely fate, yet we had rather that he was in his cold and silent tomb than to have fallen alive into the hands of parties who under no circumstances would have met us man to man. The man who has possession of my gun will confer a favor by sending it to J. P. Olive, sheriff of Williamson county, Tex., so that another d---d coward can say he handled my gun. The parties who surrounded us that night cannot be blamed for claiming that there was only eighteen of them as it looks rather dark on their side to only succeed in getting one when they had the three almost within their grasp. I heard them plan to send three of their brave men to the house to find out how matters were there. After watching them awhile I thought I had better seek a more congenial clime which I found easily done. Our horses was good property which time will prove, in fact we ride no other sort. Hoping you will give this hastily scrawled article a place in your paper I will close.

[Signed,]
"Stevens."

Appendix 5

Aside from Ed Reeves's confession, the only member of the original gang to provide testimony as to his activities was Buck Powell in the *Galveston Daily News* of July 10, 1892. The *News* took his statement from the *San Antonio Express*.

The interest in the case of "Bud" Powell, alias John Thompson, the train robber recently arrested in Montana, and who is now confined in the county jail pending his trial, which comes up next term of the Federal court at Austin, has not decreased. His story of reformation is firmly believed by those who know his traits of character, but so far the spirit of charity and generosity that is supposed to exist among church members and ministers of the gospel toward the reclaimed Christian has not been extended to him here, and beyond the words of consolation from Rev. Wickes, his friend and pastor, of Boulder, Mont., he has received no kind attention or religious ministration since his confinement in jail here.

Powell has a boyish face and is of very bashful and reticent nature. It would seem from the stormy life he has led that he would be hardened to the world and have a fearless countenance. His kindly face and mild manners plainly indicate that he was made a bad man by circumstances and not by nature. His true inclinations asserted themselves when he got in good company and his resolve to lead an upright life was never broken after once found, so far as known. He was called upon by a reporter for the Express, who requested of him a statement as to his flight from Texas after committing the Flatonia robbery. Powell consented after considerable persuasion, and here is the interview as written, word for word, by him, showing that he is by no means a poor scholar:

"I left my father's place some time in July, 1887, in company with Ed Reeves and Buck Cornet. We traveled north together to Burnet county and there we met John Barber, Bill Whitley and another man. I did not know his name; never saw him before. That was in the night. They wanted to rob another train or a bank, but I told them right there if they wanted to do anything of that kind they would have to get some one else to help them, for I was going to leave the country. They tried to persuade me to stay with them until we could make a raise, but I knew the whole country was after us, so I bade them goodbye and started. Then Ed Reeves told me if I would wait a few minutes he would go with me. He had a little talk with the other boys and then rode on and caught up with me. Ed Reeves and I traveled together to Johnson county and stayed there two or three days at his sister's house. Then we left and started toward the Indian territory.

"After we crossed Red river we separated and were to meet in Hot Springs, Ark. We did meet there, and the first night after Ed got there he got drunk, as I did not want to get drunk we separated. In fact I was afraid to get drunk, for at that time I did not want to be arrested, and thought if I stayed sober I would have a better chance to fight if I was tackled. The next morning I was very sick when I got up. I had a hard chill and fever that day, and that evening I looked around over town for Ed and could not find him. That night I went to the three-mile house. I thought I could find him out there, but could not, though I found there had been a man there of his description, so I went back to town and as I was very sick, went to bed. The next day I saw in the morning paper that the officers had arrested a big man who claimed to be a bad man from Bitter creek, and as I still did not know if it was Ed they had arrested of not, I staid [*sic*] there that day. I had a chill and fever that day again.

"That evening I was sitting in the stable where my horse was. I was sitting in a chair, with my head resting in my hands, and the first thing I knew there were five or six men all around me with their six shooters. They told me to throw up my hands. I took in the situation at a glance and told them I guessed I would. There was one man that was very nervous, and I asked the sheriff to please have that man turn that six shooter some other way, for he was liable to hurt some good man. He did as requested. Well they searched me and took my pistol from me. I asked the sheriff what the charge was. He said I would find out sooner than I wanted to, maybe, and they started down town with me and went in a store and stayed there a few minutes. The chief of police came in and he and the sheriff talked awhile together. While they were talking I made up my mind that it would never do to go to jail if I could possibly help it. When they came back across the room to where I was they searched me to see what I had in my pockets. They found about $107 in gold on me, and asked me where I got it. I told them I worked for it. They said it was rather curious that the man they arrested last night should have about the same amount of gold. I told them I knew nothing of this man they arrested. Then they said they would take me down and let me get acquainted with him. I told them then that I was sick, and if they had nothing against me but carrying a pistol I would put up what money I had for my appearance at court the next morning. Well, the sheriff and chief of police talked together a little and then said if I would put up my horse and what money I had they would turn me loose. I told them it was a go, so they turned me loose and I skipped out.

"When I left there I went up to Missouri and stayed a while, but was sick all the time, so I started to come back to Texas. When I got to Camden, Ark., I got so sick I could not travel, and I stayed there at a hotel about two weeks and then came out to a little place eleven miles from Camden, toward Texarkana, I think about seventy miles from Texarkana. I stayed there all that winter, the winter of '87, until about March of 1888. I was in partnership with a young man there in a grocery store, but I was afraid to stay there after March. I was down at Texarkana twice while I was there, in company with the telegraph operator from the station where I was living. I boarded with a man by the name of John Ingram the whole time I was there. I told them that I lived in New Mexico and was acquainted pretty well over the country and knew all the prominent men's names there was no danger of any one catching up with me on that score.

"When I left Arkansas I started for New Mexico on the train and stopped at Las Vegas for a while, but I could not get a job there that suited me. I then bought me a horse and saddle and started on west, drinking and gambling at every little town I struck until I got to William Slaughter's ranch, near the line of New Mexico and Arizona. I stopped around there, working at various places in New Mexico and Arizona until I got over about Springerville, Ariz., and there I went to work for a man by the name of Smith for a while. He was an Englishman. I went from there to Phoenix, Ariz., working with a thresher until about the 1st of June. I met a man there that used to work for A. Y. Allee down here on the Frio. I was afraid he would give me away, so about July 1, 1889, I left Phoenix and went to St. Johns, Ariz. There I met a saloonkeeper I had got acquainted with in the winter of '81. He was going north and so was I. He told me if I would go through to Salt Lake, Utah, with him he would pay all expenses. He and a doctor were going through together. They had four or five horses and I had two. We started toward Colorado, fishing and hunting along as we found game.

"While in Colorado I made up my mind I would quit my meanness and lead a different life, and the more I thought of it the stronger grew my resolution to change my way of living. I sold my pistol and said to myself, 'Here goes, old man, for a new country and a new life, and if I am caught, whatever the consequence, I will have to stand it, for I will never raise a gun against a man again, unless it be Indians, to protect myself.' We headed for Salt Lake, Utah, arriving there, I think, about the 1st of August, '89. We stayed there two or three weeks and then sold our horses and took the train for Helena, Mont. The others of the party stayed there but a short time until they left for Wyoming, but they did not like the country and came back to Salt Lake, and there I sent to them their things, which they had left with me, and I went out to Boulder, thirty-five miles from Helena, and went to work driving a four-horse team for a sawmill man. I worked there all winter, bu did not get anything for my work except what I ate. In March, 1890, I went to work for a man that lived about one mile from Boulder. I worked for him until May, 1891, when I quit him. The fall before I was breaking some horses for him and one fell and hurt my breast so I was laid up for a while. In May he wanted me to go down east of there 200 miles, where he had some 200 cattle, to ride for him that summer. I did not think I could stand it to ride. So I quit and went to work teaming, hauling ore, for two or three months, and then quit and started to school at the Helena business college September 1, 1891. I left there in January and went back to Boulder and went to work, as I was then about broke again. I was getting wood out of the mountains for a man while there. There was snow on the ground and we could use sleighs, but when the snow went off he had no use for me any more, so he paid me what he owed me, and I went up town with some boys that were 'batching' and stayed there with them for about one month and then went to work for a man by the name of Taylor, who owns a horse ranch ten miles from Boulder, and that was where I was working when arrested. I did not think they were after me when I saw them coming, and when Sheriff Halford told me there was a man there that wanted me I told him all right I was ready to go. My mind never was at rest and I wanted to get rid of this thing some way. Even if I have to work my life out in the penitentiary it is better than the way I was living."

Endnotes

Notes to Introduction

1. John E. Hallwas, *Dime Novel Desperadoes: The Notorious Maxwell Brothers* (Urbana: University of Illinois Press, 2008). Ed and Lon Maxwell were outlaws who committed the bulk of their depredations in Illinois and Wisconsin.
2. *Dayton Daily Empire,* May 9, 1865; *Cleveland Leader,* May 10, 1865.
3. *New York Herald,* January 9, 1866.
4. *Lafayette Daily Journal,* October 15, 1866.
5. Bob Alexander, *Lynch Ropes & Long Shots* (Silver City, NM: High Lonesome Press, 2006), 2.

Notes to Chapter 1

1. Jeff Burton, "'A Great Man Hunt,'—Correspondence From 'W. B. S.'—Scenes of Outlawry and Gunplay in Texas," *The Brand Book Vol. 18 1975–1976* (London, England: English Westerner's Society, 1977), 14. Hereafter cited as "Man Hunt."
2. Joe Bennett was the son of William Joseph Bennett and Mary Elizabeth Kelly. He was born in DeWitt County on May 24, 1862, according to penitentiary records, or July 19, 1861, according to some family sources. 1880 DeWitt County, Texas Census; Huntsville Penitentiary Convict Record Ledgers, Joe Bennett, No. 9245, Texas State Archives, hereafter TSA.
3. Green William Reeves was born around 1817 to David and Frances Hudgens Reeves in Georgia. When Green migrated to Alabama has not been determined, but there he married Elizabeth "Eliza" Cassandra Courtney in Montgomery County. Elizabeth was born to John Hiram Courtney and Rachel Evans in Montgomery County, Alabama, on February 4, 1830. Montgomery County, Alabama Marriage Records.
4. After the birth of Mary Francis "Fannie," there were five more children: John David in Union County, Arkansas, on June 9, 1849, Rachel Matilda in 1851, Green William Jr. on October 9, 1852, Edwin James in 1856 or 1857 at Magnolia, Arkansas, and Thomas Marion on January 18, 1858. The two children born in Bowie County were James Holloway in 1861 and Louise Penelope on October 3, 1863. 1860 Bowie County, Texas, Census.
5. Jesse Reeves married Mariah C. Hudgens on October 24, 1850, in Union County, Arkansas. The couple had several children prior to her death: Malinda V. "Mollie" in 1853; Frances Elizabeth in 1855, and Mary Frances in 1857. Coryell County, Texas Marriage Records.

6. The children of Jesse and Elizabeth C. Reeves were Jesse W., born December 23, 1867; Martha Alice, born December 18, 1870; Emma Frances born April 4, 1871; Dora born February 19, 1873; and Minnie Bell, born April 1, 1876.
7. 1870 Davis (Cass) County, Texas Census. The family was enumerated as 395. Family 396 is John D. Reeves, 21, farmer born in Arkansas and wife Nancy A., 18 born in Texas.
8. *Austin Weekly Statesman*, February 21, 1889.
9. Ellis County, Texas Marriage Records.
10. 1870 Navarro County, Texas Census.
11. Also living in the Reeves household were Sallie Wesson, an aunt of Emma Burt, and three-year-old cousin Benjamin Wesson. 1880 Ellis County, Texas Census.
12. *Austin Weekly Statesman*, February 21, 1889. The son's name has not been determined to date.
13. Hill County, Texas, Marriage Records. No divorce records for Reeves have been located to date.
14. *Austin Weekly Statesman*, February 21, 1889.
15. *Fort Worth Daily Gazette*, July 25, 1887.
16. Rusk Penitentiary Convict Register Ledgers, Ed Reeves, TSA.
17. *Galveston Daily News*, October 11, 1883.
18. Rusk Penitentiary Convict Register Ledgers, Ed Reeves, TSA.
19. *Austin Weekly Statesman*, February 21, 1889.
20. Rusk Penitentiary Convict Register Ledgers, Ed Reeves, TSA.
21. Wells Fargo & Co. circular, Adjutant General Correspondence (AGC), TSA, July 2, 1887.
22. *Fort Worth Daily Gazette*, February 15, 1887.
23. *Dallas Morning News*, February 15, 1887; *Galveston Daily News*, February 15, 1887.
24. Rusk Penitentiary Convict Register Ledgers, James Reeves, TSA. James Reeves was incarcerated as convict 1480.
25. Wells Fargo & Co. circular, AGC, TSA, July 2, 1887.
26. Samuel S. Powell was a son of Little Berry and Sarah Kerr Powell, and was born January 9, 1812, in Madison County, Kentucky. His mother, Agnes Stone, born October 10, 1820, married Samuel in Madison County on January 25, 1837. Madison County, Kentucky Record of Marriages Volume 1, 205.
27. The children born to the Powell family in Kentucky were Sarah Elizabeth, December 30, 1838; Harriet, 1839; Mary, 1840; Agnes, 1841; Delila, 1842; Houston Babbitt, 1845; William, 1847, Benjamin, August 1850 and Offa P. "Orphie" in November 1852. 1850 Madison County, Kentucky Census; 1860 DeWitt County, Texas Products of Agriculture Census.
28. The children born to the Powell family in Texas were Frances "Fannie" in 1855, Bud in 1859, and Elvira in 1863. 1870 DeWitt County, Texas Census.
29. For the definitive account of the Sutton-Taylor War see Chuck Parsons, *The Sutton-Taylor Feud: The Deadliest Blood Feud in Texas* (Denton: University of North Texas Press, 2009) *passim*. Hereafter cited as Parsons, *Sutton-Taylor*.
30. Karnes County, Texas District Court Records, Causes 1069 through 1075.
31. V. Weldon to Adjutant General W. H. King, June 20, 1887, AGC, TSA.

32. Wells Fargo & Co. circular, AGC, July 2, 1887.
33. Schneider, born April 11, 1862, to Daniel and Margarethe Schneider, was raised in Gonzales County, Texas. On August 20, 1884, he married Elveree Bascomb Powell. Four months later he was convicted of horse theft and entered the Huntsville Penitentiary on December 23, 1884. Following his escape from prison he was not recaptured until January 8, 1894. He was discharged on December 16, 1897. Schneider died on March 26, 1903, in Arizona. 1870 and 1880 Gonzales County, Texas Census; Huntsville Penitentiary Convict Record Ledgers, Reinhardt Schneider.
34. William Augustine Cloud was born in Charleston, South Carolina, on October 11, 1810, to Joseph and Martha Nettles Cloud. Records indicate that William was living in Cypress Creek, Alabama, by 1833 with his brothers John and Douglas. Both of his brothers eventually returned to South Carolina. Elizabeth Grace Kennedy was born in Maury County, Tennessee, on September 23, 1818.
35. The children of William and Elizabeth born in Alabama were James Franklin born July 23, 1837, Joseph Evander born September 17, 1839 and Mary Grace born June 16, 1840. Mary died the following day.
36. The Cloud children born in Louisiana were John Austin on November 2, 1841; Martha Ann "Mat" on November 6, 1843; Mary Jane on May 15, 1845; Elizabeth Ann on April 28, 1847; William Douglas on October 6, 1848 and Thomas Jefferson on May 8, 1850. 1840 Union Parish, Louisiana Census.
37. On June 20 Elizabeth Ann died followed nine days later by her brother William Douglas. Four days later, on July 3 Mary Jane followed them to the grave. 1850 Union Parish, Louisiana Census; family information courtesy Tom Cloud.
38. 1860 Williamson County, Texas Census.
39. 1870 Williamson County, Texas Mortality Schedule; 1870 Williamson County, Texas Census. Thomas Jefferson Cloud died February 7, 1918 in Schleicher County, Texas.
40. 1880 Williamson County, Texas Census. Penelope Ann Faulks, born August 23, 1847, to John and Rebecca Houston Faulks, married James Franklin Cloud on June 7, 1866, in Williamson County, Texas. James, born July 23, 1837, in Lowndes County, Alabama, had died on November 10, 1879, at Leander, Texas.
41. *Austin Weekly Statesman*, May 23, 1889; *Williamson County Sun*, Georgetown, Texas, July 21, 1887.
42. Burton, "Man Hunt," 14.
43. Kerr County, Texas Tax Records 1884–1887.
44. Thomas Carroll Secrest was a son of Abraham F. and Nancy Grey Secrest and was born January 12, 1819, in Tennessee. His mother was Mariah Bird Dismukes, Tennessee-born to John F. and Mary Wilson Dismukes on February 27, 1827. The couple married at Little Rock, Arkansas, on December 13, 1842. Secrest's true identity was discovered by Mike Koch who has researched the gang for years. "Sion" is pronounced "Sean." Pulaski County, Arkansas Marriage Records, 60.

45. The three oldest Secrest children were born in Arkansas: Edna around 1844, Washington Hampton on February 19, 1846, and Barbara Allen on June 20, 1848. Two months after the 1850 census, daughter Molly was born on December 22, 1850. Fayette County, Texas Census.
46. In addition to Sion the other children were Thomas Abraham "Bud," born on January 14, 1853, and John Blakemore, born on May 19, 1857. Following the 1860 census two final children were born to the couple: Isabella Saphrona "Belle" on December 10, 1852, and Maria Elizabeth "Bettie" on March 19, 1865. 1860 Fayette County, Texas Census; *Magdalena Mountain Mail*, Magdalena, New Mexico April 5, 1888.
47. 1870 Fayette County, Texas Census.
48. Guadalupe County, Texas, Marriage Records.
49. Barbara Allen Secrest had married James W. Pennington in Fayette County on February 4, 1868. Fayette County, Texas, Marriage Records.
50. 1880 Fayette County, Texas Census.
51. Iris Rose Guertin, *Navidad Country*, Vol. 1 (Sugarland, TX: Privately Published, 2009), 399.
52. Ibid., 40–41.
53. Fayette County, Texas, District Court Records, Cause 2345; 1870 Fayette County, Texas Census. Merkin was one of the children of Johann Wilhelm Ferdinand Merkin and his wife Caroline.
54. William Robert Ragsdale was the son of Charles Campbell and Sarah Scallorn Ragsdale and was born in Fayette County, Texas, on June 10, 1842. On August 30, 1865, he married Susan Prentice Robinson. The couple had five children. Ragsdale had served in the Confederate Cavalry and had been captured at the Siege of Vicksburg. Guertin, 327.
55. Ibid.
56. Ibid., 405 – 406; *Colorado Citizen*, July 1, 1880.
57. *Austin Weekly Statesman*, April 12, 1888; *San Antonio Light*, April 5, 1888; *Dallas Morning* News, April 6, 1888; *Galveston Daily News*, April 7, 1888; *Colorado Citizen*, Columbus, Texas, July 8, 1880; *Brenham Weekly Banner*, July 15, 1880.
58. *Brenham Weekly Banner*, July 8, 1880.
59. *Colorado Citizen*, August 12, 1880.
60. Burton, "Man Hunt," 14.
61. The other four Barber children were "Alcey J." (Elsie Jane?) born May 8, 1853, Sarah E., born September 17, 1854, Joel Anderson "Joe," born October 26, 1856, and Austin Callaway, born January 8, 1859. 1860 Burnet County, Texas Census.
62. Isaac Jones Barber was born in Franklin County, Virginia, on October 17, 1830, to Joseph A. Barber and Celia Jones. 1850 Carroll County, Arkansas Census.
63. Joanna Petty was a daughter of John and Elizabeth Dawson Petty and was born December 15, 1836. 1860 Burnet County, Texas Census.
64. Following the death of Samuel the Barbers had a number of children: Irena Joanna on May 13, 1863; Armenta Emma on March 15, 1865; Attia Lavisa on June 5, 1867; and Ones Ela on September 16, 1869. Following the census several more children were born: William Riley on September 15, 1871; Mary Ann on October 8, 1873; James Edgar on July 10, 1878; and Johnny

on December 14, 1879. Their youngest child, Rosa, was born sometime following the 1880 census. 1870 Williamson County, Texas Census.

65. Wells Fargo & Co. circular, July 2, 1887, AGC, TSA.
66. *Austin Weekly Statesman*, June 2, 1887. Attia Lavisa Barber married Thomas J. Hunt on November 4, 1885, in Bell County, Texas. She died on October 7, 1946, in Los Angeles, California.
67. *San Antonio Express*, September 27, 1888.
68. *Galveston Daily News*, December 8, 1889.
69. Western District Federal Court Records, Fort Smith, Arkansas, Jacket 9. It is possible that this John Barber was not John Toliver Barber. Court records note Thomas Barber as John's brother which may be how the witness knew them or may literally be true. Thomas Barber has eluded identification but may be a cousin of John Barber. The identification is far from certain.
70. 1880 Williamson County, Texas Census.
71. Barber family information courtesy Ken Drope.
72. *San Antonio Express*, September 27, 1888.
73. Wells Fargo & Co. circular, July 2, 1887, AGC, TSA.
74. Burton, "Man Hunt," 24 – 25.
75. Whitley's father, William Taylor Whitley, was the son of Jonas and Rebecca Gullick Whitley and was born February 16, 1819. Bill Whitley's mother was Elizabeth Henry, a daughter of Samuel and Margaret Hubert Henry who was born May 15, 1824, in Mississippi. Their older children were: Mary Jane, born January 29, 1841; Martha Margret, born December 31, 1842; Jonas Marion, December 12, 1844; Joseph Benton, March 11, 1847; Frances Ann, April 22, 1849; Newton Jasper, October 2, 1851; John M., December 17, 1853; James Harvey, June 24, 1856; Rebecca Angelina, December 17, 1859; and Alice Cature, August 18, 1861.
76. Mary Jane died in Alabama on March 1, 1850. Three other children died in Mississippi: John M. on September 14, 1857; James Harvey on May 30, 1858; and Frances Ann on October 10, 1860. Bill Smith Price, *Bill Whitley: Outlaw* (Austin, TX: Nortex Press, 1995), 25. Hereafter cited as Price.
77. Wells Fargo & Co. circular, July 2, 1887, AGC, TSA.
78. Newton Jasper Whitley married Mary J. Standlee in Hunt County, Texas, on March 22, 1871. He did not enjoy a savory reputation and was one of Big Bill Babb's retainers. See David Johnson, *The Horrell Wars: Feuding in Texas and New Mexico* (Denton: University of North Texas Press, 2014).
79. Price, 27. Price based this account on an interview with her aunt, Dee Jane Cox Stewart, born January 20, 1865, and died on October 31, 1953, at Sweetwater, Texas. Billie Smith Price was born August 1, 1918. Given the time lapse between the stories being related and the events, some confusion is understandable.
80. *Dallas Weekly Herald*, September 14, 1882; *Dallas Daily Herald*, September 12, 1882.
81. *Dallas Weekly Herald*, October 5, 1882. Some family histories state that Jasper was killed on May 7, 1882, but no source for this statement has been located.
82. Price, 35.

83. Williamson County, Texas Marriage Records. Cordelia was a daughter of James Christopher and Elizabeth van Winkle Cox and was born November 18, 1866.
84. Price, 29.
85. Wells Fargo & Co. circular, July 2, 1887, AGC, TSA.
86. Price, 38.
87. *San Antonio Express*, September 27, 1888.
88. Laban E. Cornett was Missouri-born to Samuel and Lucretia Pigg Cornett on April 13, 1831.
89. Cordelia Ann McGinty was a daughter of William Augustus McGinty and was born in Hancock County, Georgia, on January 9, 1844. She died in Mason, Texas, on June 16, 1930.
90. Braxton A. Cornett was born on May 22, 1844, to Samuel and Lucretia in Lafayette County, Missouri. His wife Latitia Florence Patterson was born in DeWitt County, Texas, on October 4, 1886. *The Bullion*, Las Cruces, NM, February 20, 1886; family information courtesy Lynn Cornett.
91. Jeff Burton, "The Most Surprised Man in Texas," *Frontier Times* 47, no. 2 (March 1973): 19. Hereafter cited as Burton, "Surprised."
92. 1860 Goliad County, Texas Census; 1870 Goliad County, Texas; Lynn Cornett, "Descendants of Laban E. Cornett," copy courtesy Lynn Cornett. Hereafter cited as Laban Cornett.
93. 1870 Goliad County, Texas Mortality Schedule
94. Peter M. Miller, a son of William Franklin and Phoebe Miller, was born around 1843 in either Tennessee or North Carolina. On December 14, 1865, he married Lucretia Savannah Cornett (born in Johnson County, Missouri, on November 5, 1848), one of Brack Cornett's aunts. In addition to the murder charge, Miller was indicted on March 31, 1868, for theft of a horse, theft of a mule, and theft of a mule and a colt along with other charges in DeWitt County. He died of smallpox in El Paso County on February 15, 1886. His wife died on November 25, 1932, in Fayette County, Texas. Goliad County Texas District Court Records Cause 438; DeWitt County, Texas District Court Records Causes 448, 364 and 366; Lynn Cornett to the author March 14, 2016.
95. James M. Patterson was the son of William P. Patterson and Drusilla Malinda Lockhart and was born in 1844. Drusilla later married Archibald White Templeton on July 19, 1850, in DeWitt County, Texas.
96. Goliad County, Texas District Court Records, Cause 447. James Patten "White" Miller was a younger brother of Peter M. Miller and was born February 11, 1845. Miller served during the Civil War. He was stabbed to death in Killeen, Texas, on June 15, 1884.
97. James Richard "Doc" Cornett was a younger son of Samuel Cornett and Lucretia Pigg and was born July 30, 1851, in Johnson County, Missouri. How James acquired the nickname Doc is unknown, but the 1860 census notes the nine-year-old as "Doctor Cornett." In 1885 he was charged in Frio County with exhibiting a monte bank. He died at San Antonio, Texas, of heart attack on March 9, 1924.
98. Goliad County District Court Records, Book D, Causes 1443, 1444, 1445, 1446, 1447, 1448, 1479, 1480, 1482, 1483, 1484, and 1485.

99. *Galveston Daily News*, August 18, 1878.
100. Huntsville Penitentiary Convict Record Ledgers, Brack Cornett, TSA; *Galveston Daily News*, November 8, 1878.
101. Ibid., Steve Bell.
102. Huntsville Penitentiary Convict Record Ledgers, Brack Cornett, TSA.
103. Wells Fargo & Co. circular, July 2, 1887, AGC, TSA.
104. *Daily Globe-Democrat*, Saint Louis, Missouri, February 14, 1888.
105. *Fort Worth Daily Gazette*, September 1, 1887.
106. Burton, "Surprised," 19.
107. Prison records indicate that $74.55 was spent for Cornett's recapture. The leasees paid $35 and the state $39.55. *Galveston Daily News*, December 26, 1878; No author, *Biennial Reports of the Directors and Superintendent of the Texas State Penitentiary at Huntsville, Texas with the Report of the Prison Physician, Commencing December 1, A. D. 1878, and terminating October 31, A. D. 1880* (Galveston, TX: The News Book and Job Office, 1881), 33; Huntsville Penitentiary Convict Record Ledgers, Brack Cornett, TSA; 1880 Walker County, Texas Census.
108. Huntsville Penitentiary Convict Record Ledgers, Brack Cornett, TSA.
109. *Dallas Morning News*, February 15, 1888.
110. *Daily Globe Democratic* (St. Louis, Missouri) February 14, 1888, and October 27, 1888.
111. *San Antonio Light*, August 27, 1884; *The Daily Cosmopolitan*, Brownsville, Texas, September 5, 1884.
112. *Fort Worth Daily Gazette*, September 1, 1887.
113. *Dallas Morning News*, February 15, 1888. A. M. Lewis was the son of Augustus Marion Lewis and Sarah Matilda Gorham and was born in Raleigh, North Carolina, on October 26, 1854. He married Mary Ann Jones in Caldwell County on September 8, 1857. The couple had two children, Augustus Marion born November 27, 1878, and John Churchill born September 17, 1881.
114. *Dallas Weekly Herald*, December 21, 1882.
115. *Norton's Daily Union Intelligencer*, December 24, 1882.
116. *Dallas Morning News*, February 15, 1888.
117. *Fort Worth Daily Gazette*, September 1, 1887.
118. *Galveston Daily News*, February 15, 1888.
119. Lynn Cornett to the author, March 17, 2016.
120. Burton, "Man Hunt," 14.
121. Wells Fargo & Co. circular, July 2, 1887, AGC, TSA.
122. *Fort Worth Daily Gazette*, September 1, 1887.
123. Hervey E. Chesley, *Adventuring with the Old-Timers: Trails Travelled – Tales Told* (Midland, TX: Nita Stewart Haley Memorial Library, 1979), 83. As dictated by Ira Aten.

Notes to Chapter 2

1. Western District Federal Court Records, Fort Smith, Arkansas, Jacket 282. Courtesy National Archives, Fort Smith, Arkansas.
2. Price, 38; Johnson, *The Horrell Wars, passim*.

3. 1860 Gonzales County, Texas Census. William Carroll Harrell Sr. was born to James R. and Cynthia Lee Harrell in Tennessee on January 11, 1829.
4. 1870 Gonzales County, Texas Census.
5. *Galveston Daily* News, February 3, 1885; *Dallas Weekly Herald,* February 5, 1885.
6. The confrontation took place on September 6, 1886. In what appears to have been a prearranged assault, Sheriff Fate Elder, deputies James J. Elder and John Melville, and two innocent bystanders were killed by members of the Butler faction. See John Perry, "Gunfighters and Lawmen," *Wild West,* April 2005, 10, 12, 61.
7. Western District of Arkansas, District Court Records, Jacket 282.
8. Charles L. Olmsted, *The Good, The Bad, The Butlers: Story of a Texas Pioneer Family* (Bloomington, IN: IUniverse, 2015), 293.
9. *Galveston Daily News,* January 1, 1885; Clifford R. Caldwell and Ron DeLord, *Texas Lawmen 1835–1899: The Good and the Bad* (Charleston, SC: The History Press, 2011), 139.
10. Olmsted, 60.
11. Ibid., 137.
12. Burton, "Man Hunt," 14 – 15.
13. W. C. Holden, "Law and Lawlessness on the Texas Frontier 1875–1890," *Southwestern Historical Quarterly* 44, no. 2 (October 1940): 194.
14. Burton, "Man Hunt," 14–15.
15. *New York World,* January 8, 1866; *Weekly Union,* Manchester, N. H., January 16, 1866; Rick Miller, *Rube Burrow, Desperado* (Bloomington, IN: IUniverse LLC, 2014), viii – ix. Hereafter cited as Miller, *Rube Burrow.*
16. Miller, *Rube Burrow,* ix.
17. *Lafayette Daily Journal,* Lafayette, Indiana, October 15, 1866. For the Reno brothers see Edwin J. Boley, *The Masked Halters* (Seymour, IN: Graessle Mercer Company, 1977).
18. *The Daily Argus,* Rock Island, Illinois, July 22, 1873.
19. For Sam Bass see Rick Miller, *Sam Bass & Gang* (Austin, TX: State House Press, 1999).
20. For Eugene Bunch, see Rick Miller, *The Train Robbing Bunch* (College Station, TX: Creative Publishing Company, 1983).
21. Miller, *Rube Burrow,* 23 – 26.
22. Holden, 194 – 195.
23. For the Gage train robbery and its aftermath see Bob Alexander, *Lynch Ropes & Long Shots: The Story of an Old West Train Robbery* (Silver City, NM: High Lonesome Books, 2006).
24. For the Samuels train robbery and its aftermath see Bob Alexander, *Lawmen, Outlaws, and S. O. Bs: Gunfighters of the Old Southwest* (Silver City, NM: High Lonesome Books, 2004), 10–28.
25. For Frank Jones see Bob Alexander, *Six-shooters and Shifting Sands: The Wild West Life of Texas Ranger Captain Frank Jones* (Denton: University of North Texas Press, 2015).
26. *Fort Worth Daily Gazette,* May 9, 1887.
27. *Dallas Morning News,* May 21, 1887.
28. *Dallas Daily Herald,* May 26, 1887.

29. *Galveston Daily News*, May 14, 1887.
30. *Fort Worth Daily Gazette*, May 20, 1887.
31. Burton, "Man Hunt," 15.
32. Williamson County, Texas Marriage Records.
33. Joel and Attie's children at this time were Mattie May, born November 30, 1887, Newton Toliver, born April 18, 1882, George Anderson, born March 2, 1884 and Frankie Ola, born May 18, 1886. 1860 Williamson County, Texas Census; 1870 Williamson County, Texas Census; family data courtesy Gaylon Powell, Mo Braum, and Ken Drope.
34. Burton, "Man Hunt," 15.
35. Attia Lavisa Barber married Thomas J. Hunt (1862–1909). She gave birth to a son, Dorman Chester Hunt, on November 30, 1887.
36. Ike Cloud had two sisters living in Williamson County at the time. The oldest was Eliza Catherine, born October 15, 1852, who had married Samuel Meschach Woolsey. The family lived at Hutto, Texas, at the time about nine miles east of Round Rock. It appears more likely that the pair visited Barbara Emily who married George Mitchell on December 19, 1877. Barbara, born September 21, 1849, lived with her family close to Leander near the site of the robbery.
37. Burton, "Man Hunt," 15.
38. The new moon for May 1887 occurred on May 22.
39. Burton, "Man Hunt," 15.
40. Samuel Randall Ely was born March 1866 to William H. and Mary C. E. Smith Ely. As of 1900 he was still employed by the railroads. He died March 9, 1934, in Louisiana. 1880 Walker County, Texas Census; 1900 Tarrant County, Texas Census.
41. Some sources state that there were two passengers waiting to catch the train, apparently based upon statements made by Charles W. White of Waco, one of the train's passengers. This was reported the *Dallas Morning News* among other newspapers. The *Fort Worth Daily Gazette* interviewed Rickett and the agent, both of whom stated that "they were alone in the latter's office." *Fort Worth Daily Gazette*, May 20, 1887; *Dallas Morning News*, May 20, 1887. Rickett's name has been spelled a number of ways in contemporary newspapers including J. B. Rickett, J. R. Rickett, Riggles, and Bickle. To date he has not been identified with certainty.
42. *Dallas Morning News*, May 20, 1887; *Fort Worth Daily Gazette*, May 20, 1887.
43. Burton, "Man Hunt," 15.
44. *Fort Worth Daily Gazette*, May 20, 1887.
45. *Dallas Morning News*, May 20, 1887; *Fort Worth Daily Gazette*, May 20, 1887.
46. *Fort Worth Daily Gazette*, May 20, 1887.
47. William C. Glidden was born on July 4, 1848, in Ireland. During 1885 he was living in San Antonio. He died in Williamson County, Texas, on October 31, 1899. 1880 Anderson County, Texas Census; 1885 San Antonio, Texas, City Directory; 1887 San Antonio, Texas, City Directory; death date from tombstone inscription.
48. Samuel H. Spangler was born to Joseph Josiah Cyrus Spangler and Mary A. Buchles July 8, 1858, in Jackson County, Tennessee. Samuel married Mary Benz in Jackson County on January 16, 1879. Spangler is identified as a

master mechanic in the 1900 census. He died of heart failure in Houston, Texas, on February 11, 1943. 1860 Jackson County, Illinois Census; Jackson County, Illinois Marriage Records; Harris County, 1900 Bastrop County, Texas Census; Harris County, Texas, Death Certificate 7692.

49. *Dallas Morning News*, May 20, 1887; *Fort Worth Daily Gazette*, May 20, 1887.
50. *Dallas Weekly Herald*, May 20, 1887.
51. *Dallas Morning News*, May 20, 1887; *Dallas Weekly Herald*, May 20, 1887; *Galveston Daily News*, May 20, 1887; *Luling Signal*, May 26, 1887; *Macon Telegraph*, May 22, 1887.
52. *Fort Worth Daily Gazette*, May 20, 1887. The federal indictments charged Joe Barber, John Barber, Ed Reeves, Bud Powell, Brack Cornett, Ike Cloud, Will Whitley, Charley Ross, Eli Harrell, and Will Harrell with robbing the U. S. Mail. Neither the Harrells nor Joe Barber were present at the robbery, however. Fort Smith, Arkansas, Federal Records, Indictment 282.
53. *Austin Weekly Statesman*, June 2, 1887; *Fort Worth Daily Gazette*, May 20, 1887; Burton, "Man Hunt," 15.
54. *Austin Weekly Statesman*, May 26, 1887.
55. Burton, "Man Hunt," 15.
56. *Galveston Daily News*, May 20, 1887.
57. *Austin Weekly Statesman*, June 2, 1887.
58. Ibid. W. E. Hawkins was probably the son of James E. and Paralee Self Hawkins, and was born in 1860. He died in Tarrant County on February 16, 1937.
59. *Fort Worth Daily Gazette*, May 20, 1887; Price, 49. Price based her account on some of the early reports and notes the bullet was a "stray shot" that hit Walker "in the eye."
60. *Austin Weekly Statesman*, June 2, 1887; *Fort Worth Daily Gazette*, May 20, 1887.
61. *Austin Weekly Statesman*, June 2, 1887.
62. *Austin Weekly Statesman*, May 26, 1887.
63. *Galveston Daily News*, May 20, 1887.
64. *Dallas Morning* News, May 20, 1887; *Fort Worth Daily Gazette*, May 20, 1887; *Galveston Daily News,* May 20, 1887; *Coronado Mercury*, Coronado, California, May 20, 1887; *Sacramento Daily Record-Union*, May 20, 1887; *Dallas Weekly Herald*, May 20, 1887.
65. *Austin Weekly Statesman*, June 2, 1887; *Dallas Weekly Herald*, May 20, 1887; Burton, "Man Hunt," 15.
66. *Fort Worth Daily Gazette*, May 20, 1887; *Dallas Morning* News, May 20, 1887; *The Daily Journal*, Logansport, Indiana, May 21, 1887. White was born November 15, 1844, in Amherst County, Virginia. He died in Waco on July 9, 1935, of hemiplegia and hypertension. McLennan County Death Certificate 34581.
67. Oliver Brush was the son of Seba Bogard Brush and Mary Ann Bradley and was born in Austin, Texas, on August 25, 1863. Oliver died in Birmingham, Alabama, on January 1, 1933.
68. *Austin Weekly Statesman*, May 26, 1887. George Austin Brush, who allowed the paper to publish the letter, was born December 21, 1855. He died in Austin March 2, 1907.

69. Harry Landa was a son of Joseph and Helena Friedlander Landa and was born December 20, 1863, in Comal County, Texas. In 1913 he married Hannah Frederika Mansfield. Landa died on December 12, 1951, in San Antonio, Texas. Landa was a financier, industrialist, and philanthropist. His obituary notes that he "owned the Landa Flour Mills and Landa rock crushing plant at New Braunfels. He owned the San Antonio Southern Railroad until it was purchased by Missouri-Pacific, then became a director of that line. He also had ranch holdings." 1870 Comal County, Texas Census; 1880 Comal County, Texas Census; 1900 Comal County, Texas Census; 1910 Comal County, Texas Census; 1920 Bexar County, Texas Census; 1930 Bexar County, Texas Census; 1940 Bexar County, Texas Census; *Dallas Morning News*, December 13, 1951; Texas Death Certificate 60632.
70. *Fort Worth Daily Gazette*, May 20, 1887; *Dallas Morning News*, May 20, 1887; *Dallas Weekly Herald*, May 20, 1887; *Galveston Daily News*, May 20, 1887; *Luling Signal*, May 26, 1887; *Clarksville Standard*, Clarksville, Texas, May 26, 1887; *Logansport Pharos*, May 20, 1887; *Indiana Democrat*, Indiana, Pennsylvania, May 26, 1887; Price, 40.
71. *Dallas Morning News*, May 20, 1887; *Dallas Weekly Herald*, May 20, 1887.
72. *Fort Worth Daily Gazette*, May 20, 1887; Burton, "Man Hunt," 15.
73. *Dallas Morning News* May 20, 1887; *Fort Worth Daily Gazette*, May 20, 1887; *Dallas Weekly Herald*, May 20, 1887; *Austin Weekly Statesman*, May 26, 1887.
74. *Fort Worth Daily Gazette*, May 20, 1887; *Clarksville Standard* May 20, 1887.
75. The express messenger's name is given in various newspaper accounts as Northacker, Nothacker, Northocker, Notacher, and Notchaker.
76. Burton, "Man Hunt," 15.
77. *Fort Worth Daily Gazette*, May 20, 1887.
78. Burton, "Man Hunt," 15.
79. *Austin Weekly Statesman*, May 26, 1887; *Fort Worth Daily Gazette*, May 20, 1887.
80. *Fort Worth Daily Gazette*, May 20, 1887.
81. While it has been written that Cornett demanded the sack, very likely the man in question was Ed Reeves.
82. *Dallas Morning News*, May 20, 1887; *Fort Worth Daily Gazette*, May 20, 1887.
83. Ibid.
84. *Times-Picayune*, June 2, 1887; *Austin Weekly Statesman*, June 2, 1887. Witnesses uniformly testified that the time required to complete the robbery was between twenty minutes and half an hour.
85. Burton, "Man Hunt," 16.
86. Chesley, 83.
87. Aten was born Austin Ira Aten to Austin Cunningham Aten and Kate Dunlap on September 3, 1862, at Cairo, Illinois. Bob Alexander, *Rawhide Ranger, Ira Aten* (Denton: University of North Texas Press, 2011), 11. Hereafter cited as Alexander, *Aten*. Alexander's book is the most definitive life of Aten to date.
88. Ibid., 11–12.
89. Texas Ranger Muster Rolls: Ira Aten, Texas State Archives, hereafter TSA.
90. Alexander, *Aten*, 98–99. For Hughes see Chuck Parsons, *Captain John R. Hughes: Lone Star Ranger* (Denton: University of North Texas Press, 2011).

91. John Taylor Rankin was born in 1853 to Dr. Calvin Rankin and his wife Mary T. Cole in Texas. *Brenham Banner*, September 1, 1869.
92. *La Grange Journal*, May 10, 1883.
93. *Dallas Morning News*, May 20, 1887; *Galveston Daily News*, May 20, 1887.

Notes to Chapter 3

1. John Thomas Olive was the son of Marville Mattison and Zipora Cullum Olive and was born February 28, 1850, in Lafayette County, Arkansas. The Olive family moved to Columbia County, Arkansas, prior to 1860 and to Williamson County, Texas, in the 1870s. On July 23, 1876 Olive married Frances A. Gentry in Bastrop County. Their first child, Juanita O. was born in March, 1877. At the time of the McNeil train robbery he also had several other children: Oscar Owen, born August 5, 1880; Carrie Hoxie, born July 17, 1883; and son John T., born November 1885. Two other children were born later, Bessie on December 1, 1888, and Roy A. on November 23, 1891. 1850 Lafayette County, Arkansas Census; 1860 Columbia County, Arkansas Census; 1870 Columbia County, Arkansas Census; Bastrop County, Texas Marriage Records; 1880 Williamson County, Texas Census; Sammy Tise, *Texas County Sheriffs* (Albuquerque, NM: Oakwood Printing, 1989), 544.
2. *Fort Worth Daily Gazette*, May 27, 1887.
3. *Dallas Morning News*, May 20, 1887; *Galveston Daily News*, May 20, 1887; *Dallas Weekly Herald*, May 20, 1887.
4. Ibid. James Stephen Hogg was born March 24, 1851, in Cherokee County, Texas, to Joseph Lewis and Lucanda McMath Hogg. Following the death of his parents during the Civil War, he and his brothers were raised by their sister Frances At various times he worked in the newspaper business and as a farmhand while he studied law. In 1874 he married Sarah Ann Stinson by whom he had four children. He was elected state attorney general in 1886.
5. *Austin Daily Statesman*, May 19, 1887; *Austin Weekly Statesman*, May 26, 1887.
6. Lamartine Pemberton Sieker was a son of Dr. Edward A. Sieker and Ruth Anne Gosnell and was born in Baltimore, Maryland, on April 8, 1848. During the Civil War Sieker served in Captain W. W. Parker's Company of Virginia Light Artillery from the summer of 1863 through early 1865. In 1873 he migrated to Texas where he enlisted in Company D of the Frontier Battalion on May 25, 1874. Sieker witnessed the near mutiny of Company D during the infamous Hoo Doo War. Sieker remained with the company for years, rising first to lieutenant then to captain on September 1, 1882. In 1885 he assumed the position of quartermaster for the Texas Rangers. Texas Ranger Muster Rolls, TSA.
7. Bob Alexander, *Winchester Warriors: Texas Rangers of Company D, 1874 – 1901* (Denton: University of North Texas Press, 2009), 130.
8. *Austin Daily Statesman*, May 20, 1887; *Austin Weekly Statesman*, May 26, 1887.
9. *Fort Worth Daily Gazette*, May 20, 1887; *Dallas Morning News*, May 20, 1887; *Austin Weekly Statesman*, May 26, 1887.
10. *Fort Worth Daily Gazette*, May 20, 1887.

11. *Fort Worth Daily Gazette,* May 20, 1887; *Dallas Weekly Herald,* May 20, 1887; *Fort Worth Weekly Gazette,* May 27, 1887; *Galveston Daily News,* May 20, 1887; *Austin Weekly Statesman,* May 26, 1887.
12. *Fort Worth Daily Gazette,* May 23, 1887. The article was reprinted in the *Fort Worth Weekly Gazette* on May 27, 1887.
13. *Austin Weekly Statesman,* May 26, 1887.
14. *Dallas Weekly Herald,* May 20, 1887; *Fort Worth Daily Gazette,* May 20, 1887; *Galveston Daily News,* May 20, 1887.
15. *Austin Weekly Statesman,* May 26, 1887.
16. *Dallas Weekly Herald,* May 20, 1887.
17. *Austin Weekly Statesman,* May 26, 1887; *Fort Worth Daily Gazette,* May 20, 1887; *Galveston Daily News,* May 20, 1887.
18. *Waco Daily Examiner,* May 20, 1887.
19. *Fort Worth Daily Gazette,* May 20, 1887; *Galveston Daily News,* May 20, 1887.
20. *Waco Daily Examiner,* May 21, 1887; *Austin Weekly Statesman,* May 26, 1887.
21. *Austin Weekly Statesman,* May 26, 1887; Fort *Worth Daily Gazette,* May 23, 1887.
22. *Waco Daily Examiner,* May 21, 1887.
23. *Austin Weekly Statesman,* May 26, 1887.
24. *Waco Daily Examiner,* May 21, 1887.
25. *Fort Worth Daily Gazette,* May 23, 1887.
26. *Fort Worth Daily Gazette,* May 20, 1887.
27. *Waco Daily Examiner,* May 21, 1887.
28. *Austin Weekly Statesman,* May 26, 1887. This statement was also carried in the *Fort Worth Daily Gazette* of May 20, 1887.
29. *Fort Worth Daily Gazette,* May 23, 1887.
30. *Austin Weekly Statesman,* May 26, 1887.
31. *The Daily Northwestern,* Oshkosh, Wisconsin, May 20, 1887.
32. *Fort Worth Daily Gazette,* May 20, 1887.
33. *Los Angeles Daily Herald,* May 20, 1887.
34. *Sacramento Daily Record-Union,* May 20, 1887.
35. *The Daily Journal,* Logansport, Indiana, May 21, 1887.
36. Among the Texas newspapers that carried the story were the *Luling Signal* of May 26, 1887, *The San Saba News,* May 27, 1887, and the *Clarksville Standard* on May 26, 1887. Other newspapers that covered the robbery include, but are not limited to, the *Freeborn County Standard,* Albert Lea, Minnesota, June 1, 1887, the *Indiana Democrat,* Indiana, Pennsylvania, May 26, 1887, the *Philadelphia Inquirer,* May 21, 1887, the *Kansas City Star,* Kansas City, Missouri, *Logansport Pharos,* Logansport, Indiana, May 20, 1887, and the *New York Herald* of May 21, 1887.
37. *Dallas Morning News* May 20, 1887.
38. *Fort Worth Weekly Gazette,* May 27, 1887; *Dallas Weekly Herald,* May 28, 1887.
39. *Galveston Daily News,* May 20, 1887.
40. *Galveston Daily News,* May 21, 1887; *Dallas Morning News,* May 21, 1887.
41. *Fort Worth Daily Gazette,* May 20, 1887.
42. *Dallas Morning News,* May 20, 1887.
43. *Waco Daily Examiner,* May 21, 1887; *Austin Weekly Statesman,* May 26, 1887; *Macon Telegraph,* Macon, Georgia, May 22, 1887.

44. *Fort Worth Daily Gazette*, May23, 1887.
45. Chesley, 83.
46. *Fort Worth Daily Gazette*, May 23, 1887.
47. Miller, *Burrow*, 33.
48. Chesney, 83.
49. *Fort Worth Daily Gazette*, May 20, 1887; *Fort Worth Weekly Gazette*, May 27, 1887; *Austin Weekly Statesman*, May 26, 1887.
50. *Austin Weekly Statesman*, May 26, 1887.
51. United States Federal District Court Records, Fort Smith, Arkansas, Jacket 282.
52. James E. Lucy was the son of Cornelius "Conn" Lucy and his wife Margaret Boyle, and was born May 1, 1854, at St. Clair, Missouri. In 1882 he married Virginia E. Platt. Lucy remained in Austin until his death on July 10, 1927. 1860 Franklin County, Missouri, Census; 1870 Franklin County, Missouri, Census; 1880 Travis County, Texas, Census.
53. *Fort Worth Daily Gazette*, May 20, 1887; *Fort Worth Weekly Gazette*, May 27, 1887; *Austin Weekly Statesman*, May 26, 1887; *Dallas Morning News*, May 20, 1887; *Dallas Weekly Herald*, May 20, 1887; *Galveston Daily News*, May 20, 1887. John Thomas Olive was born February 28, 1850 to Marville Mattison Olive and his wife Zepora Cullum in Lafayette County, Arkansas. Olive married Francis A. Gentry in Lee County, Texas, on July 26, 1873. Olive was elected sheriff of Williamson County in 1884 and served until 1888. He was reelected in 1890. Tise, 544; Caldwell and DeLord, *Sheriffs*, 238; *Dallas Morning News*, September 12, 1892.
54. *Dallas Morning News*, May 20, 1887; *Fort Worth Daily Gazette*, May 20, 1887, May 25, 1887; *Dallas Weekly Herald*, May 20, 1887; *Galveston Daily News*, May 20, 1887.
55. *Dallas Morning News*, May 20, 1887; *Fort Worth Daily Gazette*, May 20, 1887; *Dallas Weekly Herald*, May 20, 1887; *Galveston Daily News*, May 20, 1887; *Fort Worth Weekly Gazette*, May 27, 1887.
56. *Fort Worth Daily Gazette*, May 27, 1887,
57. *Fort Worth Daily Gazette*, May 25, 1887.
58. *Austin Weekly Statesman*, June 2, 1887.
59. Executive Clemency Record 1907: Austin C. Barber, Governor's Records, TSA.
60. Lampasas County, Texas Marriage Records.
61. Barber's children were Oliver Preston, born March 12, 1883, and Willie B., born November 1885. He was described as 5 feet 7 inches tall with brown hair and eyes. Barber was discharged on March 2, 1891. Huntsville Penitentiary Convict Record Ledgers, Austin Calloway Barber, TSA.
62. Executive Clemency Record 1907: Austin C. Barber, Governor's Records, TSA.
63. Ernest Langford, *Briggs: Brief Annals of the Times and People* (Denton, Texas: privately published, 1963), 209.
64. John Henry "Jack" Juby was the son of William and Maria Juby, and was born in Stalham, Norfolk, England, on December 2, 1850. Around 1871 Juby emigrated to the United States, settling around Briggs, Burnet County, Texas, where he engaged in ranching. On July 16, 1885, he married Fanny

Cordelia Zumpkeller. Juby died of a heart attack on April 19, 1938. *Burnet Bulletin*, April 28, 1938; 1861 England Census; 1900, 1910, 1920 and 1930 Burnet County, Texas Census.

65. Joe Btfsplk was a creation of Al Capp in the satirical comic strip *Li'l Abner*. Capp declared that Btfsplk was "the world's worst jinx" who brought disastrous misfortune to everyone around him. The main difference between John Barber and Joe was that Joe was good hearted where Barber was not.
66. *Austin Weekly Statesman*, May 26, 1887.
67. Ibid., June 2, 1887.
68. *Fort Worth Daily Gazette*, May 27, 1887.
69. *Fort Worth Daily Gazette*, May 23, 1887; *Clarksville Standard*, May 26, 1887; *Boston Journal*, Boston, Massachusetts, May 23, 1887. Several newspapers misspelled the Craft name as Croft.
70. *Fort Worth Daily Gazette*, May 23, 1887.
71. *Dallas Morning News*, May 29, 1887.
72. *Austin Weekly Statesman*, June 2, 1887.
73. A native of San Antonio, Texas, Nathaniel Lewis was born there to Nathaniel and Mary Josephine Lippeing Lewis on November 16, 1857. In 1900 Lewis was serving as district clerk. In later years he married Mabel Luella Satterwhite. He died in San Antonio on February 2, 1940. The cause of death is listed as chronic anemia combined with chronic myocarditis and bronchitis. *Austin Weekly Statesman*, June 2, 1887; 1900 Bexar County, Texas Census; Texas Death Certificate 6603.
74. *Austin Weekly Statesman*, May 26, 1887; *Fort Worth Daily Gazette*, May 20, 1887. For Sam Bass see Rick Miller, *Sam Bass & Gang* (Austin, TX: State House Press, 1999).
75. *Fort Worth Daily Gazette*, May 20, 1887 and May 23, 1887; *Boston Journal*, Boston, Massachusetts, May 23, 1887; *The Standard*, Clarksville, Texas, May 26, 1887.
76. 1860, 1870 and 1880 Guadalupe County, Texas Census.
77. Ann Elizabeth Hensley was born to Martin and Amanda Hensley on November 30, 1852 in Arkansas. 1860 Searcy County, Arkansas Census; Caldwell County, Texas Marriage Records.
78. Elizabeth Manila "Bettie" was a daughter of Chester Van Buren Ketchum and his wife Susan Ann Handcock Eustace born November 11, 1867. Caldwell County, Texas Marriage Records.
79. *San Marcos Free Press*, September 13, 1883; Victoria Dunnahoo Daywood and Peggy White Engledow, *The Bad Boys of Caldwell County, Texas, Book One, Murders in the 1800s* (Luling, TX: Ericson Books, 2011), 5–7. Hereafter cited as Daywood and Engledow, *Bad Boys* 1. See also Genealogical and Historical Society of Caldwell County, *Caldwell County Kin: The First 140 Years* (Wolfe City, TX: Hennington Publishing Co., 2000).
80. *Austin Weekly Statesman*, September 27, 1883.
81. *Galveston Daily News*, January 22, 1884; *San Marcos Free Press*, January 24, 1884; Clifford R. Caldwell and Ron DeLord, *Eternity at The End of a Rope: Executions, Lynchings and Vigilante Justice in Texas 1819 – 1923*, Santa Fe, New Mexico: Sunstone Press, 2015, 277. Hereafter cited as Caldwell and DeLord, *Eternity*.

82. *Luling Signal,* June 5, 1884.
83. Ibid., October 14, 1884.
84. Daywood and Engledow, *Bad Boys* 1, 65, 67; *Luling Signal,* June 11, 1884.
85. 1870 and 1880 Guadalupe County, Texas Census. For both the Ussery and Craft family see Daywood and Engledow, *Bad Boys* 1, and Daywood, Victoria Dunnahoo and Peggy White Engledow, *The Bad Boys of Caldwell County, Texas, Book Two, Mayhem and Mishaps in the 1800s* (Luling, TX: Printed by Ericson Books, 2011). Hereafter cited as *Bad Boys* 2.
86. *Clarksville Standard,* May 26, 1887.
87. *Times – Picayune,* June 2, 1887.
88. The San Saba County War was a bitter conflict that lasted into the 1900s. Like the Mason County "Hoo Doo" War, the conflict was never confined strictly to San Saba County and at times had both mobs and anti-mobs. The conflict began in 1869 and was not eradicated until the Texas Rangers spent intensive effort in rooting them out starting in the late 1890s.
89. *Fort Worth Daily Gazette,* May 27, 1887.
90. *Clarksville Standard,* May 26, 1887. Thomas O. Bailes was born in Giles County, Tennessee, in August 1847. Bailes came to Bell County, Texas, in 1870 and served as deputy sheriff and deputy U. S. Marshal. In later years he became involved in mines and land speculation. He died on June 12, 1917, in San Antonio, Texas.
91. *Fort Worth Daily Gazette,* May 24, 1887. The entire article is reproduced in Appendix 1.
92. *Austin Weekly Statesman,* May 26, 1887.
93. *Fort Worth Daily Gazette,* May 20, 1887.
94. *Fort Worth Daily Gazette,* May 23, 1887.
95. *Fort Worth Daily* Gazette, May 20, 1887; *Austin Weekly Statesman,* May 26, 1887.
96. *Fort Worth Daily Gazette,* May 20, 1887.
97. *Galveston Daily News,* May 20, 1887.
98. *Austin Weekly Statesman,* May 26, 1887.
99. *Galveston Daily News,* May 20, 1887.
100. *Fort Worth Daily Gazette,* May 20, 1887.
101. *Austin Weekly Statesman,* May 26, 1887.
102. *Fort Worth Daily Gazette,* May 20, 1887.
103. *Dallas Weekly Herald,* May 20, 1887; *Austin Weekly Statesman,* May 26, 1887.

Notes to Chapter 4

1. *Austin Weekly Statesman,* June 2, 1887.
2. Ibid.
3. *Times-Picayune,* June 2, 1887.
4. *Austin Weekly Statesman,* June 2, 1887.
5. Ibid.
6. Ibid.
7. *Galveston Daily News,* June 1, 1887. James C. Martin was the son of Caleb Alonzo Martin and his wife Louisa A. Crowder born May 21, 1844. He died on March 7, 1907.

8. *Austin Weekly Statesman*, June 2, 1887.
9. *Galveston Daily News*, June 1, 1887; *Austin Weekly Statesman*, June 2, 1887.
10. *Philadelphia Inquirer*, Philadelphia, Pennsylvania, June 2, 1887; *Galveston Daily News*, June 1, 1887.
11. The baby in question was Frankie Ola Barber, born May 18, 1886. Joel and Attie Barber's other children at this time were Mattie May, born November 30, 1880, Newton Toliver born April 18, 1882, and George Anderson born March 2, 1884.
12. *Austin Weekly Statesman*, June 2, 1887.
13. Ibid.
14. *Philadelphia Inquirer*, June 2, 1887.
15. *Austin Weekly Statesman*, June 2, 1887.
16. Mrs. Smart was Alcey Jane Barber, who married Brice Miller Smart. Alcey died at Collinsville, Oklahoma, on December 11, 1928.
17. Mrs. Moore was Armenta Emma Barber, who married J. D. Moore. Armenta died September 10, 1926.
18. Mrs. Hunt is Attia Barber. She married Thomas J. Hunt.
19. *Austin Weekly Statesman*, June 2, 1887.
20. *Times-Picayune*, June 2, 1887.
21. *Austin Weekly Statesman*, June 9, 1887.
22. *Galveston Daily News*, June 2, 1887; *Austin Weekly Statesman*, June 9, 1887.
23. William Martin Walton was born on January 17, 1832, to Samuel Walther and Mary Wilkerson Lee Walton in Canton, Mississippi. His father died in 1839 and his mother married B. C. Strange. In 1849 he enrolled in the University of Virginia, returning to Mississippi in 1851 where he studied law. In 1853 Walton moved to Austin, Texas, where he married Letitia A. Watkins. He served during the Civil War and was the author of *The Life of Ben Thompson*. Walton was the attorney general for Texas during 1866 and 1867. He died in Austin on July 1, 1915, of heart failure. 1860, 1870, 1880, 1900, and 1910 Travis County, Texas Census.
24. *Galveston Daily News*, June 2, 1887.
25. *Austin Weekly Statesman*, June 9, 1887. The Convict Record Ledger indicates that Charles Buckley, convict 4925, was born in 1857, 130 pounds, fair complexion, blue eyes, light hair and 5 feet 4 ½ inches tall. He was born in Arkansas. Buckley was sentenced for five years from Menard County for murder. He also was convicted for theft of a gelding in Bosque County and entered prison as convict 6120 with an eight-year sentence.
26. *Austin Weekly Statesman*, June 9, 1887; *Galveston Daily News*, June 2, 1887.
27. *Austin Weekly Statesman*, June 9, 1887.
28. Ibid.
29. *Fort Worth Daily Gazette*, June 4, 1887.
30. *Fort Worth Daily Gazette*, June 6, 1887.
31. *Austin Weekly Statesman*, June 2, 1887.
32. *Austin Weekly Statesman*, June 16, 1887.
33. *Fort Worth Daily Gazette*, June 9, 1887; *Philadelphia Inquirer*, June 6, 1887.
34. *Fort Worth Daily Gazette*, June 9, 1887. The full song is included in Appendix 2. See also Miller, *Burrow*, 8.
35. Miller, *Burrow*, 30 – 32.

36. *Fort Worth Daily Gazette*, June 10, 1887.
37. The *Fort Worth Daily Gazette* reprinted this editorial in their issue of June 10, 1887.
38. *Austin Weekly Statesman*, June 9, 1887.
39. *Austin Weekly Statesman*, June 9, 1887.

Notes to Chapter 5

1. For Schmitt see Robert W. Stephens, *Captain George H. Schmitt: Texas Ranger* (No place, 2006).
2. 1870 and 1880 Comal County, Texas Census.
3. Huntsville Penitentiary Convict Record Ledgers: Geo. Schmidt; 1860 Walker County, Texas Census. Schmidt was listed as 20 years old when he entered the penitentiary on February 5, 1859, as convict 364. The Walker County Census for 1860 also describes Schmidt as age 20 although more than a year had passed when he was enumerated on June 14, 1860.
4. Bob Alexander, *Winchester Warriors: Texas Rangers of Company D 1874 – 1901* (Denton: University of North Texas Press, 2009), 183.
5. For Jack Dean, see Bob Alexander, *One Riot, New Ranger* (Denton: University of North Texas Press, 2018.
6. Paul N. Spellman, *Captain John H. Rogers, Texas Ranger* (Denton: University of North Texas Press, 2003), 42.
7. Alexander, *Winchester Warriors*, 185; *San Antonio Daily Light*, October 22, 1883.
8. *Dallas Morning News*, June 10, 1887.
9. Wilburn H. King to George H. Schmitt, June 14, 1887, AGC, TSA.
10. King to Schmitt, June 17, 1887, AGC, TSA.
11. Burton, "Man Hunt," 16.
12. Ibid. Reeves stated that the pair hid at the Barber and Bennett homes, but it is more likely they camped away from the homes themselves. Considering how rapidly Sheriff John Olive scooped up Joe Barber, the presence of two armed men at his farm would not have gone unnoticed. Reeves undoubtedly heard this from either Barber or Whitley if not both. Price states that neither Cloud nor Ross showed up in Butler's pasture but Milton Day and John Kelley did. She also noted the presence of Will Jacobs and adds that Humphreys met them with men. Reeves's confession notes only Jacobs and Ross as being present which is far more likely. Price, 45.
13. William B. Jacobs was the son of Andrew Jackson Jacobs and his wife Mary Jane Wilcox, and was born in Mississippi on May 12, 1852.
14. *Dallas Morning News*, April 9, 1887; *Fort Worth Daily Gazette*, April 9, 1887; *Houston Post*, April 9, 1887; *Galveston Daily News*, April 9, 1887.
15. Lewis was born in Wilcox County, Alabama, to Andrew J. and his wife Elizabeth Keiser Lewis on November 27, 1849. Prior to his move to Texas, Lewis married Mary R. Campbell on December 19, 1872. Lewis moved to Milam County, Texas in 1875. In 1881 he became a deputy sheriff and was elected in 1886 as sheriff. *Houston Post*, April 13, 1887; *Galveston Daily News*, April 14, 1887; *Brenham Daily Banner*, April 15, 1887; 1850 and 1860 Coosa

County, Alabama Census; 1870 Choctaw County, Alabama Census. Lewis died in Cameron, Texas, on May 11, 1910.

16. *Fort Worth Daily Gazette*, April 13, 1887.
17. Monthly return, Company C, June 1887, TSA, AGC.
18. Burton, "Man Hunt," 16.
19. Ibid.
20. Price, 45.
21. Contemporary news accounts give the engineer's name variously as Pickers, Pickens, Pickee, Pickerin, and Pickren. Benjamin A. Pickren was born to John Aaron Pickren and his wife Bedia W. Massey in Muscogee County, Georgia, on August 17, 1847. Sometime around 1863 the family moved to Texas where Ben married Frances A. "Fannie" Saunders. In 1880 Ben and his family were living in Harris County, Texas. Fannie Pickren died on March 27, 1906. Ben lived until 1911 when he died in Miller County, Georgia, on June 2.
22. *San Antonio Daily Express*, June 19, 1887.
23. *Austin Weekly Statesman*, June 23, 1887; *Dallas Weekly Herald*, June 25, 1887; *Fort Worth Daily Gazette*, June 19, 1887; *San Antonio Daily Express*, June 19, 1887; *Gonzales Inquirer*, June 25, 1887; *Daily Morning Astorian*, Astoria, Oregon, June 19, 1887; *Phillipsburg Herald*, Phillipsburg, Kansas, June 25, 1887; *Sacramento Daily Record-Union*, June 20, 1887; *Western Kansas World*, Wakeeney, Kansas, June 25, 1887; *New York Sun*, New York, New York, June 19, 1887; *Daily Alta California*, San Francisco, California, June 19, 1887; *Reno Evening Gazette*, Reno, Nevada, June 18, 1887; The *True Northerner*, Paw Paw, Michigan, June 29, 1887; *New York Sun*, June 19, 1887; *Butte Semi-Weekly Miner*, June 22, 1887.
24. *Fort Worth Daily Gazette*, June 24, 1887.
25. *The True Northerner*, June 29, 1887.
26. Burton, "Man Hunt," 18–19. The spelling of Bill Humphreys's name has been a subject of debate—Humphreys versus Humphries. For consistency, the spelling Humphreys is used throughout except for direct quotations.
27. Ibid., 16.
28. Miller, *Burrow*, 29.
29. *San Antonio Daily* Express, June 19, 1887. Myron E. "Frank" Folger was the son of Peter Folger and Ann Louisa Parker and was born in California on May 1, 1861. He died in San Francisco on May 10, 1918.
30. Ibid.
31. *San Antonio Daily Express*, June 19, 1887; *Daily Alta California*, June 19, 1887; *Los Angeles Daily* Herald, June 19, 1887; *New York Sun*, June 19, 1887; *Dallas Daily Herald*, June 20, 1887; *Butte Semi-Weekly Miner*, June 22, 1887. James Harrison White was born February 15, 1847, to James C. and Argyra Harrison White in Portsmouth, Virginia. White first came to El Paso in 1869 and returned in 1880. He was elected as sheriff in 1884, serving until 1892. Later he became chief of police for El Paso serving for two years. During the early 1900s he went to California for his health. He died there of a heart attack on August 19, 1907.
32. *Anaconda Standard*, Anaconda Montana February 20, 1898.

33. *Omaha Daily Bee*, September 7, 1899. The article first appeared in the *New York Sun*.
34. *Dallas Weekly Herald*, June 25, 1887.
35. Price, 46.
36. *San Antonio Daily Express*, June 19, 1887; *Daily Alta California*, June 19, 1887; *Los Angeles Daily* Herald, June 19, 1887; *New York Sun*, June 19, 1887; *Butte Semi-Weekly Miner*, June 22, 1887; *Austin Weekly Statesman*, June 23, 1887; *San Saba News*, June 24, 1887; *The New North West*, Deer Lodge, Montana, June 24, 1887; *Fort Worth Daily Gazette*, June 24, 1887; *Indian Sentinel*, Muskogee, Oklahoma, June 23, 1887; *Helena Weekly Herald*, Helena, Montana, June 23, 1887; *Iola Register*, Iola, Kansas, June 24, 1887; *Bismarck Weekly Tribune*, Bismarck, N. D., June 24, 1887; *Dallas Weekly Herald*, June 25, 1887
37. *New York Sun*, June 19, 1887; *The True Northerner*, June 29, 1887.
38. *San Antonio Daily Express*, June 19, 1887.
39. *San Antonio Daily Express*, June 19, 1887; Price, 46. Neither Allen nor Lyons has been positively identified. Lyons may have been the son of Jesse and Jane M. Kincaide Lyons, and was born December 11, 1852, in Pennsylvania. Allen appears to have been Archie Nathaniel Allen, one of the children of George Washigton and Martha Jane Caldwell Allen and was born June 11, 1861, in Hardin County, Tennessee.
40. *New York Sun*, June 19, 1887; *Sacramento Daily Record-Union*, June 20, 1887; *Butte Semi-Weekly Miner*, Butte, Montana, June 22, 1887; *Austin Weekly Statesman*, June 23, 1887; *Fort Worth Daily Gazette*, June 24, 1887; *Phillipsburg Herald*, Phillipsburg, Kansas, June 25, 1887; *Western Kansas World*, Wakeeney, Kansas, June 25, 1887.
41. Ibid. Allen's description of the train's makeup indicates that the train was on a long haul. The emigrant car (or colonist car) was a passenger coach designed to provide inexpensive long-distance transportation for immigrants. They were noted for Spartan accommodations, frequently only a wooden bench along the wall. Some were freight cars temporarily fitted with wooden seats that would haul grain on the return trips.
42. Price, 46; *San Antonio Daily Express*, June 19, 1887.
43. *The True Northerner*, June 29, 1887.
44. J. H. Mitchell appears to have been John J. Mitchell listed in the voter registration for Gila County, Arizona in 1888. Mitchell was born to John and Jane Laird Mitchell around 1852 in Pennsylvania. By 1880 he had settled in Pinal County, Arizona, working as a miner. Mitchell was a newlywed, having married Patience Bennett in Tombstone on May 31, 1887. 1860 and 1870 Luzerne County Pennsylvania Census; 1880 Pinal County, Arizona Census; 1888 Arizona Voter Registration; Price, 46; *Fort Worth Daily Gazette*, June 24, 1887; *The True Northerner*, June 29, 1887; Cochise County, Arizona Marriage Records.
45. None of the spellings given have been located in the 1887 City Directory for San Francisco. This man may have been Louis Armand, a professor of Latin, Greek, and French who offered pupils a thorough preparation for "Harvard, Yale and Princeton." Louis Felix Armand was born in Louisiana around 1845 and married Celine Suzette Rachal at Natchitoches, Louisiana, on

January 2, 1867. *Fort Worth Daily Gazette*, June 24, 1887; *The True Northerner*, June 29, 1887; Price, 46; 1887 San Francisco, California City Directory.

46. Abraham Lasker was born in Prussia around 1836. Around 1860 he moved to the United States where he originally settled in Scioto County, Ohio, where the census notes him as a rabbi. Lasker became a naturalized citizen in New York City on October 23, 1860. Around 1862 he married Saleia Caroline Karger. The 1880 census notes him as a sponge merchant. At the time of the holdup Abraham and Saleia had five children. Mr. Lasker died in New York City on February 12, 1894. 1860 Scioto County, Ohio Census; Naturalization Papers: Abraham Lasker; 1863 New York Draft Registration; 1880 New York County Census; Price, 46; *Fort Worth Daily Gazette*, June 24, 1887; *The True Northerner*, Michigan, June 29, 1887.
47. Price, 46; *Fort Worth Daily Gazette*, June 24, 1887; *The True Northerner*, Michigan, June 29, 1887. A Walter Gregory is listed as a street car conductor in the 1885 San Antonio City Directory.
48. This appears to be Daniel M. Sweeney who is listed in the 1880 Census as a "moulder" and was born in Ireland around 1839. *Fort Worth Daily Gazette*, June 24, 1887; *The True Northerner*, June 29, 1887; 1880 Merced County, California Census.
49. *San Antonio Daily Express*, June 19, 1887; 1880 Galveston County, Texas Census. The census indicates that Moses Freiburg, born around 1850 in Germany, was a wholesale liquor dealer.
50. *Fort Worth Daily Gazette*, June 24, 1887.
51. *Austin Weekly* Statesman, June 23, 1887; *New York Sun*, June 19, 1887; *Sacramento Daily Record-Union*, June 20, 1887; *Butte Semi-Weekly Miner*, Butte, Montana, June 22, 1887; *Phillipsburg Herald*, Phillipsburg, Kansas, June 25, 1887; *Western Kansas World*, Wakeeney, Kansas, June 25, 1887. Stokes has not been further identified.
52. *Fort Worth Weekly Gazette*, June 24, 1887; *Los Angeles Daily Herald*, June 19, 1887; *Sacramento Daily Record-Union*, June 20, 1887; *Helena Weekly Herald*, June 23, 1887; *Iola Register*, June 24, 1887; *Daily Alta California*, June 19, 1887; *Butte Semi-Weekly Miner*, June 22, 1887; *Indian Signal*, June 23, 1887; *San Saba News*, June 24, 1887.
53. *Galveston Daily News*, June 19, 1887.
54. *Austin Weekly Statesman*, June 23, 1887; *Dallas Daily Herald*, June 20, 1887.
55. *The New North West*, Deer Lodge, Montana, June 24, 1887.
56. William Newberger was the son of Raphael Newburger and Adelheid Friedberger, and was born January15, 1846, in Wurttemberg, Germany. He is listed on the 1870 New York Census as a merchant. On February 27, 1870, he married Mary "Marie" Bauer. His wife Marie gave her age as 19 at the time. By 1880 the family had moved to Baltimore, Maryland. Newberger died in New York on December 21, 1891. *Austin Weekly Statesman*, June 23, 1887; *Iola Register*, June 24, 1887; *Phillipsburg Herald*, June 25, 1887; *Western Kansas World*, June 25, 1887; *New York Sun*, June 19, 1887; *Indian Sentinel*, June 23, 1887; 1870 New York Census; 1880 Maryland Census; New York Marriage Licenses.
57. Price, 47.
58. *The True Northerner*, June 29, 1887.

59. *Indian Sentinel,* Muskogee, Oklahoma, June 23, 1887; *Iola Register,* Iola, Kansas, June 24, 1887; *Western Kansas World,* Wakeeney, Kansas, June 25, 1887; *Phillipsburg Herald,* Phillipsburg, Kansas, June 25, 1887.
60. *Austin Weekly Statesman,* June 23, 1887; *New York Sun,* June 19, 1887. Robert Lewis Armistead was the son of William Blair and Mary Robina Woods Armistead and was born May 7, 1847, in Nashville, Tennessee. His father was a well-to-do merchant, noted in the 1850 census as having property valued at $7,000. Armistead married Nancy Minor Humphreys on April 21, 1875, and the couple had a number of children at the time of the robbery. The 1910 Census lists Armistead's profession as "Tobacco Firm." He died of pneumonia in Nashville on February 24, 1924. 1850 Davidson County, Tennessee Census; 1910 Davidson County, Tennessee Census; Tennessee death certificate 136.
61. Price, 50; *Austin Weekly* Statesman, June 23, 1887; *Fort Worth Daily Gazette;* June 24, 1887; *Daily Alta California,* San Francisco, California, June 19, 1887; *Los Angeles Daily Herald,* June 19, 1887; *Sacramento Daily Record-Union,* June 20, 1887; *Butte Semi-Weekly Miner,* June 22, 1887; *Indian Sentinel,* June 23, 1887; *Helena Weekly Herald,* June 23, 18887; *Iola Register,* June 24, 1887.
62. Louis A. Mayer was a son of Morris Leopold and Rose Goodhart Mayer and was born in Cincinnati, Ohio on February 7, 1848. The 1880 Census notes that he was a dealer in wholesale goods. He died in Cincinnati on October 7, 1929, of cancer complicated by pneumonia. *New York Sun,* June 19, 1887; 1880 Hamilton County, Ohio, Census; Ohio Certificate of Death 57391.
63. *Fort Worth Daily Gazette,* June 24, 1887. William Francis Beers was born November 6, 1852, in New Orleans to Jonathan Sturges Beers and Mary Elizabeth Illsley. The 1880 census for Galveston County, Texas, notes him as an insurance agent. Beers married Mary Iola Elizabeth Barnes in New York City on August 21, 1880. Beers died in Galveston on August 20, 1934.
64. *Austin Weekly Statesman,* June 23, 1887; *San Antonio Daily Express,* June 19, 1887.
65. *Fort Worth Daily Gazette,* June 24, 1887; *San Saba News,* June 24, 1887; *Daily Alta California,* June 19, 1887; *Los Angeles Daily Herald,* June 19, 1887; *Sacramento Daily Record-Union,* June 20, 1887; *Austin Weekly Statesman,* June 23, 1887.
66. *Austin Weekly Statesman,* June 23, 1887; *Fort Worth Daily Gazette,* June 24, 1887.
67. Ibid.
68. *Austin Weekly Statesman,* June 23, 1887.
69. *Fort Worth Daily* Gazette, June 24, 1887.
70. Burton, "Man Hunt," 16.
71. Beach was probably Joseph A. Beach, born August 31, 1845. The 1900 Sumter County, Florida Census describes him as a farmer. Beach died on March 15, 1910.
72. Lionel S. Hohenthal was born in New York City to Solomon L. and Charlotte Hohenthal on October 18, 1856. Hohenthal was described as a "well known steamship agent" at the time of his death. Hohenthal collapsed on a street in Houston and was rushed to a hospital but died on November 29, 1916. The

cause of his death was acute edema probably due to congestive heart failure. *Houston Post*, December 1, 1916; Texas Death Certificate 255776.

73. *Fort Worth Daily Gazette*, June 24, 1887.
74. Ibid., *San Saba News*, June 24, 1887.
75. *Fort Worth Daily Gazette*, June 24, 1887.
76. *San Antonio Daily Express*, June 19, 1887.
77. Wells Fargo Circular, July 2, 1887, AGC.
78. *San Antonio Daily Express*, September 22, 1887.
79. Wells Fargo Circular, July 2, 1887, AGC.
80. *San Antonio Daily Express*, June 19, 1887.
81. Price, 64.
82. Burton, "Man Hunt," 16; Price, 46, *San Antonio Daily Express*, June 19, 1887.
83. Burton, "Man Hunt," 16.
84. *Fort Worth Daily Gazette*, June 24, 1887.
85. Price, 46.
86. Burton, "Man Hunt," 18–20.
87. Price, 48.
88. Wells Fargo & Co. Ledger Excerpt, courtesy Cliff Caldwell. Among the newspapers who reported significantly higher numbers of outlaws was the *New York Sun* of June 19, 1887 who reported "eight or ten men" in addition to those who had boarded the train. This was echoed by the *Daily Alta California*, June 19, 1887; the *Reno Evening Gazette*, June 18, 1887, and the *Daily Morning Astorian*, Astoria, Oregon, June 19, 1887. See also *Los Angeles Daily Herald*, June 19, 1887; *Butte Semi-Weekly Miner*, June 22, 1887; *Indian Sentinel*, June 23, 1887; *Iola Register*, June 24, 1887; *Salt Lake Herald*, June 24, 1887; *Bismarck Weekly Tribune*, Bismarck, North Dakota, June 24, 1887; *Philipsburg Mail*, Philipsburg, Montana, June 23, 1887; *Western Kansas World*, June 25, 1887; *Phillipsburg Herald*, Phillipsburg, Kansas, June 25, 1887, and the *Great Falls Tribune*, Great Falls, Montana, June 23, 1887. The *Macon Telegraph* in Macon, Georgia reported the number of outlaws at thirteen in the June 22, 1887 issue.
89. *Fort Worth Daily Gazette*, May 24, 1887.

Notes to Chapter 6

1. *Londonderry Sifter*, Londonderry, Vermont, June 23, 1887.
2. *Fort Worth Daily Gazette*, June 24, 1887.
3. *New York Sun*, June 19, 1887.
4. *Fort Worth Daily Gazette*, June 24, 1887.
5. *The True Northerner*, June 29, 1887.
6. Among the papers that carried a vastly inflated amount were the *Phillipsburg Herald*, June 25, 1887, who placed the loss somewhere between \$75,000 and \$100,000. A nearly identical story was carried by the *Western Kansas World*, June 24, 1887.
7. Typical examples of this can be found in *Alexandria Gazette and Virginia Advertiser*, Alexandria, D. C. (not Virginia), June 18, 1887; *Reno Evening Gazette*, June 18, 1887; *Daily Morning Astorian*, June 19, 1887; *Essex County Herald*, Guildhall, Vermont, June 24, 1887; *New York Sun*, June 19, 1887; *Daily Alta*

California, June 19, 1887; *Los Angeles Daily Herald*, June 19, 1887; *Press and Daily Dakotaian*, Yankton, Dakota Territory (S. D.), June 29, 1887; *Columbus Journal*, June 22, 1887; *Butte Semi-Weekly Miner*, June 22, 1887; *Emporia Semi-Weekly News*, June 23, 1887; *Iola Register*, June 24, 1887; *Salt Lake Herald*, June 24, 1887; *Alma Record*, Alma, Michigan, June 24, 1887, among many others.

8. *Lake Charles Commercial*, Lake Charles, Louisiana, June 25, 1887; *Austin Weekly Statesman*, June 23, 1887; *Los Angeles Daily Herald*, June 19, 1887; *Daily Alta California*, San Francisco, California, June 19, 1887; *Logansport Journal*, Logansport, Indiana, June 19, 1887.
9. Burton, "Man Hunt," 16.
10. *Daily Alta California*, June 18, 1887.
11. *Los Angeles Daily Herald*, June 19, 1887.
12. *Sacramento Daily Record-Union*, June 20, 1887.
13. *Helena Weekly Herald*, June 23, 1887.
14. *Butte Semi-Weekly Miner*, June 22, 1887.
15. *Indian Sentinel*, June 23, 1887.
16. *Iola Register*, June 24, 1887.
17. *The New North West*, June 24, 1887.
18. *Fort Worth Daily Gazette*, June 20, 1887. The entire article is included in Appendix 3.
19. *Falkirk Herald*, Edinburgh, Scotland, June 25, 1887.
20. *The Sydney Mail and New South Wales Advertiser*, Sydney, Australia, July 20, 1887; *Western Gazette*, Somerset, England, June 24, 1887.
21. *Thames Advertiser*, Shortland and Grahamstown, Thames, New Zealand, July 26, 1887; *Poverty Bay Herald*, Poverty Bay, New Zealand, July 29, 1887; *Auckland Star*, Auckland, New Zealand, July 23, 1887.
22. Burton, "Man Hunt," 17.
23. Miller, *Rube Burrow*, 30–33.
24. *Austin Weekly Statesman*, June 23, 1887.
25. *Fort Worth Daily Gazette*, June 24, 1887; *Austin Weekly Statesman*, June 23, 1887.
26. *Daily Alta California*, June 19, 1887.
27. The Hoo Doo War was a conflict in central Texas that began over cattle in the early 1870s but swiftly degenerated into a blood feud. See David Johnson, *The Mason County "Hoo Doo" War, 1874–1902* (Denton: University of North Texas Press, 2006).
28. Townsend died while in office on November 14, 1894. His family was embroiled for a time in the Reese-Townsend Feud in Colorado County, Texas. For more on Townsend see James C. Kearney, Bill Stein, and James Smallwood, *No Hope for Heaven, No Fear of Hell* (Denton: University of North Texas Press, 2016), and Tula Townsend Wyatt, *The Seven Townsend Brothers of Texas, 1826 – 1838: A Genealogy* (Austin, TX: Privately published, Austex Duplications, 1974). *San Saba News*, June 24, 1887; *Brenham Banner*, November 15, 1894; Tise, 117.
29. Following Zapp's retirement in 1894 he entered private business for several years. In 1904 Zapp was appointed to fill the unexpired term of County Treasurer R. T. Bradshaw. He was later elected to the office and held it for

eighteen years. Zapp died at La Grange on December 7, 1926, of a lingering illness. Tise, 183; *La Grange Journal*, December 9, 1926

30. *Austin Weekly Statesman*, June 23, 1887; *San Antonio Daily Express*, June 19, 1887, *Fort Worth Daily Gazette*, June 24, 1887.
31. *Fort Worth Daily Gazette*, June 24, 1887.
32. *Los Angeles Daily Herald*, June 19, 1887.
33. *Austin Weekly Statesman*, June 23, 1887.
34. *Fort Worth Daily Gazette*, June 24, 1887.
35. *Fort Worth Daily Gazette*, June 24, 1887.
36. *San Antonio Daily Express*, June 21, 22, 1887.
37. *Alexandria Gazette and Virginia Advertiser*, June 20, 1887; *St. Paul Daily Globe*, St. Paul, Minnesota, June 21, 1887; *Mitchell Capital*, Mitchell, South Dakota, June 24, 1887.
38. Karnes County, Texas Death Certificate 3722; England Births and Christenings, 1538–1975, GS Film 1526654. Only Rudd's mother's name appears in the record: Elizabeth. For Rudd see also Mrs. G. C. Mayfield, "Interesting Narrative of Capt. W. L. Rudd, Ex-Ranger," Hunter's *Frontier Times* 10, no. 3 (December 1932).
39. Texas Ranger Muster Rolls, TSA.
40. Following his retirement, Rudd worked as a lumber dealer in De Witt County for a time. Rudd had immigrated to the United States around 1872. He was first appointed sheriff on September 9, 1886, and was subsequently reelected in November of that year. He served through November 1888. Rudd died in Karnes County on January 9, 1941. Tise, 296; 1900 DeWitt County, Texas Census; Karnes County, Texas Death Certificate 3722.
41. *San Antonio Daily* Express, June 22, 1887; *Mitchell Capital*, Mitchell, South Dakota, June 24, 1887; *St. Paul Daily Globe*, St. Paul, Minnesota, June 21, 1887; *Alexandria Gazette and Virginia Advertiser*, Alexandria, D. C., June 20, 1887.
42. W. H. King to William Scott, Commanding Co. F, June 19, 1887, AGC, TSA.
43. Frontier Battalion Operations, Company B, June 1887, AGC, TSA; Miller, *Rube Burrow*, 33.
44. Frontier Battalion Operations, Company C, June 1887, AGC, TSA. Captain George Schmitt's report states that the company hunted the McNeil train robbers from June 12 through June 27, 1887.
45. Miller, *Rube Burrow*, 33.
46. *Sacramento Daily Record-Union*, June 20, 1887.
47. *Waco Daily Examiner*, June 21, 1887.
48. *San Antonio Daily Light*, June 21, 1887. The resolution was signed by J. P. Smith, President, and P. Alexander, Secretary.
49. *Fort Worth Daily Gazette*, June 21, 1887.
50. *San Antonio Daily Light*, June 21, 1887.
51. *Fort Worth Daily Gazette*, June 21, 1887; *Dallas Morning News*, June 23, 1887; *San Antonio Daily Express*, June 23, 1887. John Otho was the son of Antone Otho and Amanda Mimms and was born February 12, 1866, in Halletsville, Texas. He died at Waelder, Texas, on December 18, 1932, of heart failure. Clark and Smith have not been identified with certainty.
52. *Alexandria Gazette and Virginia Advertiser*, June 22, 1887.

53. Emancipation Day is observed in many former European colonies in the Caribbean and areas within the United States to commemorate the emancipation of enslaved people. In Texas, Emancipation Day is celebrated on June 19.
54. Archibald Jacob Smothers was born in Lavaca County, Texas, during December 1844 to William and Cynthia Kelly Smothers. Smothers served as sheriff from 1882 through 1888. His father had been sheriff of Lavaca County from 1860 through 1862. Around 1905 he moved to Gonzales County. He was found dead in a barn behind his farm on May 25, 1906, apparently having committed suicide using strychnine. *Weimar Mercury*, May 26, 1906; Tise, 324.
55. *San Antonio Daily Express*, June 23, 1887.
56. Ibid.
57. *Gonzales Inquirer*, June 25, 1887. George Crockett Shoaf was born in Lockhart, Texas, on January 1, 1854, to George Washington Shoaf and his wife Melissa Jane Dillard. He died in San Antonio, Texas, on March 6, 1939, of a cerebral hemorrhage. Bexar County, Texas: Death Certificate 11222. At one time Shoaf had served as marshal of Luling, Texas.
58. *Fort Worth Daily Gazette*, June 23, 1887. The identical article was also published in the *Fort Worth Weekly Gazette*, June 24, 1887.
59. *San Antonio Daily Light*, June 23, 1887; *Fort Worth Daily Gazette*, June 23, 1887; *Dallas Morning News*, June 23, 1887; *San Antonio Daily Express*, June 24, 1887.
60. *Fort Worth Daily Gazette*, June 30, 1887.
61. *Los Angeles Daily Herald*, June 22, 1887; *Salt Lake Herald*, June 22, 1887; *Titusville Herald*, Titusville, Pennsylvania, June 24, 1887; *Wheeling Register*, Wheeling, West Virginia, June 24, 1887; *Wichita Eagle*, Wichita, Kansas, June 24, 1887; *The Republican*, Waukesha, Wisconsin, June 24, 1887; *Memphis Appeal*, Memphis, Tennessee; *Rock Island Daily Argus*, Rock Island, Illinois, June 22, 1887; *Logansport Pharos*, Logansport, Indiana, June 22, 1887; *Daily Evening Bulletin*, Maysville, Kentucky, June 23, 1887.
62. *Fort Worth Daily Gazette*, June 23, 1887; *Gonzales Inquirer*, June 25, 1887.
63. *San Antonio Daily Light*, June 21, 1887.
64. *Fort Worth Daily Gazette*, June 22, 1887.
65. *Los Angeles Daily Herald*, June 19, 1887.
66. *Fort Worth Daily Gazette*, June 25, 1887.
67. *Gonzales Inquirer*, June 25, 1887.
68. *Fort Worth Daily Gazette*, June 28, 1887; *Dallas Morning News*, June 23, 1887; *San Antonio Daily Light*, June 23, 1887.
69. *Austin Weekly Statesman*, June 30, 1887.
70. Vachel Weldon died abruptly on September 12, 1896. L. E. Daniell, *Personnel of the Texas State Government, with Sketches of Distinguished Texans, Embracing The Executive and Staff, Heads of the Departments, United States Senators and Representatives, Members of the Twenty-First Legislature* (Austin: Smith, Hicks & Jones, State Printers, 1889), 312-313; *Houston Daily Post*, September 13, 1896.
71. Vachel Weldon to Adjt. Gen. King, June 20, 1887, AGC, TSA. Reinhardt Schneider was the son of Daniel and Justina Margaretha Schneider and was born November 4, 1862, in Texas. He drew five years for horse theft in 1884

from Fayette County. Schneider died on March 26, 1903. He was a brother-in-law of Bud Powell, having married Powell's sister Elvira.

72. *Magdalena Mountain Mail*, Magdalena, New Mexico, April 5, 1888.
73. Burton, "Man Hunt," 16–17.
74. Allee was born on May 3, 1855, to Alfred Alonzo Lee and Julia Wilcox in DeWitt County, Texas. Like Brack Cornett he was raised during the savage Sutton-Taylor War. There is no biography of Allee available at the present time.
75. *Saint Louis Republic*, July 15, 1891.
76. *Galveston Daily News*, December 31, 1876.
77. Ibid., February 21, 1877.
78. *San Antonio Daily Express*, June 25 and 26, 1887, and August 21, 1887.
79. Wells, Fargo & Co. Circular, AGC, TSA.
80. Burton, "Man Hunt," 18–19.
81. 1870 De Witt County, Texas Census.
82. Convict Record Ledger, Huntsville, Walker County. W. M. Day was convicted in Lavaca County on August 17, 1883, entering the penitentiary on September 7, 1883, as convict number 654. Penitentiary records describe him as six feet tall, 155 pounds, having brown hair and blue eyes. Day had a bullet-scarred thigh and was described as having a limited education. He both smoked and drank. He had received a sentence of two years for robbery and two for burglary. Day was discharged on April 22, 1887.
83. Burton, "Man Hunt," 17.
84. Ibid.
85. J. Waldo to W. Snyder, General Manager of the Gulf, Colorado & Santa Fe Railroad, July 5, 1887, AGC, TSA.
86. Those railroads accepting the proposal were Gulf, Colorado & Santa Fe, the Houston & Texas Central, the Houston East & West Texas, the St. Louis Arkansas & Texas, and the Texas & Pacific.
87. J. Waldo to W. Snyder, General Manager of the Gulf, Colorado & Santa Fe Railroad, July 5, 1887, AGC, TSA.
88. H. L. Morrill, Gen. Mgr. St. Louis and San Francisco Railway Co. to J. Waldo, July 11, 1887, AGC, TSA.
89. C. L. Frost to J. Waldo, July 12, 1887, AGC, TSA.
90. J. Waldo to Governor L. S. Ross, July 14, 1887, AGC, TSA.
91. J. Waldo to Adjutant General King, July 11, 1887, AGC, TSA.
92. J. Waldo to L. S. Ross, July 13, 1887, AGC, TSA; Adjutant General W. H. King to J. Waldo, July 16, 1887, AGC, TSA.
93. Alexander Pope to L. S. Ross, July 2, 1887, AGC, TSA.
94. Tom O. Bailes, Deputy U. S. Marshal to W. H. King, July 9, 1887, AGC, TSA.
95. A. B. Coffee to W. H. King, July 8, 1887, AGC, TSA. According to Coffee, "When John Barber was here two years ago [1885] on a horse case, Johnston says he proposed to him to rob the bank and a store and when Austin Barber was in jail he says John Barber sent up $500 to bribe me or the Sheriff or Dist. Atty. and get Austin out. Money was returned."
96. *Galveston Daily News*, July 10, 1892.
97. Burton, "Surprised," 21; Burton, "Man Hunt," 20.

Notes to Chapter 7

1. George H. Schmitt to W. H. King, July 5, 1887.
2. George H. Schmitt to L. P. Sieker, July 5, 1887, AGC, TSA.
3. George H. Schmitt to W. H. King, July 8, 1887; George H. Schmitt to L. P. Sieker, July 8, 1887, AGC, TSA.
4. George H. Schmitt to W. H. King, July 11, 1887, AGC, TSA.
5. John York Bell was a son of James Madison and Miriam G. York Bell and was born August 30, 1846, at Cuero, DeWitt County, Texas. Bell married Eliza Ann "Annie" Wofford (born in Tennessee on February 4, 1848) on March 1, 1870. They had two children: Myrtle, born February 10, 1871, and William Albert, born September 3, 1875. John Y. Bell died in DeWitt County on June 14, 1910. Annie died in Harris County, Texas, on December 23, 1934.
6. V. Weldon to W. H. King, July 11, 1887, AGC, TSA.
7. V. Weldon to W. H. King, July 12, 1887, AGC, TSA.
8. George H. Schmitt to W. H. King, July 13, 1887, AGC, TSA.
9. B. F. Yoakum to Geo. H. Schmitt, July 13, 1887, AGC, TSA.
10. George H. Schmitt to W. H. King, July 14, 1887, AGC, TSA.
11. Wells, Fargo & Co. Circular, AGC, TSA.
12. Ibid.
13. *Taylor County News*, Abilene, Texas, July 2, 1887.
14. J. C. Martin to Governor L. S. Ross from Manchaca, Texas, July 17, 1887, AGC, TSA. Red Rock lies about 12 miles southwest of Bastrop.
15. Wm. Safford to W. H. King from Seguin, Texas, July 17, 1887, AGC, TSA. August G. Startz was a long-time resident of Comal County, born there on August 25, 1855, to Heinrich Severus Startz and his wife Johnne Louise Artzt. Startz died of natural causes in San Antonio on July 29, 1937.
16. James E. Hollingsworth to Governor L. S. Ross, July 18, 1887, AGC, TSA.
17. George H. Schmitt to W. H. King, July 18, 1887, AGC, TSA.
18. *Fort Worth Daily Gazette*, July 25, 1887; *San Saba News*, July 29, 1887. This was not the only false lead during the hunt for the outlaws. R. R. Gilbert of Calhoun County wrote to Adjutant General King that John and Will Bickford (*sic*: Brickford), the latter of whom was believed to be Captain Dick, were in Port Lavaca around this time. R. R. Gilbert to W. H. King, July 23, 1887, AGC, TSA.
19. *Brenham Daily Banner*, August 2, 1887.
20. *Fort Worth Daily Gazette*, July 29, 1887.
21. Price, 51; *Waco Daily Examiner*, July 28, 1887; *San Antonio Express*, July 27, 1887.
22. *Dallas Morning News*, July 29, 1887.
23. *Poverty Bay Herald*, Poverty Bay, New Zealand, July 29, 1887; *Auckland Star*, Auckland, New Zealand, July 23, 1887.
24. *Thames Advertiser*, Shortland and Grahamstown, Thames, New Zealand, July 26, 1887.
25. *The Sydney Mail and New South Wales Advertiser*, Sydney, Australia, July 20, 1887.
26. W. H. King to William Scott, August 2, 1887, AGC, TSA.
27. George H. Schmitt to W. H. King, August 3, 1887, AGC, TSA.

28. Sam McMurry to W. H. King, August 6, 1887, AGC, TSA.
29. Ira Aten to L. P. Sieker, August 6, 1887, C. L. Sonnichsen Collection, University of Texas at El Paso. Sonnichsen is quoting the Webb papers.
30. For N. O. Reynolds, see Chuck Parsons and Donaly E. Brice, *Texas Ranger N. O. Reynolds: The Intrepid* (Denton: University of North Texas Press, 2014).
31. Wolf was the son of Jacob and Adaline Faulkner Wolf, and was born March 9, 1851, in Rusk County, Texas. He was tragically killed in 1892 by constable John Taylor. Taylor confronted Wolf over the arrest of Taylor's son and shot Wolf in the leg, severing an artery. Wolf died on May 12, 1892. Caldwell and DeLord, *Texas Lawmen 1835–1899*, 44–45; Tise, 76; 1860, 1870 and 1880 Burnet County, Texas Census.
32. Ira Aten to L. P. Sieker, August 7, 1887, C. L. Sonnichsen Collection, University of Texas at El Paso. Sonnichsen is quoting the Webb papers.
33. William J. Stanley was born to Thomas Edward and Holland West Gaitlin Stanley on May 4, 1833, in Mississippi. He married Martha Ann Grumbles in Travis County, Texas, on June 21, 1855. The couple had eight children. 1840 Tippah County, Mississippi Census; 1850 Travis County, Texas Census; 1860 Bastrop County, Texas Census; 1870 and 1880 Williamson County, Texas Census; Caldwell and DeLord, *Texas Lawmen 1835–1899*, 237.
34. *Brenham Daily Banner*, August 9, 1887.
35. *Temple Weekly Times*, Temple, Texas, August 13, 1887.
36. Price, 27.
37. *Galveston Daily News*, August 9, 1887; *Wichita Eagle*, August 9, 1887; *Waco Daily Examiner*, August 9, 1887; *San Antonio Daily Express*, August 8, 1887; *The Daily Times*, Trenton, New Jersey, August 9, 1887; Price, 53.
38. *Austin Weekly Statesman*, August 11, 1887.
39. *Fort Worth Daily Gazette*, August 9, 1887; *The Weekly Mineola Monitor*, Mineola, Texas, August 13, 1887.
40. Schmitt to King, August 7, 1887, AGC, TSA.
41. King to Schmitt, August 8, 1887.
42. Schmitt to L. P. Sieker, August 9, 1887, AGC, TSA.
43. Schmitt to King, August 17, 1887, AGC, TSA.
44. Schmitt to King, August 19, 1887, AGC, TSA.
45. Schmitt to King, August 26, 1887, AGC, TSA.
46. O. D. Baker from Batesville, Texas to L. S. Ross, August 11, 1887, AGC, TSA.
47. Hall & Waller's Detective Agency to L. S. Ross, August 9, 1887, AGC, TSA. The principals in this Waco-based detective agency were Frank Hall and J. W. Waller.
48. Executive Requisitions: L. S. Ross for John Barber and Bill Whitley, August 30, 1887, TSA.
49. John W. Insall was born in Lavaca County, Texas, to Richard Noel and Carolyn Mims Insall on July 25, 1857. The Insall family was living in Kendall County by 1870 where Richard is listed as a farmer. By 1880 he was listed as a stock raiser in Kimble County. John had two daughters: Clara Josephine, born on January 13, 1879, and Francis Alice, born December 20, 1885. His wife's name was Josephine E. "Jennie" Linscomb, but some family stories name the mother of his second daughter as Annie. The matter is unresolved.

1870 Kendall County, Texas Census; 1880 Kimble County, Texas Census; Mary Beth Marchant to the author, July 9, 2017.

50. *Galveston Weekly News*, June 1, 1882.
51. *Galveston Daily News*, October 23, 1883.
52. *Austin Daily Statesman*, September 11, 1887.
53. *Galveston Daily News*, December 19, 1887.
54. Mary Beth Marchant to the author, July 9, 2017.
55. For Jack Helm see Chuck Parsons, *Captain Jack Helm: A Victim of Texas Reconstruction Violence* (Denton: University of North Texas Press, 2018).
56. Executive Clemency Records: Henry Peter Kelly, TSA. This information was provided by D. W. Nash in a note affixed to the records.
57. Burton, "Man Hunt," 21.
58. Burton, "Surprised," 19.
59. *Titusville Morning Herald*, August 30, 1887. Thompson's Switch was a small station some 77 miles from Houston. The *Dallas Morning News*, August 30, 1887, mentions that the gang had been seen at Thompson's Switch but makes no mention of their spree.
60. Thomas Monroe Williford was a son of William Walton and Mary Daughterty Williford, and was born November 16, 1865, in Jefferson County, Texas. By 1870 the family was living in Wharton County but moved to Harris County prior to 1880. Williford died of a cerebral hemorrhage in Houston on November 30, 1931. *Dallas Morning News*, August 30, 1887; *Titusville Morning Herald*, August 30, 1887; 1870 Wharton County, Texas Census; 1880 Harris County, Texas Census.
61. George W. Ellis was born to George and Martha Tucker Ellis in De Soto County, Mississippi. The family moved to Texas during the early 1850s. Following father George's death in 1857, Martha married Judge William Ellison. In 1861 George W. enlisted in the Caldwell County Rangers, later Company B, 26th Texas Cavalry. He was later transferred to the Second Texas Field Battery. On October 20, 1869, Ellis married Louisa Jane Warren. He was elected sheriff of Harris County in 1886 and served until 1894. Afterwards he served as police chief of Houston, clerk of the criminal district court, and county commissioner. Ellis died of natural causes in Houston on January 2, 1927.
62. Albert Erichson (also Erickson) was born on March 17, 1855, to Gustavus and Maria Barbara Boniz Erickson. In 1894 he was elected sheriff of Harris County to replace the retiring George W. Ellis. He served until 1898. Newspapers of the time use the spelling Erichson, which is used here throughout.
63. Ben Kegans was a son of Hamilton and Margaret Hodge Kegans, and was born June 7, 1854.
64. *Dallas Morning News*, August 30, 1887.
65. Ibid.
66. *Titusville Morning Herald*, August 30, 1887. The *Dallas Morning News* of August 30, 1887, stated that none of the posse was injured.
67. *Titusville Morning Herald*, August 30. 1887; *Dallas Morning News*, August 30, 1887.
68. *Dallas Morning News*, August 30, 1887.

Notes to Chapter 8

1. *Dallas Morning News,* August 30, 1887.
2. *Fort Worth Daily Gazette,* September 1, 1887.
3. *Titusville Morning Herald,* August 30. 1887.
4. Thomas Sewell McDade was a son of James Wilkins and Caroline F. "Tennessee" Cooper McDade and was born in Montgomery County, Alabama, on July 19, 1829. Thomas McDade married Margaret J. Bouldin. McDade was first elected sheriff of Waller County in 1876 and served until shortly before his death in 1888. McDade was murdered on November 26, 1888. The murderer was never identified with certainty. Waller County, Texas 1860, 1870, and 1880 Census; Tise, 520; Caldwell and DeLord, *Texas Lawmen 1835–1899,* 226; *San Antonio Daily Express,* November 28, 1888; *Dallas Morning News,* August 31, 1887.
5. *Fort Worth Daily Gazette,* September 1, 1887.
6. *Galveston Daily News,* September 4, 1887.
7. Ibid.
8. Henry Weidener Baylor was the son of John Robert Baylor and Emily J. Hanna and was born in Fayette County, Texas, on November 27, 1848. Baylor served as sheriff there from 1884 through 1906. He died on October 12, 1932, of kidney failure. 1850 Fayette County, Texas Census; 1870 Lavaca County, Texas, Census, 1880 Uvalde County, Texas Census; Uvalde County, Texas death certificate 44463; Tise, 503.
9. *Dallas Morning News,* September 4, 1887; *Galveston Daily News,* September 4, 1887.
10. *Dallas Morning News,* September 11, 1887.
11. *Galveston Daily News,* September 11, 1887; *Dallas Morning News,* September 11, 1887; *Dallas Weekly Herald,* September 17, 1887. Thomas Green Martin, born April 1, 1840 in Springfield, Missouri, and James C. Martin born May 21, 1844, were the sons of Caleb Alonzo and Louisa A. Crowder Martin. Frank Martin, son of Thomas and Delilah Hooper Martin, was born in September 1865.
12. *Galveston Daily News,* September 12, 1887; *Dallas Weekly Herald,* September 17, 1887.
13. Ibid. Albert Francis Field was the son of Henry Hill and Mary Calvin Field and was born six miles south of Lockhart on June 6, 1856. Field served under Leander H. McNelly and Lee Hall from 1876 through January 3, 1878. He was appointed first deputy under Sheriff A. Y. Larremore, serving until 1882 when Larremore retired and he was elected sheriff of Caldwell County. He married Kate McDowell the same year. Field served as county sheriff through November 1892. Field also served as mayor of Lockhart from 1908 through 1911. He died in Lockhart on the evening of January 25, 1912. Tise, 79; *Plum Creek Almanac* 26, no. 1 (Spring 2008): 70; Karla Field, "Albert Francis Field," *Plum Creek Almanac* 34, no. 2 (Fall 2016): 133–135; No author, *Record of Southwest Texas* (Chicago: Goodspeed Brothers, Publishers, 1894), 364–365.
14. Jones was born in Texas on May 30, 1860, to Hamilton Jones and his wife Elizabeth Stevens. He died March 2, 1936, in Leon County of heart failure

compounded with bronchitis and asthma. Jones served as sheriff of Gonzales County from 1884 through 1890 and again from 1894 to 1896. Tise, 209; Leon County, Texas death certificate 16130.

15. Brassell died in Hays County, Texas, on March 13, 1947. 1870 DeWitt County, Texas Census; 1880 Gonzales County, Texas, Census; Hays County, Texas Death Certificate 12291.
16. *Dallas Morning News*, September 15, 1887.
17. *Dallas Morning News*, September 12, 1887; *Galveston Daily* News, September 12, 1887; *San Saba News*, September 16, 1887.
18. *Wheeling Register*, Wheeling, West Virginia, September 14, 1887; *Newark Daily Advocate*, Newark, Ohio, September 16, 1887.
19. John Fines Crisswell was born in Tennessee to Leroy V. and Elizabeth McMicken Crisswell on December 25, 1845. Crisswell was married to Margaret R. Jackson in 1868 and had seven children at the time of his arrest.
20. Henry "Buck" Hamilton was a well-respected lawman who served as sheriff of Bandera County from 1875 until his death of a lingering illness on July 23, 1888. Hamilton was born to William Hamilton and Sarah Moore in Wheatley County, Tennessee, on April 15, 1833. The family moved to Texas in 1859. *Bandera Enterprise*, July 26, 1888; Earl Hardin, Jr., "Sheriffs and Rangers," *Bandera County Historian* 22, no. 3 (Fall 2001): 3, 4.
21. *Austin Weekly Statesman*, September 15, 1887.
22. *San Antonio Daily Express*, September 13, 14, 15, 1887; *Austin Daily Statesman*, September 13, 14, 15, 1887.
23. Herrin has eluded positive identification, but records place his birth around 1864. A notation in the prison records states that Herrin was "Ex-convict 787," but designation 787 was for a William Gibson convicted in the late 1860s. The most promising theory is that Herrin was the stepson of William Looney. The census places him working on a farm for his stepfather and gives the name of his mother as Elizabeth. The matter remains unresolved. Huntsville Penitentiary Convict Record Ledgers: James Herrin; 1880 Randolph County, Arkansas Census.
24. *Dallas Morning News*, September 15, 1887.
25. Reverend Benjamin Franklin Dixon was born December 14, 1849, in Louisiana to Shadrach Tootle Dixon and his wife Judith Covington. He was the first pastor of the McNeil Creek Baptist Church. Dixon died January 3, 1917, of "general debility" in Lubbock County, Texas. Lubbock County Death Certificate 2387; Chuck Parsons and Pat Parsons, *A History of the Prairie Lea Baptist Church* (Gonzales, TX: Reese's Print Shop, 2017), 97.
26. A son of Sylvester and Catherine "Kitty" Baker, Andrew Jackson Rife was born February 2, 1831. Rife married Mary Story in Oktibbeha County, Mississippi, on October 7, 1856. In 1862 Rife joined the Confederate forces at West Point, Mississippi, serving in Company G, 35th Regiment Mississippi Infantry. Following the war but prior to 1869, he and his wife moved to Lamar County, Texas. In 1872 he moved his family to Caldwell County where he was an early settler in the Lytton Springs area and built the first store, Rife Mercantile, there. Rife died in Caldwell County on March 23, 1902. His obituary characterized him as a "kind and gentle man." His wife survived him by thirty years, dying on October 7, 1932. Frances R. Condra,

"A. J. Rife, Early Lytton Springs Settler," *Plum Creek Almanac* 9, no. 1 (Spring 1991): 40–44; *Historical Caldwell County: Where Roots Intertwine* (Caldwell County, TX: The Mark Withers Trail Drive Museum, 1984), entry by Lois Masur, 127; 1850 and 1860 Oktibbeha County, Mississippi Census; 1870 Lamar County, Texas Census.

27. *Austin Weekly Statesman*, September 15, 1887; *Galveston Daily News*, September 14, 1887.
28. George H. Schmitt to W. H. King, August 31, 1887, AGC, TSA.
29. *Galveston Daily News*, September 5, 1887.
30. A. C. Grimes, Sgt. Co. C to W. H. King, September 7, 1887, AGC, TSA.
31. George H. Schmitt to L. P. Sieker, September 10, 1887, AGC, TSA.
32. Burton, "Man Hunt," 18.
33. Ibid., 18 – 20.
34. *Dallas Morning News*, April 9, 1887; *Galveston Daily News*, April 9, 1887.
35. Wells Fargo Circular, July 2, 1887, AGC, TSA.
36. Huntsville Penitentiary Texas Convict Record Ledgers, TSA: Will Jacobs.
37. *Dallas Morning News*, September 15, 1887.
38. *Austin Daily Statesman*, September 13, 1887; *Ballinger Eagle*, September 13, 1887.
39. *Galveston Daily News*, September 14, 1887. The horses were held by S. G. Martin at Kyle, Texas.
40. *Waco Daily Examiner*, September 15, 1887.
41. *Canadian Free Press*, Canadian, Texas, September 21, 1887.
42. *San Saba News*, September 16, 1887.
43. Ibid., September 17, 1887.
44. *Fort Worth Gazette*, November 26, 1887.
45. *Galveston Daily News*, September 12, 1887.
46. *Canadian Free Press*, September 21, 1887; *Waco Daily Examiner*, September 15, 1887.
47. Huntsville Penitentiary Convict Record Ledgers. Kelly was convict 4755 and Day 4756.
48. *Austin Weekly Statesman*, September 29, 1887; *Fort Worth Daily Gazette*, September 29, 1887; *San Saba News*, October 7, 1887.
49. *Brenham Daily Banner*, September 11, 1880, and August 21, 1881.
50. Brown entered the penitentiary at Huntsville on November 10, 1881, as convict 9831. Penitentiary records describe him as 5-feet, 10-inches tall, 35-years-old and 160 pounds, fair complected with blue eyes and brown hair. He gave his birthplace as Virginia. On January 1, 1883, he was transferred to the Rusk Penitentiary as convict 710. Brown was pardoned on March 5, 1886. Huntsville Penitentiary Convict Record Ledgers: George Brown; Rusk Penitentiary Convict Record Ledgers: George Brown.
51. *Austin Weekly Statesman*, September 15, 1887.
52. *Fort Worth Daily Gazette*, September 14, 1887; *Waco Daily Examiner*, September 15, 1887.
53. *Dallas Morning News*, September 18, 1887; *Waco Daily Examiner*, September 15, 1887.
54. *Austin Weekly Statesman*, September 29, 1887.
55. *Waco Daily Examiner*, November 22, 1887.

56. *Dallas Morning News*, December 14, 1887.
57. Burton, "Man Hunt," 20.
58. *Fort Worth Daily Gazette*, September 29, 1887.
59. *Galveston Weekly News*, March 9, 1882.
60. *Dallas Morning News*, September 18, 1887; Burton, "Man Hunt," 23.
61. William Henry Cornett was one of the children of William M. Cornett and Matilda Melvina Greer and was born May 11, 1857, in Goliad County. He married Llano County native Triphenie Etta Lewis, a daughter of Jackson Owen Lewis and Averiles Catherine Pruitt in Llano County on October 2, 1884. Triphenie was born February 12, 1866. At the time of Brack's arrival they had two children: Joseph, born in January 1886 and Daniel born in September 1887. William Henry Cornett died in Dawson County, Texas, on December 4, 1943.
62. Roger Cornett to the author, November 28, 2016.
63. *Dallas Morning News*, October 1, 1887.
64. Ibid., October 5, 1887.
65. *Austin Weekly Statesman*, October 6, 1887.
66. Ibid., February 21, 1889; *Bay City Times*, Bay City Michigan, February 21, 1889.
67. Burton, "Man Hunt," 20.
68. *Galveston Daily News*, July 19, 1882. Powell's entire confession is included as Appendix 5.
69. Kinch Harrison Hamilton was born January 1852 in Arkansas to Robert and Rebecca Ann Hayes Hamilton. He married Rachel Matilda Reeves in Cass County, Texas March 19, 1871. Rachel Reeves Hamilton died October 24, 1918, of influenza. Kinch Hamilton died March 28, 1919, at Port Arthur, Jefferson County, Texas.
70. *Galveston Daily News*, October 7, 1887; *Dallas Herald*, October 7, 1887.
71. *Galveston Daily News*, October 11, 1887. John H. Boyd was born in Laurens County, South Carolina, sometime during March 1846, the son of John Hamilton and Elizabeth Hudgens Boyd. Boyd was elected continuously as sheriff of Johnson County, Texas from 1882 through 1888, his final term expiring in 1890. He also served as assistant superintendent of the Huntsville Penitentiary for a time. He died of pneumonia at Clovis, New Mexico, on February 29, 1912. Tise, 291; *Cleburne Morning Review*, March 3, 1912.
72. J. Waldo to W. H. King, October 1, 1887, AGC, TSA.
73. *Dallas Daily Herald*, October 15, 1887; *El Paso Times*, October 15, 1887; *Dallas Herald*, October 15, 1887; *Galveston Daily News*, October 15, 1887; *Fort Worth Daily Gazette*, October 15, 1887; *Palo Pinto Star*, Palo Pinto, Texas, October 22, 1887.
74. Burton, "Man Hunt," 20–21.

Notes to Chapter 9

1. F. R. Graves, County Attorney, to W. H. King, October 18, 1887, AGC, TSA.
2. *Galveston Daily News*, October 25, 1887; *Austin Weekly Statesman*, October 27, 1887.

3. Huntsville Penitentiary Convict Record Ledgers, Henry Kelly and Martin Day, TSA.
4. *Atlanta Constitution*, October 27, 1887.
5. *Austin Weekly Statesman*, October 27, 1887. The El Paso robbery referred to involved two men attempting to rob a train near there. J. E. Smith, the express messenger, killed them both. *El Paso Times*, October 15, 1887.
6. Ira Aten to L. P. Sieker, from Lampasas, Texas, October 29, 1887, AGC, TSA.
7. *Daily Globe-Democrat*, October 27, 1888; Price 51.
8. F. R. Graves, County Attorney, to W. H. King, November 4, 1887, November 4, 1887, AGC, TSA.
9. *Ballinger Leader*, Ballinger, Texas, November 7, 1887.
10. Alexander, *Aten*, 137–138, 372; Burton, "Man Hunt," 25.
11. *Fort Worth Gazette*, November 26, 1887.
12. Ibid., December 11, 1887. The identical article appeared in the *Clarksville Standard* of December 15, 1887.
13. *Galveston Daily News*, December 11, 1887.
14. Ibid.
15. Ira Aten to Capt. L.P. Sieker from Belton, Texas, December 13, 1887, AGC, TSA.
16. Miller, *Rube Burrow*, 42 – 46, 54 – 56.
17. *Dallas Morning News*, December 20, 1887.
18. *Dallas Herald*, December 26, 1887.
19. Burton, "Man Hunt," 27. While Queen's nickname has been given as Kelp, family sources list it as "Kep," which is used throughout the text.
20. *Dallas Morning News*, December 26, 1887; *Wichita Daily Eagle*, December 27 and 28, 1887; *Clarksville Standard*, January 6, 1888.
21. Frederick Wilkins, *The Law Comes to Texas* (Austin, TX: State House Press, 1999), 278.
22. Mike Cox, *The Texas Rangers: Wearing the Cinco Peso* (New York: Tom Doherty Associates,), 330.
23. L. C. Alexander to Governor L. S. Ross, January 3, 1888, AGC, TSA. Alexander was part of the law firm of Alexander, [John G.] Winter & [L. R.] Dickinson based in Waco, Texas.
24. Van Hall and J. M. Waller to Governor L. S. Ross, January 13, 1888; George Clark to Governor L. S. Ross, January 18, 1888, AGC, TSA. George Clark was a partner in Clark and [Thomas L.] Dyer Attorneys at Law in Waco.
25. *Brenham Banner*, January 15, 1888.
26. *Galveston News*, January 13, 1888.
27. *Fort Worth Daily Gazette*, January 31, 1888. The article also appeared in both the *San Antonio Daily Express* and the *Denver Rocky Mountain News* on January 31, 1888.
28. William C. Daugherty was born to William Daugherty and Matilda Stanley on March 12, 1842, in Van Buren County, Arkansas. Daugherty served as sheriff from 1882 through 1890. He died on August 3, 1927, in Culberson County, Texas.
29. *Austin Daily Statesman*, February 14, 1888; *Austin Weekly Statesman*, February 16, 1888; *Galveston Daily News*, February 14, 1888.
30. *Galveston Daily News*, February 14, 1888.

31. *Daily Globe-Democrat*, February 14, 1888; *San Antonio Daily Express* February 14, 1888; *San Antonio Daily Times* February 17, 1888.
32. *San Antonio Daily Express* February 14, 1888.
33. *Fort Worth Daily Gazette*, February 14, 1888.
34. *Dallas Morning News*, February 14, 1888; *Galveston Daily News*, February 14, 1888.
35. *Dallas Morning News*, February 14, 1888.
36. Mallie White, "The True Story of Brack Cornett's Death," courtesy Roger Cornett.
37. M. L. Cornett to the author, September 8, 2018.
38. *Dallas Morning News*, February 15, 1888; *Galveston Daily News*, February 14, 1888.
39. M. L. Cornett to the author, September 8, 1888.
40. *Galveston Daily News*, February 14, 1888.
41. *San Francisco Bulletin*, February 16, 1888.
42. *Austin Weekly Statesman*, February 16, 1888.
43. *Fort Worth Daily Gazette*, February 14, 1888.
44. *The Palatka Daily News*, Palatka, Florida, February 15, 1888
45. *Dallas Morning News*, February 15, 1888.
46. *Austin Weekly Statesman*, February 16, 1888.
47. *Fort Worth Daily Gazette*, February 16, 1888.
48. Ibid.
49. *New York Times*, February 17, 1888.
50. Ibid.
51. 1860 Lampasas County, Texas Census; 1870 Williamson County, Texas Census; 1880 Williamson County, Texas Census; Williamson County, Texas Marriage Records, Book 5.
52. Bell County, Texas District Court Records, Cause 2108.
53. The Saga of "Kep" Queen related by Wendel Lawler as recalled by family members, transcribed by Reba Lawler. Copy in author's files.
54. John M. Oskison, "Young Henry and the Old Man," *McClure's Magazine* 31 (May–October, 1908), 237–239. The story deals with the capture of Kep Queen and his gang in 1884. No independent substantiation has been located to date.
55. Western District Federal Court Records, Fort Smith, Arkansas, Jacket Number 158.
56. Price, 61.
57. 1880 Bell County, Texas Census.
58. Bell County, Texas, District Court Records Cause 1947.
59. Huntsville Penitentiary Convict Record Ledger, Bill Jones, Number 2889.
60. Rusk Penitentiary Convict Record Ledger, Bill Jones, Number 735.
61. Western District Federal Court Records, Fort Smith, Arkansas, Jacket Number 158.
62. *Fort Worth Daily Gazette*, February 16, 1888; *Brenham Weekly Banner*, February 23, 1888.
63. James Knox Schmick was the second-longest-serving sheriff in Eastland County. A son of Casper and Mary Mansker Schmick, he was born in Randolph County, Arkansas, on December 5, 1844. In 1868 he moved to

Eastland County. He was elected sheriff in 1882 and served until 1892. Schmick died of influenza on February 20, 1934, in Eastland County.

64. *Fort Worth Daily Gazette*, February 17, 1888.
65. Ibid.
66. Ibid.
67. *Fort Worth Daily Gazette*, February 18, 1888.
68. Henry Scott Sisk was a native of Kentucky, born in Hopkins County on March 27, 1840, to Daniel Harrison Sisk and his wife Louisa Reynolds. By 1850 the Sisk family had relocated to Parker County where Daniel was listed as "Assessor & Collector." Henry, then twenty, was listed as a trader. The following year Sisk enlisted in the 5th Texas Cavalry and served through the end of the war. In 1868 he married Sarah A. K. Virginia "Jennie" Bounds. Henry returned to farming until 1886 when he was elected sheriff of Parker County. Sisk would serve for three terms of office until 1892 and later became involved with the prison system. Sisk moved to Houston in before 1903. His wife died in 1912. Sisk died of pneumonia in the Confederate Home in Austin on November 19, 1930. He is buried in Houston. 1850 Hopkins County, Kentucky Census; 1860, 1870, 1880, 1900 Parker County, Texas Census; Confederate Pension File 38920; Tise, 406; 1903 Houston City Directory; 1910 Harris County, Texas Census; Harris County, Texas, Death Certificate 55610.
69. Price, 63.
70. *Fort Worth Daily Gazette*, February 18, 1888.
71. Mike Buck to the author, February 9, 2016.
72. Author's interview with Terry Wooten, November 20, 2016.
73. *Fort Worth Daily Gazette*, February 24, 1888; *Austin Weekly Statesman*, March 1, 1888.
74. Alexander, *Ira Aten*, 142.

Notes to Chapter 10

1. *Fort Worth Daily Gazette*, February 17, 1888.
2. Ibid.
3. *Dallas Morning News*, February 22, 1888; *Press and Daily Dakotaian*, Yankton, Dakota Territory (S. D.), February 24, 1888.
4. *Magdalena Mountain Mail*, Magdalena, New Mexico, April 5, 1888.
5. *Galveston Daily News*, April 7, 1888.
6. *Magdalena Mountain Mail*, Magdalena, New Mexico, April 5, 1888.
7. *San Antonio Daily Light*, April 5, 1888.
8. *Dallas Morning News*, April 6, 1888.
9. *Austin Weekly Statesman*, April 12, 1888; *Dallas Morning News*, April 6, 1888.
10. Guertin, 401, photographic copy of an unknown newspaper.
11. Wells Fargo Circular, July 2, 1887, AGC, TSA.
12. *Magdalena Mountain Mail*, April 5, 1888.
13. *Fort Worth Daily Gazette*, February 18, 1888. T. K. Furlong was the chief detective of the Missouri Pacific Railway.
14. *Fort Worth Daily Gazette*, February 21, 1888.
15. *Fort Worth Daily Gazette*, February 24, 1888.

16. Price, 45.
17. Sheriff A. J. Lewis of Milam Co. to W. H. King, March 20, 1888, AGC, TSA.
18. W. H. King to Sheriff A. J. Lewis, March 22, 1888, Letters sent October 24, 1887–May 24, 1888, AGC, TSA.
19. *San Antonio Daily Express*, March 22, 1888.
20. Hussey Manuscript, courtesy Gowen Research Foundation, Lubbock, Texas.
21. James M. Ferris to W. H. King, March 30, 1888, AGC, TSA.
22. *Galveston Daily News*, July 19, 1892.
23. Brice Miller Smart was born February 13, 1845, in Wright County, Missouri, to John and Mary Bybee Smart. He married Ailcy, possibly a phonetic spelling of Elise, Jane Barber on March 21, 1871. Ailcy was born May 8, 1853, in Caldwell County Texas. Both of the Smarts died in Oklahoma, Brice on July 29, 1932, and Ailcy on December 11, 1928.
24. *Galveston Daily News*, April 27, 1888; *Plain Dealer*, Cleveland, Ohio, April 26 and 28, 1888; *Fort Worth Daily Gazette*, April 27, 1888.
25. *Austin Weekly Statesman*, October 4, 1888.
26. Price, 72.
27. Langford, *Briggs*, 207.
28. *Austin Weekly Statesman*, October 4, 1888.
29. Price, 73.
30. Mike Buck to the author, September 30, 2016.
31. *Galveston Daily News*, May 30, 1888.
32. *Waco Evening News*, September 28, 1888.
33. *Austin Weekly Statesman*, October 4, 1888; *Waco Evening News*, September 28, 1888; *Times-Picayune*, September 28, 1888.
34. Western District Federal Court Records, Fort Smith, Arkansas, Jacket 282, April 28, 1888.
35. Price, 72, 73.
36. *Dallas Morning News*, May 10, 1888.
37. *Galveston Daily News*, June 17, 1888.
38. *Indian Chieftain*, Vinita, I. T., June 21, 1888; *Galveston Daily News*, June 17, 1888; *Fort Worth Daily Gazette*, June 17, 1888.
39. *Indian Chieftain*, Vinita, I. T., June 21, 1888.
40. *Galveston Daily News*, June 17, 1888.
41. Western District Federal Court Records, Fort Smith, Arkansas, Court Declaration, testimony of J. H. Holloman. Hereafter cited as Court Declaration.
42. *Galveston Daily News*, June 17, 1888.
43. *Austin Weekly Statesman*, June 21, 1888; *The Daily Journal*, Freeport, Illinois, June 17, 1888.
44. Court Declaration: Testimony of Wallace H. Rasback. Rasback was the youngest child of John M. Rasback and his wife Rosanna DeLong and was born in New York on June 18, 1843. Rasback's mother died in 1849 and his father in 1854 after which he was raised by his older brother William. He served in the Civil War as a private in Company L of the 8th Illinois Cavalry. Rasback was married to Lena Keller. He died on November 13,

1893. 1850 Herkimer County, New York Census; 1860 Herkimer County, Illinois Census; 1865 Herkimer County, New York State Census.

45. Ibid.
46. *Galveston Daily News,* June 17, 1888.
47. *Austin Weekly Statesman,* June 21, 1888.
48. Court Declaration: Testimony of Wallace H. Rasback.
49. *Galveston Daily News,* June 17, 1888.
50. Ibid. Testimony of Willis P. Colton. While newspapers of the day called him Charles Colton and William Collon, he was born Willis Payson Colton on June 2, 1855, to Lewis James and Mary Ann Phelps Colton in Priceton, Illinois. Colton married Lena Electra Brown on December 24, 1883, in Dupage, Illinois. Colton died on January 26, 1926, at Kansas City, Kansas. At the time of the holdup he was living in Fort Scott, Kansas.
51. Ibid. Testimony of Wallace H. Rasback.
52. Ibid. Testimony of Willis P. Colton.
53. Ibid.
54. *Galveston Daily News,* June 17, 1888.
55. *Galveston Daily News,* June 17, 1888; *Fort Worth Daily Gazette,* June 17, 1888. The express agent's name is given variously as A. B. Codding and Bart Coddington. In court he gave his name as A. B. Codding.
56. Court Declaration: Testimony of A. B. Codding.
57. *Fort Worth Daily Gazette,* June 17, 1888. Nelson Covert Blanchard was a real estate broker born in Rock County, Wisconsin, on August 15, 1855, to William and Mary J. Blanchard. At the time of the holdup Blanchard was married to Louvinia Nellis and had three daughters: Irene, Belle, and Lulu. Blanchard later moved to California where he died on May 17, 1941, at Fresno. 1860 and 1870 Rock County, Wisconsin, Census; 1885 and 1895 Palo Alto, Iowa State Census.
58. *Austin Weekly Statesman,* June 21, 1888. Clark has not been identified with certainty.
59. Court Declaration: Testimony of J. T. Holloman.
60. *Galveston Daily News,* June 17, 1888.
61. Henry Ryan has eluded positive identification, but there was a Henry Dettmer Ryan born January 27, 1878, to John Nevins Ryan and his wife Ella Weston. In later years Ryan was an engineer for the Southern Pacific. He died in Oregon on January 31, 1949. The identification remains tentative. 1880 Pottawatomie, Kansas Census;
62. Court Declaration: Testimony of Harry Ryan. This is at variance with Sterling Clark's statement that Ryan and Ben Tarver were ordered back into the railroad car before the outlaw fired at them.
63. *Indian Chieftain,* June 21, 1888.
64. *Galveston Daily News,* June 17, 1888.
65. *The Daily Journal,* Freeport, Illinois, June 18, 1888.
66. *Galveston Daily News,* June 17, 1888.
67. Court Declaration: Testimony of Harry Ryan.
68. Benjamin Castleman Tarver was the son of Albert George Tarver and his wife Perscilla Elizabeth Sinclair and was born around 1856 in Mississippi. 1870 Leake County, Mississippi Census; 1880 Falls County, Texas Census.

69. William Perry White was born in February 1851 to Elija and Juliet E. Jones White. He died on August 1, 1923, in McLennan County, Texas.
70. Court Declaration: Testimony of William Perry White.
71. *Galveston Daily News,* June 17, 1888.
72. See Note 57 in this chapter for identification of Blanchard.
73. *Fort Worth Daily Gazette,* June 17, 1888.
74. Ibid.
75. *Austin Weekly Statesman,* June 21, 1888.
76. *Galveston Daily News,* June 17, 1888.
77. *Indian Chieftain,* Vinita, I. T., June 21, 1888; *Galveston Daily News,* June 17, 1888; *Fort Worth Daily Gazette,* June 17, 1888.
78. *Indian Chieftain,* June 21, 1888.
79. *Galveston Daily News,* June 17, 1888.
80. *Austin Weekly Statesman,* June 21, 1888.

Notes to Chapter 11

1. *Galveston Daily News,* June 17, 1888.
2. *Fort Worth Daily Gazette,* June 20, 1888; *Our Brother in Red,* Muskogee, Oklahoma, June 23, 1888; *Indian Journal,* Eufala, Oklahoma, June 19, 1888; Glenn Shirley, *Heck Thomas: Frontier Marshal* (Norman: University of Oklahoma Press, 1981), 112.
3. In contrast to accounts of the atrocity at Flatonia, newspaper coverage in other states was brief. The *Newark Daily Advocate,* Newark, Ohio, and *Hamilton Daily Democrat,* Hamilton, Ohio, both dated June 18, 1888, carried two-line accounts of the affair as did the *Jackson Journal* in Maquoketa, Iowa, on July 28. The *Wellsboro Agitator* in Wellsboro, Pennsylvania, devoted three lines to the robbery on July 3, 1888.
4. William Robert Dawson was born August 31, 1866, in Tarrant County, Texas, to Francis Marion and Julia Ann Sutter Dawson. Dawson was cleared on the charges and later married Frances Lavinia Foreman. In later years he ranched near Talala, Oklahoma, and had interests in oil leases. Dawson died in December 1950.
5. Oscar Coulter was wanted in Arkansas for murder in addition to whiskey peddling charges against him in federal court. *Our Brother in Red,* August 31, 1889.
6. The Dustins have not been identified with certainty.
7. Leif Ernst, "The Kelp Queen Gang," *Oklahoma Outlaws Lawmen History Association* 9, no. 1 (Spring 2012): 4.
8. Western District Federal Court Records, Fort Smith, Arkansas, Jacket 158.
9. For Heck Thomas see Glenn Shirley, *Heck Thomas: Frontier Marshal* (Norman: University of Oklahoma Press, 1981). The biography, originally published in 1962, is now sadly outdated.
10. Western District Federal Court Records, Fort Smith, Arkansas, Jacket 158.
11. *Our Brother in Red,* August 31, 1889.
12. *Austin Weekly Statesman,* July 5, 1888; *San Antonio Daily Express,* July 5, 1888.

13. For Frank Jones see Bob Alexander, *Six-Shooters and Shifting Sands: The Wild West Life of Texas Ranger Captain Frank Jones* (Denton: University of North Texas Press, 2015).
14. Frank Jones to W. H. King, July 31, 1888, AGC, TSA.
15. *Galveston Daily News*, July 10, 1892.
16. Price, 85.
17. Wester District Federal Court Records, Jacket 158.
18. *Fort Worth Daily Gazette*, February 18, 1888.
19. Duval West was born November 13, 1861, in Austin, Texas, to Florence Duval and her husband Charles Shannon West. During the winter of 1879–1880 he was part of an expedition to the Chinati Mountains of the Big Bend. He later became a deputy U. S. Marshal and afterwards studied law. As assistant U. S. Attorney he presented the case against O. Henry (William Sydney Porter) for embezzlement.
20. J. S. McNeil has not been identified with certainty.
21. William H. Van Riper was born in New York in 1847 to Garry and Matilda J. Marshall Van Riper. By 1860 the family had moved to Bexar County, Texas. Van Riper served as a deputy sheriff for a number of years before becoming a Deputy U. S. Marshal. Van Riper eventually left the marshal service due to an increasing interest in spiritualism. The 1900 Census lists him as a magnetic healer. He died of a stroke in San Bernardino, California, on May 9, 1924. 1860 Bexar County, Texas census; 1900 Bexar County, Texas Census; San Diego Union May 11, 1924.
22. J. J. Kelly has not been identified with certainty.
23. New York-born Daniel H. Toomey was the son of Daniel H. and Ann Lenihan Toomey and was born November 17, 1848. He died in San Antonio of Bright's disease on October 18, 1912.
24. *Waco Evening News*, September 24, 1888.
25. The fireman may have been John Glaisor, born around 1859 in Louisiana. The 1880 Harris County, Texas Census lists him as a brakeman on the railroad. The identification is far from certain.
26. Ibid. Elmer Ellsworth Shackford was born September 9, 1862, in Massachusetts and died June 14, 1938. He was buried in Crown Point Cemetary, Kokomo, Indiana.
27. *Luling Signal*, September 27, 1888; *Waco Evening News*, September 24, 1888.
28. *Gonzales Inquirer*, September 27, 1888.
29. Henry Jacob Labatt was born January 13, 1832, in New Orleans. In his day he was a well-known attorney. He was killed during the hurricane that destroyed Galveston on September 8, 1900.
30. *Galveston Daily News*, September 24, 1888.
31. *San Antonio Daily Times*, September 24, 1888.
32. *Galveston Daily News*, September 24, 1888.
33. *Gonzales Inquirer*, September 27, 1888.
34. *San Antonio Daily Times*, September 24, 1888.
35. *Galveston Daily News*, September 24, 1888.
36. *Waco Evening News*, September 24, 1888; *Luling Signal*, September 27, 1888; *Galveston Daily News*, September 24, 1888.
37. Price, 88.

38. *Springfield Republican*, Springfield, Massachusetts, September 23, 1888.
39. *Galveston Daily News*, September 24, 1888.
40. *Waco Evening News*, September 24, 1888; *Luling Signal*, September 27, 1888; *Galveston Daily News*, September 24, 1888.
41. Burton, "Man Hunt," 28.
42. *Galveston Daily News*, September 24, 1888; *Salt Lake Herald*, September 25, 1888.
43. *San Antonio Daily Times*, September 24, 1888.
44. *Galveston Daily News*, September 24, 1888.
45. *San Antonio Daily Express*, September 25, 1888; *Austin Weekly Statesman*, September 27, 1888. Addison D. Kilgore, son of James Thomas Kilgore and Caroline Elizabeth Bookwalter, served as sheriff of DeWitt County from 1886 through 1888. He was born in DeWitt County on March 14, 1884. Kilgore died in San Antonio on August 13, 1929, of stomach cancer.
46. *San Antonio Daily Express*, September 26, 1888; *Galveston Daily News*, September 27, 1888; *Dallas Morning News*, September 27, 1888.
47. *Dallas Morning News*, September 27, 1888.
48 *San Antonio Express*, September 27, 1888.
49. *San Antonio Daily Express*, September 26, 1888.
50. *Muskegon Chronicle*, Muskegon, Michigan, September 26, 1888; *San Antonio Daily Express*, September 26, 1888; *Laredo Times*, September 27, 1888; *Logansport* (Indiana) *Pharos*, September 27, 1888; *Waukesha Freeman*, Waukesha, Wisconsin, October 4, 1888.
51. *New York Herald-Tribune*, September 27, 1888.
52. *San Antonio Daily Express*, September 27, 1888; *Dallas Morning News*, September 27, 1888; *Galveston Daily News*, September 27, 1888.
53. *San Antonio Daily Express*, September 27, 1888.
54. Hussey Manuscript: Statement attributed to Willie Mae "Billie" Smith Price regarding the events of her grandfather's death on September 25, 1888:
55. *Dallas Morning News*, September 27, 1888; *Galveston Daily News*, September 27, 1888.
56. Ibid. William Harrell married Leah Burkett in Atascosa County.
57. *San Antonio Daily Light*, September 28, 1888.
58. Hussey Manuscript.
59. *Austin Weekly Statesman*, October 4, 1888; *Philadelphia Inquirer*, October 1, 1888; *San Antonio Daily Express*, September 27, 1888; *Dallas Morning News*, September 27, 1888.
60. *Dallas Morning News*, September 27, 1888; San Antonio Express, September 27, 1888; *Galveston Daily News*, September 27, 1888.
61. *Dallas Morning News*, September 27, 1888.
62. *Dallas Morning News*, September 27, 1888; *San Antonio Express*, September 27, 1888; *Galveston Daily News*, September 27, 1888.
63. *Dallas Morning News*, September 27, 1888.
64. *Austin Weekly Statesman*, October 4, 1888; *San Antonio Daily Light*, September 28, 1888; *Galveston Daily News*, September 28, 1888.
65. *Austin Weekly Statesman*, October 4, 1888.
66. *San Antonio Daily Light*, September 28, 1888; *Galveston Daily News*, September 28, 1888.

67. *San Antonio Daily Light*, September 28, 1888.
68. *Dallas Morning News*, October 2, 1888.
69 *San Antonio Express*, September 27, 1888.
70. *Galveston Daily News*, September 28, 1888.
71. *Galveston Daily News*, September 27, 1888.
72. *Dallas Morning News*, September 27, 1888.
73. Robert T. Rogers was born in Leon County to J. Tipton Rogers and his wife Nancy Jane Dotson in August 1862. Following her husband's death, Nancy married Francis Marion "Frank" Bell. Rogers grew up in Leon County. 1870 and 1880 Leon County, Texas Census.
74. *Galveston Daily News*, October 5, 1888. Bell was the son of Joseph Jefferson and Nancy Childress Bell. He was later sent to the penitentiary for the killing.
75. W. C. Dougherty was first elected sheriff of Frio County on November 7, 1882. He served until November 4, 1890. Prior to his election, the 1880 census indicates that he was a stock raiser and was born around 1832 in Arkansas. Tise, 199; 1880 Frio County, Texas Census.
76. Lewis served four years as Bexar County sheriff, being elected on November 2, 1886, and serving until November 6, 1890. Tise, 43.
77. There is an error in the newspaper account concerning Everett. The sheriff of Milam County during 1888 was A. J. Lewis. Tise, 374.
78. *New York Herald*, September 30, 1888; *Austin Weekly Statesman*, October 4, 1888; *The Ledger*, Warren, Pennsylvania, October 5, 1888.
79. Federal District Court Records, Cause 42.
80. Federal District Court Records, Cause 262.
81. Email from Margaret Lindly dated May 16, 2003. Courtesy Cloud family.
82. Tom Cloud to the author, February 4, 2017.
83. Ibid.
84. *Waco Evening News*, November 6, 1888; *Fort Worth Weekly Gazette*, November 9, 1888.
85. The 1860 Coryell County, Texas census indicates that Noah Neff was a 34-year-old farmer and his wife Isabella, 28, a teacher. Both were born in Virginia. Samuel was their third child. The Neff family had a combined personal and real estate value of $8,900. The family's fortunes were not diminished significantly by the Civil War. In 1870 they still had substantial holdings to the amount of $6000. Samuel Neff was still living with his family in 1880 when he was noted as "works on farm." 1860 Coryell County, Texas Census; 1870 Coryell County, Texas Census; 1880 Coryell County, Texas Census.
86. Lampasas County, Texas Marriage Records.
87. *Indian Chieftain*, Vinita, I. T., November 22, 1888.
88. William Edward "Ed" Sanders was a prominent lawman and public figure born April 2, 1861, to Eli and Elmira Eldridge Sanders. Sanders was educated in the Cherokee Public Schools. He was first elected sheriff in the Cherokee Nation in 1885. Over the years he served in a number of positions. Sanders died on October 14, 1939.

89. *Indian Chieftain*, November 22, 1888; *New York Times*, November 18, 1888; *Bangor Daily Whig & Courier*, Bangor, Maine, November 19, 1888; *Fort Smith Elevator*, Fort Smith, Arkansas, November 23, 1888.
90. *Fort Smith Elevator*, Fort Smith, Arkansas, November 23, 1888; *Indian Chieftain*, November 22, 1888.
91. *Fort Smith Elevator*, Fort Smith, Arkansas, November 23, 1888; *Indian Chieftain*, November 22, 1888.
92. Ibid.
93. *Indian Chieftain*, November 22, 1888.
94. Ibid., November 29, 1888.
95. Those interested in Belle Starr should see Glenn Shirley, *Belle Starr and Her Times: The Literature, the Facts and the Legends* (Norman: University of Oklahoma Press, 1982); Carl R. Green and William R. Sanford, *Belle Starr* (New York: Enslow Publishers, Inc., 2009).
96. *Fort Worth Daily Gazette*, December 12, 1888. The full text of Stephens's letter is included as Appendix 4.

Notes to Chapter 12

1. *San Antonio Daily Express*, December 1 and 2, 1888.
2. *Dallas Morning News*, December 1, 1888.
3. *San Antonio Daily Express*, December 1, 1888.
4. Ibid., December 4 and December 5, 1888; *San Antonio Daily Light*, December 5, 1888; *Dallas Morning News*, December 6, 1888.
5. *San Antonio Daily Light*, December 5, 1888; *San Antonio Daily Express*, December 6, 1888; *Dallas Morning News*, December 6, 1888.
6. *Dallas Morning News*, December 6, 1888.
7. Ohio Penitentiary Register of Prisoners, courtesy Ohio State Archives, Columbus, Ohio, Volume 15: Convict 21117, Samuel H. Neff.
8. *Dallas Morning News*, December 6, 1888.
9. *Fort Smith Elevator*, December 14, 1888.
10. Western District Court Records, Cause 170.
11. Western District Court Records, Cause 42.
12. *Austin Weekly Statesman*, February 21, 1889; *Bay City Times*, Bay City, Michigan, February 21, 1889; *The Salem Daily News*, Salem, Ohio, February 22, 1889; *The News*, Frederick, Maryland, February 22, 1889; *Pittsburg Gazette*, Pittsburgh, Pennsylvania, February 22, 1889; *The Athens Messenger*, Athens, Ohio, February 28, 1889; *Jackson Citizen Patriot*; Jackson, Michigan, February 22, 1889; *Lima Daily Democratic Times*, Lima, Ohio, February 23, 1889.
13. *Austin Weekly Statesman*, February 21, 1889.
14. *Austin Weekly Statesman*, May 16, 1889.
15. Western District Court Records, Probate; *Fort Smith Elevator*, September 27, 1889.
15. Gary Tharp to the author, October 9, 2017.
16. *The Canadian Free Press*, Canadian, Texas, August 30, 1889.
17. Western District Court Records, Cause 158, National Archives.
18. *Indian Chieftain*, April 4, 1889.

19. *Our Brother in Red,* December 14, 1889; *The Telephone,* Tahlequah, I. T., December 19, 1889.
20. *Arkansas Gazette,* Little Rock, Arkansas, September 5, 1889.
21. *Indian Chieftain,* September 12, 1889.
22. *Dallas Morning News,* September 26, 1889.
23. *Dallas Morning News,* September 27, 1889.
24. *Galveston Daily News,* December 8, 1889; *The Indian Chieftain,* December 12, 1889; *The Telephone,* December 19, 1889.
25. *The Telephone,* December 19, 1889.
26. *Fort Smith Elevator,* December 20, 1889.
27. Ernst, 7.
28. *Indian Chieftain,* November 28, 1889.
29. Ibid.
30. *Galveston Daily News,* December 8, 1889; *Dallas Daily Times-Herald,* December 9, 1889; *San Antonio Light,* December 9, 1889; *Logansport Pharos,* December 10, 1889; *Logansport Reporter,* December 10, 1889; *The Fort Smith Elevator,* December 13, 1889; *The Saturday Herald,* Decatur, Illinois, December 14, 1889; *Our Brother in Red,* December 14, 1889.
31. *Indian Chieftain,* December 12, 1889.
32. *Newark Daily Advocate,* Newark, Ohio, April 8, 1897.
33. Guertin, 395.
34. *Anaconda Standard,* Anaconda, Montana, July 7, 1892.
35. *Galveston Daily News,* July 9, 1892.
36. *San Antonio Daily Light,* July 9, 1892.
37. *Anaconda Standard,* July 7, 1892.
38. Ibid.
39. *Red Lodge Picket,* Red Lodge, Montana, July 16, 1892.
40. *Livingston Enterprise,* Livingston, Montana, July 16, 1892.
41. *The Weekly Tribune,* Great Falls, Montana, July 16, 1892.
42. *Livingston Enterprise,* Livingston, Montana, July 16, 1892; *The Weekly Tribune,* July 16, 1892.
43. *Galveston Daily News,* July 10, 1892.
44. See Appendix 5.
45. *San Antonio Daily Light,* July 23, 1892; *Galveston Daily News,* August 21, 1892.
46. *New York Times,* February 23, 1893.
47. Medina County, Texas, death certificate 22114.
48. *The Telephone,* Tahlequah, I. T., December 19, 1889.
49. William Shakespeare, *Julius Caesar,* Act 3, Scene 2.
50. Bernard "Barney" Connelly was born around 1849 to Henry and Sarah Conley in Greene County, Pennsylvania. By 1877 he was living in Benton County, Arkansas, where he married Mattie E. Powell. The marriage produced one child: Ada A., born around 1879. 1850 Greene County, Pennsylvania Census; Benton County, Arkansas Marriage Records, 1880 Benton County, Arkansas Census.
51. *Cherokee Telephone,* Tahlequah, I. T. August 27, 1891, *Oklahoma Democrat,* El Reno, I. T., August 29, 1891.
52. Busby was born in Wayne County, Kentucky, around 1833 to Steven Sheppard Busby and his wife Mary Polly McIlwaint. By 1858 he had moved

to Illinois. He served for the Union during the Civil War. 1870 Stoddard County, Missouri Census; *Arkansas Gazette*, Little Rock Arkansas April 28, 1892.

53. *Brenham Daily Banner*, September 13, 1892; *Galveston Daily News*, September 13, 1892.
54. *Anaconda Standard*, Anaconda, Montana, February 20, 1898.
55. Ibid.
56. Adam Joseph Barthelow born to Jefferson and Sarah Josefek Barthelow on January 3, 1852.
57. *The Daily Herald*, Brownsville, Texas, August 24, 1896.
58. *Dallas Morning News*, January 22, 1897.
59. *San Antonio Express*, September 3, 1915.
60. *Springfield Republican*, Springfield, Massachusetts, November 19, 1897.
61. *El Paso Daily Times*, December 4, 1897
62. *Brenham Daily Banner*, December 10, 1897; *Dallas Morning News*, December 18, 1897; *Abilene Reporter*, Abilene, Texas, December 21, 1897.
63. *Brenham Daily Banner*, January 12, 1898.
64. *Houston Daily Post*, June 7, 1898; *Shiner Gazette*, Shiner, Texas, June 18, 1898.
65. Bexar County, Texas Death Certificate 5370.
66. *Dallas Morning News*, March 27, 1891.
67. *Caldwell News-Courier*, Caldwell, Texas, April 29, 1898.
68. *Dallas Morning News*, October 9, 1901; *Rockdale Messenger*, Rockdale, Texas, October 10, 1901; *Houston Daily Post*, October 9, 1901.
69. *Laredo Weekly Times*, April 2, 1911.
70. *Beaumont Enterprise*, Beaumont, Texas, April 1, 1911; *Laredo Weekly Times*, April 2, 1911.
71. *Laredo Weekly Times*, April 2, 1911.
72. *San Diego Union*, May 11, 1924.
73. Bexar County, Texas Death Certificate 21131; *Dallas Morning News*, May 15, 1949.
74. *Omaha Daily Bee*, September 7, 1899.
75. *Fort Worth Daily Gazette*, September 11, 1890.

Select Bibliography of Sources Consulted

Books

—. *Historical Caldwell County: Where Roots Intertwine*. Caldwell County, Texas: The Mark Withers Trail Drive Museum, 1984. Entry by Lois Masur.

—. *Biennial Reports of the Directors and Superintendent of the Texas State Penitentiary at Huntsville, Texas with the Report of the Prison Physician, Commencing December 1, A. D. 1878, and terminating October 31, A. D. 1880*. Galveston, Texas: The News Book and Job Office, 1881.

—. Record of Southwest Texas. Chicago: Goodspeed Brothers, Publishers, 1894.

Alexander, Bob. *Lawmen, Outlaws, and S. O. Bs: Gunfighters of the Old Southwest*. Silver City, NM: High Lonesome Books, 2004.

———. *Rawhide Ranger, Ira Aten*. Denton: University of North Texas Press, 2011.

———. *Lynch Ropes and Long Shots: The Story of an Old West Train Robbery*. Silver City, NM: High Lonesome Books, 2006.

———. *Six-Shooters and Shifting Sands: The Wild West Life of Texas Ranger Captain Frank Jones*. Denton: University of North Texas Press, 2015.

———. *Winchester Warriors: Texas Rangers of Company D, 1874 – 1901*. Denton: University of North Texas Press, 2009.

Boley, Edwin J. *The Masked Halters*. Seymour, IN: Graessle Mercer Company, 1977.

Caldwell, Clifford R., and Ron DeLord. *Eternity at The End of a Rope: Executions, Lynchings and Vigilante Justice in Texas 1819–1923*. Santa Fe, NM: Sunstone Press, 2015.

———. *Texas Lawmen 1835–1899: The Good and the Bad*. Charleston, SC: The History Press, 2011.

Chesley, Hervey E. *Adventuring with the Old-Timers: Trails Travelled—Tales Told*. Midland, TX: Nita Stewart Haley Memorial Library, 1979.

Cox, Mike. *The Texas Rangers: Wearing the Cinco Peso*. New York: A Tom Doherty Associates Book, 2008.

Daniell, L. E. *Personnel of the Texas State Government, with Sketches of Distinguished Texans, Embracing The Executive and Staff, Heads of the Departments, United States Senators and Representatives, Members of the Twenty-First Legislature.* Austin: Smith, Hicks & Jones, State Printers, 1889.

Daywood, Victoria Dunnahoo, and Peggy White Engledow. *The Bad Boys of Caldwell County, Texas, Book One, Murders in the 1800s*. Luling, TX: Privately published, printed by Ericson Books, 2011.

———. *The Bad Boys of Caldwell County, Texas, Book Two, Mayhem and Mishaps in the 1800s*. Luling, TX: Privately published, printed by Ericson Books, 2011.

Genealogical and Historical Society of Caldwell County. *Caldwell County Kin: The First 140 Years*. Wolfe City, TX: Hennington Publishing Co., 2000.

Green, Carl R., and William R. Sanford. *Belle Starr*. New York: Enslow Publishers, Inc., 2009.

Guertin, Iris Rose. *Navidad Country*, vol. 1. Sugarland, TX: Privately Published, 2009.

Johnson, David. *The Horrell Wars: Feuding in Texas and New Mexico*. Denton: University of North Texas Press, 2014.

———. *The Mason County "Hoo Doo" War, 1874–1902*. Denton: University of North Texas Press, 2006.

Kearney, James C., Bill Stein, and James Smallwood. *No Hope for Heaven, No Fear of Hell*. Denton: University of North Texas Press, 2016.

Langford, Ernest, *Briggs: Brief Annals of the Times and People*. Denton, TX: Privately published, 1963.

Miller, Rick. *Rube Burrow, Desperado.* Bloomington, IN: IUniverse LLC, 2014.

———. *Sam Bass and Gang*. Austin, TX: State House Press, 1999.

———. *The Train Robbing Bunch*. College Station, TX: Creative Publishing Company, 1983.

Olmsted, Charles L. *The Good, The Bad, The Butlers: Story of a Texas Pioneer Family*. Bloomington, IN: IUniverse, 2015.

Parsons, Chuck, and Donaly E. Brice. *Texas Ranger N. O. Reynolds: The Intrepid*. Denton: University of North Texas Press, 2014.

Parsons, Chuck and Pat Parsons. *A History of the Prairie Lea Baptist Church*. Gonzales, TX: Reese's Print Shop, 2017.

Parsons, Chuck. *The Sutton-Taylor Feud: The Deadliest Blood Feud in Texas*. Denton: University of North Texas Press, 2009.

Price, Bill Smith. *Bill Whitley: Outlaw*. Austin, TX: Nortex Press, 1995.

Shirley, Glenn. *Belle Starr and Her Times: The Literature, the Facts and the Legends*. Norman: University of Oklahoma Press, 1982.

———. *Heck Thomas: Frontier Marshal*. Norman: University of Oklahoma Press, 1981.

Spellman, Paul N. *Captain John H. Rogers, Texas Ranger.* Denton: University of North Texas Press, 2003.

Stephens, Robert W. *Captain George H. Schmitt: Texas Ranger*. No place, 2006.

Tise, Sammy. *Texas County Sheriffs*. Albuquerque, NM: Oakwood Printing, 1989.

Wilkins, Frederick. *The Law Comes to Texas*. Austin, TX: State House Press, 1999.

Wyatt, Tula Townsend. *The Seven Townsend Brothers of Texas, 1826–1838: A Genealogy*. Austin, TX: Privately published, Austex Duplications, 1974.

Articles

Burton, Jeff. "'A Great Man Hunt' – Correspondence From 'W. B. S.': Some Scenes of Outlawry and Gunplay in Texas." *The Brand Book Vol. 18 1975 – 1976*. London, England: English Westerner's Society, 1977.

———. "The Most Surprised Man in Texas," *Frontier Times* 47, no. 2 (Feb.– March, 1973).

Condra, Frances R., "A. J. Rife, Early Lytton Springs Settler," *Plum Creek Almanac* 9, no. 1 (Spring 1991): 40 – 44.

Ernst, Leif. "The Kelp Queen Gang." *Oklahoma Outlaws Lawmen History Association* 9, no.1 (Spring 2012): 2–11.

Field, Karla. "Albert Francis Field." *Plum Creek Almanac* 34, no. 2 (Fall 2016): 133–135.

Fitzgerald, Hugh Nugent. "Mild-Mannered Captain Lucy." *Frontier Times* 21, no. 11 (August 1944).

Hardin, Earl Jr. "Sheriffs and Rangers." *Bandera County Historian* 22, no. 3 (Fall 2001): 1–5.

Holden, W. C. "Law and Lawlessness on the Texas Frontier,1875–1890." *Southwestern Historical Quarterly* 44, no. 2 (October 1940): 188–203.

Mayfield, Mrs. G. C. "Interesting Narrative of Capt. W. L. Rudd, Ex-Ranger." Hunter's *Frontier Times* 10, no. 3 (December 1932).

Oskison, John M. "Young Henry and the Old Man." *McClure's Magazine* 31 (May–October, 1908): 237–239.

Perry, John. "Gunfighters and Lawmen." *Wild West*, April 2005, 10, 12, 61.

Whittington, Mary. "The Great Train Robberies of 1885 and 1887." *Plum Creek Almanac* 19, no. 2 (Fall 2001): 140–144.

United States Census

Alabama

Coosa	1850, 1860
Choctaw	1870
Arizona	
Pinal	1880
Arkansas	
Benton	1880
Carroll	1850
Columbia	1860, 1870
Lafayette	1850
Randolph	1880
Searcy	1860

California	
Merced	1880
Illinois	
Jackson	1860
Iowa State Census	
Palo Alto	1885, 1895
Kansas	
Pottawatomie	1880
Kentucky	
Hopkins	1850
Madison County	1850
Louisiana	
Union Parish	1840, 1850
Mississippi	
Leake County	1870
Oktibbeha	1850, 1860
Tippah	1840
Missouri	
Franklin County	1860, 1870
Stoddard	1870
New York	
Herkimer	1865 State Census
Herkimer	1850, 1860
New York	1870, 1880
Ohio	
Hamilton	1880
Scioto County	1860
Pennsylvania	
Greene	1850
Luzerne	1860, 1870
Tennessee	
Davidson	1850, 1910

Texas

Anderson	1880
Bastrop	1860, 1900
Bell	1880
Bexar	1860, 1900, 1920, 1930, 1940
Bowie	1860
Burnet	1860, 1870, 1880, 1900, 1910, 1920, 1930
Comal	1870, 1880, 1900, 1910
Coryell	1860, 1870, 1880
Davis (Cass)	1870
DeWitt	1870, 1880, 1900
Ellis	1880
Falls	1880
Fayette	1850, 1860, 1870, 1880
Frio	1880
Galveston	1880
Goliad	1860, 1870
Guadalupe	1860, 1870, 1880
Harris	1880, 1910
Kendall	1870
Kimble	1880
Lamar	1870
Lampasas	1860
Lavaca	1870
Leon	1870, 1880
Parker	1860, 1870, 1880, 1900
Travis	1860, 1870, 1880, 1900, 1910
Uvalde	1880
Waller	1860, 1870, 1880
Wharton	1870
Texas Mortality Schedule	1870
Gonzales	1860, 1870, 1880

Navarro	1870
Tarrant	1900
Walker	1860, 1880
Williamson	1860, 1870, 1880
Wisconsin	
Rock	1860, 1870
International Census	
England	1861

Legal Sources

1863 New York Draft Registration

1885 San Antonio City Directory

1887 San Francisco, California City Directory

1888 Arizona Voter Registration

Adjutant General Correspondence, Texas State Archives, Austin, Texas

Arizona Department of Health Death Certificates

Convict Record Ledgers, Huntsville Penitentiary, Texas State Archives, Austin, Texas

Convict Record Ledgers, Rusk Penitentiary, Texas State Archives, Austin, Texas

England Births and Christenings, 1538 – 1975, GS Film 1526654

Executive Clemency Records, Texas State Archives, Austin, Texas

Executive Requisition Records, Texas State Archives, Austin, Texas

Governor's Correspondence, Texas State Archives, Austin, Texas

Naturalization Papers: Abraham Lasker

Ohio Death Certificates

Ohio Penitentiary Register of Prisoners

Tennessee Death Certificates

Texas State Board of Health: Death Certificates

Western District Federal Court Records, Fort Smith, Arkansas, National Archives, Fort Smith, Arkansas

County Records

Alabama

Montgomery County Marriage Records

Arizona

Cochise County Marriage Records

Arkansas

Benton County, Arkansas Marriage Records

Pulaski County Marriage Records

Illinois

Jackson County Records

Kentucky

Madison County Record of Marriages

New York

New York County Marriage Licenses

Texas

Bastrop County Marriage Records

Bell County District Court Records

Caldwell County Marriage Records

Coryell County Marriage Records

Ellis County Marriage Records

Fayette County District Court Records

Fayette County Marriage Records

Goliad County District Court Records

Guadalupe County Marriage Records

Hill County Marriage Records

Karnes County District Court Records

Kerr County Tax Records 1884 – 1887

Lampasas County Marriage Records

Williamson County Marriage Records

Unpublished Source Material

1885 San Antonio, Texas, City Directory

1887 San Antonio, Texas, City Directory

1903 Houston City Directory

Barber Family Data, copy courtesy Ken Drope

C. L. Sonnichsen Collection, University of Texas at El Paso

Cloud family genealogy material

Cornett, Lynn, "Descendants of Laban E. Cornett," copy courtesy Lynn Cornett.

Hussey Manuscript, courtesy Gowen Research Foundation, Lubbock, Texas

Personal correspondence: Lynn Cornett, Ken Drope

Saga of "Kep" Queen related by Wendel Lawler as recalled by family members, transcribed by Reba Lawler.

Texas Ranger Muster Rolls, Adjutant General Files, Texas State Archives

Wells Fargo & Co. Ledger

White, Mallie, "The True Story of Brack Cornett's Death."

Newspapers

Arkansas

Arkansas Gazette, Little Rock

Fort Smith Elevator, Fort Smith

Australia

Sydney Mail and New South Wales Advertiser, Sydney, Australia

California

Coronado Mercury, Coronado

Daily Alta California, San Francisco

Los Angeles Daily Herald

Sacramento Daily Record-Union, Sacramento

San Diego Union

San Francisco Bulletin

Colorado

Denver Rocky Mountain News

District of Columbia

Alexandria Gazette and Virginia Advertiser, Alexandria, D. C.

England

Western Gazette, Somerset, England

Florida

The Palatka Daily News, Palatka

Georgia

Atlanta Constitution

Macon Telegraph, Macon

Illinois

Daily Journal, Freeport

Rock Island Daily Argus, Rock Island

Saturday Herald, Decatur

Indiana

Lafayette Daily Journal, Lafayette

Logansport Journal, Logansport

Logansport Pharos, Logansport

Logansport Reporter, Logansport

Iowa

Jackson Journal, Maquoketa

Kansas

Emporia Semi-Weekly News

Iola Register, Iola, Kansas

Phillipsburg Herald, Phillipsburg, Kansas

Western Kansas World, Wakeeney, Kansas

Wichita Eagle, Wichita, Kansas

Kentucky

Daily Evening Bulletin, Maysville

Louisiana

Lake Charles Commercial, Lake Charles

Times-Picayune, New Orleans

Maine

Bangor Daily Whig & Courier, Bangor

Maryland

The News, Frederick

Massachusetts

Boston Journal

Springfield Republican

Michigan

Alma Record, Alma

Bay City Times, Bay City

Jackson Citizen Patriot; Jackson

Muskegon Chronicle, Muskegon

The True Northerner, Paw Paw

Minnesota

Freeborn County Standard, Albert Lea

St. Paul Daily Globe, St. Paul

Missouri

Daily Globe Democrat, St. Louis

Kansas City Star, Kansas City

Saint Louis Republic

St. Louis Globe-Democrat

Montana

Anaconda Standard, Anaconda

Butte Semi-Weekly Miner

Great Falls Tribune, Great Falls

Helena Weekly Herald

Livingston Enterprise, Livingston

Philipsburg Mail, Philipsburg

Red Lodge Picket, Red Lodge

The New North West, Deer Lodge

The Weekly Tribune, Great Falls

Nebraska

Omaha Daily Bee

Columbus Journal, Columbus, Nebraska

Nevada

Reno Evening Gazette

New Hampshire

Weekly Union, Manchester

New Jersey

The Daily Times, Trenton

New Mexico

Magdalena Mountain Mail, Magdalena

The Bullion, Las Cruces

New York

New York Herald

New York Herald-Tribune

New York Sun

New York Times

World, New York, New York

New Zealand

Auckland Star, Auckland, New Zealand

Poverty Bay Herald, Poverty Bay, New Zealand,

Thames Advertiser, Shortland and Grahamstown, Thames, New Zealand,

North Dakota

Bismarck Weekly Tribune

Ohio

Athens Messenger, Athens

Lima Daily Democratic Times, Lima

Newark Daily Advocate, Newark

Salem Daily News, Salem

Plain Dealer, Cleveland

Hamilton Democrat, Hamilton

Oklahoma
Indian Chieftain, Vinita
Indian Journal, Eufala
Indian Sentinel, Muskogee
Oklahoma Democrat, El Reno
Our Brother in Red, Muskogee
The Telephone, Tahlequah
Oregon
Astorian, Astoria, Oregon
Pennsylvania
Indiana Democrat, Indiana
Philadelphia Inquirer
Pittsburg Gazette, Pittsburgh
The Ledger, Warren
Titusville Herald, Titusville
Wellsboro Agitator in Wellsboro
Scotland
Falkirk Herald, Edinburgh, Scotland
South Dakota
Mitchell Capital, Mitchell
Press and Daily Dakotaian, Yankton
Tennessee
Memphis Appeal
Texas
Abilene Reporter, Abilene
Austin Daily Statesman
Austin Weekly Statesman
Ballinger Leader, Ballinger
Bandera Enterprise, Bandera
Beaumont Enterprise, Beaumont
Brenham Banner, Brenham
Burnet Bulletin

Canadian Free Press, Canadian
Clarksville Standard, Clarksville
Cleburne Morning Review
Colorado Citizen, Columbus
Daily Cosmopolitan, Brownsville
Daily Herald, Brownsville
Dallas Herald
Dallas Times-Herald
Dallas Morning News
Dallas Weekly Herald
El Paso Times
Fort Worth Daily Gazette
Fort Worth Weekly Gazette
Galveston Daily News
Gonzales Inquirer, Gonzales
Houston Post
La Grange Journal, La Grange
Laredo Times
Luling Signal, Luling
Mineola Monitor, Mineola
Norton's Daily Union Intelligencer
Palo Pinto Star, Palo Pinto
Rockdale Messenger, Rockdale
San Antonio Daily Times
San Antonio Express
San Antonio Light
San Marcos Free Press
San Saba News, San Saba
Shiner Gazette, Shiner
Taylor County News, Abilene
Temple Weekly Times, Temple
Waco Daily Examiner

Weimar Mercury, Weimar
Williamson County Sun, Georgetown
Utah
Salt Lake Herald
Vermont
Essex County Herald, Guildhall
Londonderry Sifter, Londonderry
West Virginia
Wheeling Register
Wisconsin
Daily Northwestern, Oshkosh
The Republican, Waukesha
Waukesha Freeman, Waukesha

Index

A

Abingdon, Illinois, 35
Adair, Iowa, 23, 24
Albany, Texas, 145, 148
Alexander, J. L., 151
Alford, Joe, 183
Allee, Alfred Young (deputy sheriff), xiii, 69, 94, 95, 123, 124, 140, 141, 152, 174, 194, 195, 197, 239 note 74
Allen, A. N., xv, 73, 74, 76
Amarillo, Texas, 196
Anderson, James, 63
Anglin, -----, 39, 45
Applewhite, -----, 88
Armand, Louis (misidentified as Armaroux, Pamaroux and P. A. Maroux), 75, 232, 233 note 45
Armaroux. *See* Armand, Louis
Armistead, R. L., 77, 234 note 60
Armstrong brothers, 194
Armstrong, -----, 137
Armstrong, Bill, 15
Arnold, R. H., 32
Atascosa County, Texas, 19, 22, 68, 117
Aten, Austin Ira (Texas Ranger), xiii, xviii, 20, 34–36, 43, 44, 49, 107, 108, 134–136, 164, 223 note 87; *photo insert*
Atoka, Oklahoma, 137
Austin, Texas, 38, 47, 58, 129, 130, 134, 135, 149, 151, 177, 195

B

Bagdad, Texas, 9
Bailes, Thomas O. (U. S. Deputy Marshal), xiii, 49, 98, 118, 120, 149, 228 note 91; *photo insert*
Bailey, W. C. (Railroad detective), xiii, 49, 135
Baird, Texas, 145, 146
Baker, -----, 118
Ballinger, Texas, 106, 129, 145
Bandera County, Texas, 121, 126
Barber, Attie Lee Swinney, 26
Barber, Austin Calloway, 45, 46, 59
Barber, Isaac Jones, 12, 27, 47, 216 notes 61 and 62, 63, 64
Barber, Joanna, 12
Barber, Joel, 26, 44–47, 49, 52–59, 62–64, 69, 95, 104, 155, 221 note 33, 226 note 61, 229 note 11
Barber, John (son of John T. Barber and B. Palmer), 184
Barber, John Toliver, xii, 2, 8, 9, 12–16, 22, 23, 26, 28, 30, 34, 44, 45, 47, 56, 57, 64, 70–72, 75, 78, 80, 93, 95, 96, 98, 99, 101, 103–111, 112, 123, 125, 129, 134, 135, 137, 142, 144, 147, 148, 151–155, 164, 165, 174, 176, 177, 179, 180, 184–188
Barber, Samuel D., 12
Barber, Sarah, 12
Barber, Tom, 13
Barnes, A. T., 89
Barnhart, -----, 39
Barthelow, Joseph, 195, 258 note 56
Bass, Sam, xvi, 23, 47, 93, 116
Baylor, Henry W., 118, 243 note 8
Beach, A. J., 79, 234 note 71
Beadle, Erastus, xvi
Beers, W. F., 78, 234 note 63

Bell County, Texas, 144, 145
Bell, John T, 177
Bell, John Y., 101, 240 note 5, 255 note 74
Bell, Steve, 17, 18
Bell, W. J. (U. S. Deputy Marshal), xiii, 49, 62–64, 88, 95
Bellevue, Texas, 23, 43
Bennet, W. E. 174
Bennett, Joe, xii, 2, 69, 104, 110, 111, 174, 213 note 2, 230, 248
Bentley, J. T., xv, 167
Bently, George, 119
Bexar County, Texas, 47, 62, 63, 127, 177
Bickett, Jonathan H., 151
Billy the Kid, xvi
Bishop, -----, 167
Bishop, J. N., 155, 156
Blake, T. R., 143
Blanchard, N. C., 158, 160, 161, 251 note 57, 252 note 72
Blanco, Texas, 104
Bonnell, W. H. (Missouri Pacific detective), xiii, 49
Bosque County, Texas, 62, 125, 127
Boulder, Montana, 192
Bowie County, Texas, 3
Boyce, Rube, 128
Boyd, John H. (Sheriff of Johnson County), xiii, 130, 134, 135, 139, 155, 246 note 71
Bracken, -----, 39, 45
Brady, C. J. (City Marshal of Georgetown) xiii, 39
Brassell, John Morgan, 120, 125, 126
Brassell, Phillip Haddox, 120, 244 note 15
Breckenridge, Texas, 5–6, 145
Brickford, ----- 105, 240 note 18
Brock, Leonard, 137, 138
Brooks, J. A., 165
Brown, John (or George), xii, 81, 121, 124, 127, 128
Brown, Sam, 48, 127, 128
Brownwood, Texas, 70, 109, 111, 145, 146
Brush, George, 31, 222 note 68
Brush, Oliver, 31, 36, 222 note 67
Buckley, Charles, 47, 49, 59–63, 126, 229 note 25
Bunch, Eugene, xvii, 23
Burnet County, Texas, 12, 39, 46, 99, 104, 142, 153
Burnet, Texas, 26, 51, 99
Burney, John, 115
Burns, Robert B., 88
Burrow, Jim, 137
Burrow, Rube, xvi, 23, 43, 86, 89, 131, 137, 138
Burt, Emma (Inez), 3–5
Burt, John, 4
Burt, Margaret Jane Abbey, 4
Busby, Shepherd, 194, 256 note 52
Butler, Adeline Riggs Burris, 22
Butler, Emmett, 22
Butler, Newton Green "Newt," xii, 22, 69, 70, 79, 94–96, 100, 103, 111, 151, 166, 174
Butler, William Green, 6, 22

C

Caldwell County, Texas, 47, 48, 121
Calhoun, -----, 39
Camden, Arkansas, 153
Carroll County, Arkansas, 12
Carroll, John, 183
Carson County, Texas, 32
Carson, Kit, xvi
Carthage, Missouri, 181
Cass County, Texas, 3
Cassidy, Butch, xvi
Cherokee County, Texas, 5
Chickasaw Nation, 111
Cincinnati, Ohio, 77
Cisco, Texas, 89, 143, 145, 148, 149 156, 174, 185
Claremore, Oklahoma, 179
Clark, Ed, 90–92
Clark, Sterling, 157, 158, 161, 162
Clark, William A. (Sheriff of Caldwell County), 48

Clarksville, Texas, 49
Clay County, Texas, 23
Cline, Frank, 103
Cloud, Elizabeth Kennedy, 8
Cloud, George, 9
Cloud, Isaac Kennedy "Ike," xii, 2, 8, 9, 23, 26, 27, 29, 32, 34, 39, 44, 51, 69, 94, 99, 111, 129, 142, 150, 165, 177, 178, 184–185, 215 notes 34, 35, 36, 37, 40, 221 note 36
Cloud, James, 9
Cloud, Mary, 8
Cloud, Penelope, 9
Cloud, Thomas, 9
Cloud, William, 9
Cloud, William Augustine, 8
Codding, A. B., xv, 158, 251 note 55
Cody, Buffalo Bill, xvi
Coffee, A. B., 98
Cohen, -----, 136
Coleman, Texas, 145
Collier, Wes, 35
Colorado River, 101, 102
Colter, Bertie, 157, 161
Colton, Willis P., xv, 157, 158, 251 note 50
Columbus, Rogers "One-eyed," 163
Comal County, Texas, 67, 104
Comanche, Texas, 145, 147
Connelly, Barney (Deputy U. S. Marshal), xiii, 184, 188, 194, 256 note 50
Cook, -----, 110
Cook, William, xiv, 28, 29, 33, 54
Coombs, L. G. (Sheriff of Washington County), 185
Cooper, J. E., 55
Copps, -----, 61
Cornett, Braxton A., 17, 19, 218 note 90
Cornett, Braxton E. "Brack," xii, 2, 12, 16, 18–20, 23, 24, 26–28, 32–34, 40, 43, 44, 47, 54, 69–71, 73, 77, 80, 94, 95, 99, 101, 103, 104, 110, 112, 113, 117, 121, 123, 125, 128, 129, 131, 140–142, 149, 174, 194, 195, 197; *photo insert*
Cornett, Cordelia Ann McGinty, 16, 218 note 89
Cornett, Cordelia Lucretia, 17
Cornett, Elizabeth Agnes, 16
Cornett, James Richard "Dock," 17, 142, 218 note 97
Cornett, John William, 16, 142; *photo insert*
Cornett, Joseph, 142
Cornett, Laban E., 16, 17, 218 note 88
Cornett, Mary Elizabeth Wooten, 16
Cornett, Matilda Malvina "Mallie," 128
Cornett, Sarah, 16
Cornett, William Henry, 128, 129, 246 note 61; *photo insert*
Corsicana, Texas, 43, 44
Coryell County, Texas, 14, 179
Cotulla, Texas, 109
Coulter, Oscar, 164, 185, 252 note 5
Cox, Cordelia Lucinda, 107, 152, 173–176, 218 note 83; marries Bill Whitley, 16
Cox, John Thomas, 173
Cox, Samuel, 153
Cox, Tom, 107, 152
Craft, Archalaous, 48
Craft, Archalaous "Cheed," 47, 48, 49, 51, 60, 62, 63, 127
Craft, John, 47, 48, 49, 51, 60, 62, 63, 127
Crevisson, John, 189
Crisswell, John, xii, 81, 121, 124, 126–128, 244 note 19
Crowder, W. A., 56, 58
Crowell, John, 81
Cruz, Citarino, 78
Cuero, Texas, 2, 16, 22, 95, 96, 101, 102, 104, 110, 174
Cypress, Texas, 115, 117

D

Daileyville, Texas, 22
Dallas, Texas, 26, 157, 196

Daniel, D. D., 147
Daugherty, William C. (Sheriff of Frio County), xiii, 139, 247 note 28
Dawson,William R., 164, 165, 185, 252 note 4
Day, Frances A. Lowe, 96
Day, John Washington, 97
Day, Martin (aka Milton Day, born Winfield Martin Day), xii, 72, 81, 96, 99, 104, 105, 110, 112, 119, 120, 124, 126, 133, 239 note 82
Day, Short, 11
De Witt County, Texas, 2, 7, 96, 101, 110, 112
Deal, Robert, 12
Dean, Jack, 67
Deer, -----, 57
Denison, Texas, 137
Dickson, Hamilton "Vic," 11
Dixon, Ben, 121, 244 note 25
Dougherty, W. C. (Sheriff of Frio County), 177, 255 note 75
Drake, Sherman, 31
Dustin, John, 164, 165, 185
Dustin, Tobe, 164, 165, 185

E

Earp, Wyatt B. S., xvi, 35
Eastland, Texas, 145
Edwards County, Texas, 165
El Paso, Texas, 150
Ellis County, Texas, 3, 5
Ellis, George W. (Sheriff of Harris County), xiii, 91, 113, 116–118, 242 note 61
Ely, Samuel R., xiv, 27, 28, 29, 36, 43, 51, 221 note 40
Emmetsburg, Iowa, 160
Erichson, Albert (Deputy Sheriff of Harris County), xiii, 113, 114, 117, 118, 121, 196, 242 note 62
Espizer, Manuel, 6
Eureka, Texas, 113–115, 117, 118, 125
Evans, Jack, 5
Evans, James W. (Sheriff of Fannin County), xiii, 135
Everett, Giles, 177
Everett, Milton, xv, 167

F

Faulkner, A., 91
Fayette County, Alabama, 14
Fayette County, Texas, 10, 22, 25, 35, 87, 90
Field, Albert Francis, 120, 243 note 13
Finny, John W., 12
Flatonia, Texas, 18, 22, 25, 70, 71, 75,59, 81, 84, 85, 87, 88, 90–93, 99, 101, 103, 106, 120, 123, 125, 126, 132–134, 138, 140, 150, 151, 164, 172, 177, 187, 193
Flens, S. F., 174
Florence, Texas, 55, 57, 58, 108, 109, 171, 172, 185
Folger, M. E. "Frank," xv, 72, 73, 76, 80, 88, 106, 231 note 29
Fort Gibson, Oklahoma, 157
Fort Smith, Arkansas, 183, 194
Fort Worth, Texas, 160
Fredericksburg, Texas, 96
Freiburg, Mose, 76, 233 note 49
Fricke, Paul, 190, 191
Frio County, Texas, 139, 141, 165, 174, 177
Frost, C. L., 97
Furlong, T. K. (Chief Detective Missouri Pacific), xiii, 151

G

Gainesville, Texas, 148
Galbraith, F. P. (Sheriff of Benton County), 185
Galveston, Texas, 76, 154, 155
Gay, Mary Ann, 120
Georgetown, Texas, 57, 58
Ghio, John, 151
Gissoway, -----, 39, 45
Gleason, George, 127
Glidden, William, xiv, 28, 221 note 47

Goliad County, Texas, 16, 17
Goliad, Texas, 16, 17, 94, 105
Gonzales County, Texas, 8, 21, 101, 120
Gordon, Texas, 23
Goree, Col. -----, 62
Graves, F. R., 132, 133, 135
Grayson, Jim, 115
Green, -----,189
Greeser (Glaisor, John?), xv, 166, 169, 174, 253 note 25
Gregory, Walter, 75, 233 note 47
Grimes, Albert C. (Texas Ranger), xiii, 110, 123
Grimshaw, John, 137
Grizzard, Jim, 195, 196
Guadalupe County, Texas, 48
Guadalupe River, 126

H

Haas, William, 188, 189
Hall, ----- 86
Hall, Jesse Lee, 45, 95, 117, 118
Hall, John, 61, 62, 91
Hall, Van, 138
Hallettsville, Texas, 11
Hamilton, Henry "Buck" (Sheriff of Bandera County), 121, 244 note 20
Hamilton, Kinch, 130, 246 note 69
Hamilton, Margaret, 179
Hamilton, Sheriff Henry "Buck," 121
Hardin, John Wesley, 129
Hargraves, Levi, 116
Hargrove, T. J., 19
Harrell, Eli Y., xii, 7, 21, 44, 70, 94, 95, 103, 151, 166, 171, 173, 182, 183
Harrell, Leah, 173
Harrell, M. J., 21
Harrell, William Carroll "Will," xii, 21, 44, 94, 95, 103, 151, 166, 171–173, 185, 254 note 56
Harrell, William Carroll (father of Will and Eli), 21, 220 note 3
Harris County, Texas, 196
Hart, -----, xv
Harwood, Texas, 165–167, 175, 177, 178, 183, 196
Hatfield, Elizabeth, 181
Hawkins, W. E., xiv, 29, 30, 53, 54, 222 note 58
Hays, Jack, 67
Hays, Texas, 3
Hearne, Texas, 39, 45
Helena, Montana, 190
Helena, Texas, 6, 22, 100, 109, 110, 111, 132, 135
Helm, Jack, 7, 112
Hendrix, Bob, 183
Hensley, Annie Elizabeth, 48, 227 note 77
Herrin, Jim, xii, 121, 128, 244 note 23
Hickok, Wild Bill, xvi
Hill County, Texas, 4
Hilliare, H. P., 148
Hogan, Hugh, 161
Hogg, James Stephen (State Attorney General), xiii, 37, 39, 43, 64, 224 note 4
Hohenthal, Lionel, 79, 234 note 72
Hollingsworth, James E., 104
Holloman, J. H., xii, 165, 185, 188
Holmes, H. H., alias of Herman Webster Mudgett 193
Holt, Walter, 35
Hoo Doo War, 86, 107
Horn, Marion, 186
Hornsby, William M. (Sheriff of Travis County) xiii, 59, 119
Horrell-Higgins War, 107
Horrell family, 21
Hot Springs, Arkansas, 130
Houston, Texas, 88, 113, 116–118, 131, 155
Hughes, -----, 126
Hughes, John R. (Texas Ranger), xiii, xviii, 35, 43, 44, 49
Hume, James B. (Wells Fargo detective), xiii, 87
Humphreys, William, xii, 72, 81, 120,

124, 126–128
Hunt, Attie Barber, 13, 26, 56, 60, 64, 217 note 66, 221 note 35
Hutchinson, A. C., 98

I

Insall, John, xii, 112, 114, 119, 125, 126, 135, 137, 196, 241 note 49
Irby, James, 147
Ireland, John (governor of Texas), 68, 123
Itawamba County, Mississippi, 14

J

Jack the Ripper, 193
Jackson, Jim, 93
Jackson, W. R., 56
Jacobs, Will, xii, 8, 68, 69, 70, 72, 81, 93, 100, 101, 124, 151, 152, 165, 167, 184, 230 note 13
James-Younger gang, 23, 24, 142
James, Frank, 40, 41
James, Jesse, xvi, 83
Jamison, John, 153
Jenkins, Lee,151
Jenks, -----, 158
Johnson County, Texas, 139
Johnson family, 86
Johnson, ----- 61
Johnson, Charles, xv, 77
Johnson, Laura, 90
Johnson, O. H., 187
Johnston, S. S., 98
Jones, Elisha, 145
Jones, Frank, 165
Jones, Frank (Texas Ranger), xiii, 24
Jones, Mark, 136
Jones, Tom (alias Tom Montgomery), xii, 72, 81, 120, 124, 126–128
Jones, William E. (Sheriff of Gonzales County), xiii, 120, 170, 171, 2433 note 14
Juby, John Henry, 46, 226 note 64

K

Karnes County, Texas, 2, 7, 8, 19, 69, 88, 89, 94, 95, 100, 106, 110,111, 122, 132, 151
Kasiner, --- 114
Kegans, Ben (Deputy Sheriff of Harris County), xiii, 113, 117, 118, 196, 242 note 63
Kelly, Henry Peter, xii, 72, 81, 112, 119–121, 124–126, 133
Kelly, J. J., 166
Kelly, Will, 8, 93, 101
Kendrick, Malinda Emeline, 145
Kennedy, John, 57
Kerr County, Texas, 9
Kerrville, Texas, 34
Ketchum, Elizabeth Manila, 48, 227 note 81
Kilgore, Addison (Sheriff of De Witt County), 95, 170, 174, 254 note 45
Kimble County, Texas, 112
Kinement, ----- 136
King, Dick, 35
King, Wilburn H. (Adjutant General), xiii, 39, 43, 44, 66, 68, 89, 93, 98, 100, 101, 107, 109, 110, 122–124, 132, 135, 151–153, 165
Kirk, Steve, 57
Kniffe, -----, 114
Kyle, Texas, 119

L

Labatt, Henry J., 167–169, 253 note 29; *photo insert*
LaGrange, Texas, 25, 149, 190
Lamar, ----- 57
Lampasas County, Texas, 12, 21, 43, 44, 107–109, 151, 174, 178, 179, 182
Lampasas, Texas, 46, 147
Lancaster, S. J., 130
Landa, Harry, 31, 36, 42, 43, 233 note 69
Langford, Ernest, 46, 154
Laredo, Texas, 172, 195

Lasker, Abraham, 75, 233 note 46
Laughlin, Peter, 15
Lavaca County, Texas, 12, 101, 120
Leary, Edgar, 22
Ledbetter, Texas, 134
Lee County, Texas, 40
Leon County, Texas, 165
Leveaux, F. C., 143, 148
Lewis, A. A. 164, 165
Lewis, A. M. "Gus," 19, 219 note 113
Lewis, A. S. 185, 188
Lewis, Andrew Jackson (Sheriff of Milam County), xiii, 69, 151, 152, 230 note 15
Lewis, Charles, 39
Lewis, Dan, 177
Lewis, Nathaniel (Sheriff of Bexar County), xiii, 47, 62–64, 88, 91, 227 note 73, 255 note 76
Lewis, R. E., 115
Linn, George, 131
Llano, Texas, 128, 190
Lockhart, Texas, 120,122
Lodge, Sophia, 93
Logan County, Arkansas, 184
Long, J., 93
Lubbock, Dave, 114
Lubbock, Tom, 115
Lucy, James E. (City Marshal of Austin) xiii, 37, 38, 40, 41, 44, 50, 55, 56, 59, 119, 226 note 52; *photo insert*
Luling, Texas, 47, 49, 61, 122
Lyons, Buck, 94
Lyons, Jesse K., xv, 71, 73, 75, 76, 78, 88

M

Magdalena, New Mexico, 149
Malsch, Walter, 196
Manchaca, Texas, 104, 118, 119
Mansfield, Leon, 90
Mapes, William R., 17
Marble Falls, Texas, 26, 104
Marlin, Texas, 160
Maroux, P.A. *See* Armand, Louis
Martin, -----, 189
Martin, Frank, 119, 243 note 11
Martin, James C., 56, 104, 119, 228 note 7, 243 note 11
Martin, Tom, 119, 243 note 11
Mason County, Texas, 107, 142
Mathews, Lucinda Mathis, 48
Mayer, Lou, 77, 234 note 62
McCarty, A., 17
McClatchy, J. F., 91
McDade, Thomas S. (Sheriff of Waller County), xiv, 116, 243 note 4
McGraw, John, 21
McLaue, S. B., 55
McMurray, Sam (Texas Ranger), xiv, 89, 107
McNeil, J. S. (Deputy U. S. Marshal), xiv, 166
McNelly, Leander H., 89
Medina City, Texas, 121
Menafee, Tom, 25
Menard County, Texas, 62
Merced, California, 76
Mercer, Tom, 124
Merkin, Samuel, 11, 216 note 53
Metcalf, J. M. (Sheriff of Bosque County), 125
Milam County, Texas, 151, 160, 177
Miller, Chris, 62
Miller, James P., 17, 218 note 96
Miller, Peter M., 17, 94, 218 note 94
Millett, -----, 140
Miner, Bill, xvii
Mitchell, Barbara Emily Cloud, 26
Mitchell, J. H., 75, 232 note 44
Mobeetie, Texas, 32
Montgomery, Tom. *See* Jones, Tom
Montgomery County, Alabama, 3
Montgomery County, Texas, 115
Montgomery, -----, 39, 45
Moore, Armenta Emma, 60, 229 note 17
Morrill, H. L., 97
Mueller, Dietrich, 35
Munden, George W., 98

Muskogee, Oklahoma, 155, 159

N

Nashville, Tennessee, 77
Navarro County, Texas, 4
Navasota, Texas, 113
Neff, Charles, 179
Neff, Noah, 178, 255 note 85
Neff, Pat Morris, 179
Neff, Samuel Herbert, xii, 170, 178, 182, 183
New Braunfels, Texas, 104, 128
Newburger, William, 76, 94, 233 note 56
Newton County, Georgia, 164
Nichols, J. W., 88
Norman, James, 178
Northacker, A. J., xv, 33, 34, 43, 54

O

Oldham County, Texas, 153
Olive, John Thomas (Sheriff of Williamson County), xiv, 37, 39–41, 45, 55–59, 64, 107, 108, 135, 140, 174, 194, 224 note 1, 226 note 53
Otho, John, 90, 92, 237, note 51
Owens, Chad, 177
Owens, M. B., 143

P

Paddock, Martha M., 10
Palatka, Florida, 79
Palmer, -----, 38, 45
Palmer, B., 180, 184
Palo Pinto County, Texas, 15, 23
Pamaroux. *See* Armand, Louis
Parker, Isaac, 163
Paschell, Perry, 145
Patterson, James, 17, 218 note 95
Patton, Harry, 21, 22
Patton, William, 153
Pearsall, Texas, 140, 142, 177
Perkins, Olivia, 35
Petty, Jane Ann, 144
Pfeuffer, George, 123
Phipps brothers, 163
Pickren, Ben, xv, 71, 72, 231 note 21; *photo insert*
Pike, Zebulon, 155
Platt, Jake, 39, 45
Platt, Sam (Deputy Sheriff Travis County), xiv, 38, 45
Pleasants, John T., 174
Pleasonton, Texas, 19
Pool, Lee, 69, 124, 152, 184
Powell, Agnes Stone, 7
Powell, James Asberry "Bud," xii, 2, 6–8, 23, 26, 30, 31, 34, 40, 45, 69, 71, 72, 75, 80, 93, 96, 99, 103–105, 111, 123, 129, 130, 142, 153, 165, 186, 188, 190–192, 208–212
Powell, Samuel S., 7, 214 notes 26, 27, 28
Price, Tom, 147
Putnam, Texas, 145

Q

Quanah, Texas, 107
Queen, Nancy, 180
Queen, Samuel David, 144
Queen, Samuel DeKalb "Kep," xii, 137, 144, 145, 147, 156, 157, 164–166, 179, 180, 183, 185, 186
Quintos, Colonel -----, 78

R

Ragland, W.T., 137
Ragsdale, James, 11
Ragsdale, Robert, 11, 150, 216 note 54
Rankin, John Taylor (U. S. Marshal), xiv, 34–36, 38, 44, 45, 51, 87, 90, 91, 166–168, 171, 172, 174, 178, 194–196, 224 note 91
Rankin, W., 91
Rasback, Wallace H., xv, 156, 157, 250 note 44
Red Rock, Texas, 104
Reeves, Edwin James "Ed," xii, 1–5, 8, 9, 13, 16, 19, 22–24, 27, 29, 31–34, 40, 43, 44, 69, 70, 72, 72,

80, 81, 84, 94, 96, 99, 103–106, 111, 123, 129, 130, 134, 139, 150, 153, 155, 165, 174, 179, 184, 186, 188, 189, 192, 208
Reeves, Elizabeth Courtney, 3
Reeves, Green William, 3, 213 notes 3, 4
Reeves, James H., 4, 5, 6
Reeves, Jesse Winchester, 3, 5, 213 note 5, 214 note 6
Reeves, Mary Francis "Fannie," 3
Reeves, Rachel Matilda (wife of Kinch Hamilton), 3, 4
Reno brothers, xvii
Reno, John, 23, 24
Reno, Simeon, 23, 24
Reynolds, George T., 148
Reynolds, N. O. (Sheriff of Lampasas County / former Texas Ranger), xiv, 107, 178, 183
Rhodes, Frank, 69
Richardson, Tillman, 91, 92
Rickett, J. B., 27, 29, 51
Riddleville, Texas, 105
Rife, Andrew Jackson, 121, 244 note 26
Rigney, Henry, 13
Rising Star, Texas, 146, 147, 151
Roberts, Dan, 45
Robinson (Robertson), ----- 39
Robinson, Walter, 39, 45
Rockdale, Texas, 69
Roe, Bob, 136
Rogers, Bob, xii, 165, 177, 185, 255 note 73
Ross, Charley. *See* Secrest, Sion Searcy
Ross, Lawrence Sullivan "Sul" (Governor), xiii, 43, 69, 85, 89, 96–98, 104, 111, 138, 140, 147, 149
Round Rock, Texas, 3, 34, 45, 57, 61
Rudd, William L. (Sheriff of Karnes County/former Texas Ranger), xiv, 6, 88, 89, 100, 123, 237 note 40
Ruggles, -----, 53
Rundell, -----, 38, 45
Russ, George, 183
Ryan, Henry, xv, 159–161, 251 note 61

S

Sacramento, California, 46
San Angelo, Texas, 129
San Antonio River, 70, 105
San Antonio, Texas, 26, 43, 61, 62, 75, 79, 88, 90–92, 100, 121, 139, 140, 149, 155, 167, 172, 190, 196
San Francisco, California, 75, 87
San Saba County War, 65, 227 note 88
San Saba County, Texas, 49
San Saba, Texas, 144
Sanders, Ed (Sheriff of Cherokee Nation, Oklahoma), xiv, 179, 183, 255 note 88
Sandoval, -----, 88
Saran, Ed, xv, 167
Sayle, D. P., 146
Schmick, James K. (Sheriff of Eastland County), 145, 146, 248 note 63
Schmitt, George (Texas Ranger), xiv, 67–70, 89, 100–102, 105, 107, 109–111, 122, 123, 131–135, 137–139, 165, 197
Schneider, Reinhardt, 8, 93, 100, 101, 215 note 33; *photo insert*
Scott, William (Texas Ranger), xiv, 68, 89, 106
Secrest, Abraham Francis, 9
Secrest, Barbara Allen, 10
Secrest, Mariah Bird Dismukes, 10
Secrest, Sion Searcy (alias Charley Ross), xii, 2, 9, 10–12, 19, 22, 23, 27, 28, 32–34, 39, 44, 51, 69, 70, 94, 99, 111, 129, 142, 149–151, 153, 165, 188–190, 215 note 44, 216 notes 45, 46, 47
Secrest, Thomas Abraham "Bud," 11, 12
Secrest, Thomas Carroll, 10

Seguin, Texas, 167
Seven Star (alias Jim Stop), 177
Seymour, Indiana, 23
Shackford, E. E., xv, 166, 167, 253 note 26
Sharp, ----- 120
Shea, J. B., 39
Shely, W. W. (Sheriff of Starr County), 195
Shepherd, Isabella Eleanor, 178, 179
Shirley, John, 181
Shoaf, George, 91, 92, 238 note 57
Shoffner, ----- 57
Shulenberg, Texas, 86
Sieker, Lamartine P. (Texas Ranger quartermaster), xiv, 38, 100, 123, 134, 136, 224 note 6
Sisk Henry S. (Sheriff of Parker County) 146, 249 note 68
Sisson, Harry, 163
Sloan, ----- 86
Smart, Alcey Jane Barber, 60, 153, 229 note 16
Smart, Brice M., 153, 250 note 23
Smith, August, 90, 92
Smith, Nancy Adeen, 144
Smothers, A. J. (Sheriff of Lavaca County), xiv, 91, 238 note 54
Sneed, Thomas, 59
Snow, J. D., 5
Spangler, Samuel H., xv, 28, 221 note 48
Sparkes, Frank, 23, 24
Spaulding, S. R., xv, 30, 33, 50, 53, 54
Stair, A. F., 148
Standley, Eugene, xiii, 186
Standley, Hamp, xiii, 186
Stanley, William (Deputy Sheriff of Williamson County), xiv, 107–110, 172, 241 note 33
Stapp, Ida Elizabeth, 46
Starr, Belle (alias of Myra Maybelle Shirley), 181
Startz, August G., 104, 128, 240 note 15
Stephens, Jim, xiii, 137, 147, 164, 165, 179–181, 185, 186, 206, 207; alias of William J. Jones?, 145
Stevens, Ed (Constable in San Antonio), xiv, 88, 120
Stevenson, -----, 105
Stokes, Max, 76
Stringtown, Oklahoma, 137
Sundance Kid, xvi
Sutton-Taylor War, 7, 17, 96, 112, 129
Sweeney, Dan, 76, 233 note 48
Sweet Home, Texas, 120

T

Tahlequah, Oklahoma, 188, 193
Tarver, Ben, 160, 161, 182
Tarver, Benjamin C. 251 note 68
Tascosa, Texas, 32
Taylor, Amanda Jane, 112
Taylor, Texas, 37, 43, 68
Tevis (Tivvis?), Sarah, 90, 93
Texarkana, Texas, 136, 153
Thacker, John (Wells Fargo detective), xiv, 87
Thomas, J. J., 174
Thomas, Henry Andrew "Heck" (Deputy U. S. Marshal), xiv, 164, 185
Thomas, J. T., 143, 145
Thomas, Lovick Pierece, 164
Thomas, Martha Ann Fullwood Bedell, 164
Thorp, -----, 39
Tombstone, Arizona, 75
Toomey, Dan, xv, 166, 168–170, 253 note 23
Townsend, James Light (Sheriff of Colorado County), xiv, 86, 87, 236 note 28
Travis County, Texas, 47, 118
Turner, Sarah Eliza Ann, 93

U

Union Parish, Louisiana, 8
Ussery, Abner Mastin, 47, 48, 49, 51, 60, 62, 63, 127

Ussery, Catherine "Kitty," 48
Ussery, James Welcome, 47, 48, 49, 51, 60–63, 127
Ussery, Mastin, 48
Ussery, Sarah Jane, 48
Uvalde County, Texas, 118

V

Van Riper, William (U. S. Deputy Marshals), xiv, 49, 166, 171, 172, 197, 253 note 21
Villa, Pancho, 190

W

Waco, Texas, 25, 151
Waites, ----- 114
Waldo, J., 96, 97, 98, 130
Walker, C. D., xv, 30, 36
Walker, Gus, 18
Walker, J. E., 130
Waller County, Texas, 116
Waller, J. M., 138
Walton, William M., 62, 229 note 23; *photo insert*
Ward, John, 183
Waxahachie, Texas, 5
Weatherford, Texas, 146, 148
Weimar, Texas, 90
Weldon, Abram Brewer, 93
Weldon, Vachel, 93, 94, 101, 102, 238, 239 notes 70, 71; *photo insert*
West, C. H., 81
West, Duval (Deputy U. S. Marshal), xiv, 166, 170–172, 197, 253 note 19; *photo insert*
Westfield, Texas, 116
Whaley, Agnes, 142
White, Barbara, 78, 79
White, Charles W., 30, 31, 34, 222 note 66
White, Ham, 90
White, James H. (Sheriff of El Paso County), 73, 78, 79, 231 note 31
White, S. C., 188
White, William P., 160, 252 note 69
Whitley, Elizabeth Henry, 14
Whitley, Jasper, 14, 15, 108, 217 notes 78, 81
Whitley, Joe, 153, 154
Whitley, Minnie Margaret "Eliza," 16
Whitley, Richard, 196
Whitley, Temperance Alice, 16
Whitley, William Henry "Bill," xii, xviii, 2, 13, 14, 21–24, 30, 31, 34, 69, 70, 72, 75, 76, 80, 99, 101, 103–108, 110–112, 123, 125, 129, 134, 135, 137, 142, 144–148, 151, 153–155, 164, 166, 168–174, 177, 180, 183, 186, 187; *photo insert*
Whitley, William Taylor, 14, 217 notes 75, 76
Wichman, Charles, 114
Wickes, Reverend ----- 192
Wilburn, ----- 61
Williamson County, Texas, 9, 12, 13, 16, 25, 26, 37, 47, 105, 107, 108, 144, 172, 174, 178
Williford, Tom, 113, 114, 121, 242 note 60
Wolf, John W. (Sheriff of Burnet County), xiv, 107, 241 note 31
Woods, Bud, 92
Woods, J. S., xv, 29, 30, 33, 36, 44
Wright, S. L., xv, 72
Yarbrough, G. C., 124
Yeary, John M. (Sheriff of Karnes County), 94
Yglesis, Eugene (Deputy U. S. Marshal), xiv, 171, 172, 197
Yoakum, B. F., 102
Young, R. L., 122

Z

Zapp, Brutus Lytt (Sheriff of Fayette County), xiv, 87, 90, 91, 149, 150, 236 note 29; *photo insert*
Zapp, Maria J. H. H., 87
Zapp, Robert, 87
Zork, H., 91